REGIONAL FLASHBACKS

THE REGIONAL FLASHBACKS SERIES IS PUBLISHED BY THE
EUROPEAN ETHNOLOGICAL RESEARCH CENTRE
CELTIC & SCOTTISH STUDIES
UNIVERSITY OF EDINBURGH
50 GEORGE SQUARE
EDINBURGH EH8 9LH

TITLES IN THE REGIONAL FLASHBACK SERIES:

Stranraer Lives
Voices in Trust

Edited by Caroline Milligan and Mark A. Mulhern

TITLES IN THE FLASHBACK SERIES:

The Making of *Am Fasgadh*
An Account of the Origins
of the Highland Folk Museum by its Founder

Isabel Frances Grant MBE, LLD

From Kelso to Kalamazoo
The Life and Times of George Taylor

Edited by Margaret Jeary and Mark A. Mulhern

Scotland's Land Girls
Breeches, Bombers and Backaches

Edited by Elaine M. Edwards

An Orkney Boyhood
Duncan Cameron Mackenzie

Showfolk
An Oral History of a Fairground Dynasty

Frank Bruce

Galoshins Remembered
'A penny was a lot in these days'

Edited by Emily Lyle

From Land to Rail
Life and Times of Andrew Ramage 1854–1917

Edited by Caroline Milligan and Mark A. Mulhern

| REGIONAL FLASHBACKS |

Whithorn: An Economy of People, 1920–1960

Edited by
Julia Muir Watt

THE EUROPEAN ETHNOLOGICAL RESEARCH CENTRE
AND NMS ENTERPRISES LIMITED – PUBLISHING
NATIONAL MUSEUMS SCOTLAND

GENERAL EDITOR
Mark A. Mulhern

Published in Great Britain in 2018 by
European Ethnological Research Centre
Celtic & Scottish Studies
University Of Edinburgh
50 George Square
Edinburgh EH8 9LH

and

NMS Enterprises Limited – Publishing
NMS Enterprises Limited
National Museums Scotland
Chambers Street
Edinburgh EH1 1JF

Text © European Ethnological
Research Centre 2018

Figure 2 © Dumfries and Galloway
Libraries, Information and Archives
All other images © Whithorn
Photographic Group 2018

No reproduction permitted without
written permission to the publishers in
the first instance.

ISBN 978-1-910682-19-7

*No part of this publication may be
reproduced, stored in a retrieval system
or transmitted, in any form or by any
means, electronic, mechanical, photocopy-
ing, recording or otherwise, without the
prior permission of the publishers.*

The rights of Julia Muir Watt as editor
and all named contributors to be identified as the authors of this book have
been asserted by them in accordance
with the Copyright, Designs and Patents
Act 1988.

**British Library Cataloguing in
Publication Data**
A catalogue record of this book is
available from the British Library.

Cover design by Mark Blackadder.
Cover photograph: Whithorn main
 street (front); Grapes Hotel with
 Denton's worker in foreground
 (back) © Whithorn Photographic
 Group 2018.

Internal text design by
 NMS Enterprises Ltd – Publishing.
Printed and bound in Great Britain by
 Bell & Bain Ltd, Glasgow.

For a full listing of related NMS titles
please visit:
www.nms.ac.uk/books

CONTENTS

Whithorn Manse by Alistair Reid VII
Acknowledgements VIII
Preface IX
Editorial note XI
List of Illustrations XIV
Introduction 1

WHITHORN: AN ECONOMY OF PEOPLE, 1920–1960

1 **Leaving and Returning: Nostalgia of the Writers** 11
   Time and Money I: Eden and the Fall 11

2 **Outside-In: The Rural Town** 28
   Time and Money II: The Patient Economy 28
   The Language of Locality: Shops 30
   Up and Down: Top and Bottom of the Town 48
   Time and Money III: Credits and Debits 54
   Giving and Taking 58
   Outside In: Working the Margins 60
   Self-Help and Helping Yourself 72
   Inside Out: The Houses 74

3 **Outside: The Farms** 87
   The Rhythm of Work 87
   Horse-power 93
   The Circulation of Milk 109
   Inside-Outside: Farmhouses 142

4 **Work and Rest: The Timing of Pleasures** 148

5 **Up and Down: Wealth and Poverty** 159
   Upstairs-Downstairs 159
   Down and Out 177

6	**IHere and There**	188
	'Gaun Folk'	196
	People Who Left	201
	People Who Came	202
	Coming and Staying	205
7	**Here and Hereafter**	209
	In Sickness and Health	218
	Cleanliness and Godliness	225
	Established and Free	226
	Insiders and Outsiders: The Catholic Church	229
	Hereafter	240
8	**Incursion and Dispersion: Second World War**	245

Index 268

WHITHORN MANSE

I knew it as Eden,
that lost walled garden,
past the green edge
of priory and village;
and, beyond it, the house,
withdrawn, white,
one window alight.

Returning, I wonder,
idly, uneasily,
what eyes from inside
look out now, not in,
as once mine did,
and what might grant me,
a right of entry?

Is it never dead, then,
that need of an Eden?

Even this evening,
estranged by age,
I ogle that light
with a child's greed,
wistfully claiming
lost prerogatives
of homecoming.

Alistair Reid

from *Inside Out – Selected Poetry and Translations* (© Polygon, 2008).
Reproduced with permission of Birlinn Limited via PLSClear.

ACKNOWLEDGEMENTS

My thanks go to all those people of Whithorn and district who gave their time to be interviewed, sometimes more than once; they have contributed to a permanent record of the world which was, and to some extent still is, Whithorn.

I am grateful to Mark Mulhern and Alison Burgess for making the Dumfries and Galloway study possible and for patience as my workload elsewhere added to the time taken to edit the typescript.

My thanks above all to my mother who understood that what is small and little known is obscure only because of our inability to see and not because of any inherent lack of significance and interest.

This book is dedicated to David Ehrich Goebel, another of Whithorn's cognoscenti.

Julia Muir Watt
Whithorn 2018

PREFACE

This work is an addition to the long-standing series of oral histories, memoir and diary accounts of lives published by the European Ethnological Research Centre (EERC) in association with NMSE Publishing – *Flashbacks*. It is the second such work to be published based upon the work undertaken by the EERC in its research programme, Dumfries and Galloway: A Regional Ethnology. This study is part of a wider research programme being conducted by the EERC – The Regional Ethnology of Scotland Project (RESP).

One of the main strands of this research programme is the conduct of new fieldwork using recorded oral interview as a means of inquiry. The particular approach adopted by the EERC has been to train the people of Dumfries and Galloway to conduct this work themselves with the guidance and support of the EERC and Alison Burgess, Local Studies Officer with Dumfries and Galloway Council Libraries and Archives. The interviews which form this work come from the work of Julia Muir Watt, who interviewed a total of 29 individuals from Whithorn and its hinterland.

The RESP is seeking to build up an understanding of life and society across Scotland at a local and regional level. To do so it was considered important that space was left for the people of the regions – in this case Dumfries and Galloway – to give *their* view as to what was and is of importance to them. The contention being that, by allowing the people of Dumfries and Galloway to establish for themselves what was and is important, allows for the synthesis of a more nuanced and complete understanding of lives in a time and place. The manner in which we worked towards meeting this objective was by enabling to people of Dumfries and Galloway to interview each other without being directed as to what they should discuss.

Thus far this approach has encouraged participation of 49 volunteer fieldworkers who have interviewed over 300 individuals. The range of topics discussed is extensive and provides, to some extent, a statement about what life and society in Dumfries and Galloway during the twentieth century was and how those who lived those lives felt about that time and about the places in which they lived, worked and spent time. In what follows, just such an account of life in and around

Whithorn is provided. That account is set out thematically. The balance of material presented is a reflection of the level of detail on a given theme contained within the interviews. It also reflects the response of the editor to the content of the recordings. It is notable that the fieldworker who generated the recordings and the editor of this work are the same individual, Julia Muir Watt. This work is therefore a considered reflection on the experience of creating the recordings and of then reflecting on what they say as a collection about this part of the Machars. Julia is also a long-term resident of Whithorn so it is true to say that what follows is a product of Whithorn and its surroundings.

Such is the richness of recorded oral interviews that there remains scope for others to look at these interviews to seek information on other aspects of being which are of interest to them. The EERC will further enable such inquiry by, in due course, establishing a freely available repository of the interview recordings – both in audio and in transcription.

An important aspect of our approach is to provide opportunities for members of the community who become involved in our work to extend their participation as fully as they feel able to. In Julia's case this involved her not only interviewing 29 people, but working with the EERC to shape those interviews, as editor, into this book. Julia, and other volunteer participants, have also extended their participation by presenting accounts of their findings at a series of three conferences held by the EERC in 2016. An aspiration of the RESP is that we enable the communites of regions to build up a picture of life and society that touches on the themes that are important or notable to them. By enabling those who become involved to go beyond interviewing, it is hoped that this aspect of our approach is enhanced. In this instance, what follows is a considered account of life and society in Whithorn in the early to mid-twentieth century from the perspective of one who is active and engaged with the people of the town and its hinterland.

This work is the culmination of much work on the part of the EERC, Dumfries and Galloway Libraries and Archives and Julia Muir Watt. Most importantly, however, it is a representation of the contribution made by those interviewed to our understanding of a place within a place. This is ultimately a work of the people of Whithorn and the Machars. A work in their own voice in which they tell us what it is they know and understand about their place and about themselves.

Mark A. Mulhern
General Editor

EDITORIAL NOTE

This series of interviews, undertaken between 2012 and 2013 under the auspices of the European Ethnological Research Centre, involved those in Whithorn and district, whose memories related largely to the period from 1920 to 1960, with the Second Word War, which, with its disruption of the small world of Whithorn, acts as a natural close to the book.

The subject matter of the interviews offered the chance to examine the belonging together of landscape, dwelling and technology, and how a particular world, now largely gone, was spaced and timed. All of the following people generously offered their insights into this world:

Guy (Gavin) Brown
Born Port William
Interviewed in Port William
22 August 2012

Judy Brown
Born Isle of Whithorn
Interviewed in Isle of Whithorn
6 September 2012

Margerie Clark
Born London, 1956
Interviewed in Whithorn
22 August 2013

Kennedy Donnan
[no photograph]
Born Glenluce
Interviewed in Glenluce
3 November 2012

Cathy Doughty
Born Whithorn area
Interviewed in Whithorn
16 June 2012

Robert Galashan
Born Perth
Interviewed in Whithorn
26 May 2013

WHITHORN: AN ECONOMY OF PEOPLE, 1920–1960

Alex Haswell
Born Whithorn
Interviewed in Whithorn
29 September 2013

Margaret (Greta) Hawthorn
Born Glasserton estate
Interviewed in Whithorn
26 June 2012

Jenny Jolly
Born Ireland
Interviewed in Whithorn
12, 19, 26 June 2012

Robin Kinnear
Born Port William
Interviewed in Port William
30 August 2012

Betty McBratney
Born Glasserton
Interviewed in Whithorn
1 June 2013

Tom McCreath
Born Broughton Mains,
near Garlieston
Interviewed in Whithorn
21 and 28 June 2012

Jessie McLean
Born Whithorn, 1918
Interviewed in Whithorn
25 June 2012

Jock McMaster
Born Port William
Interviewed in Port William
22 August 2012

Andrew McNeillie
Born North Wales
Interviewed in Wigtown
7 October 2012

Elsie McShane
Interviewed in Isle of Whithorn
31 October 2013

Cathy Miller
Born Garrarie, near
Monreith
Interviewed near Whithorn
25 September 2012

Betty Murray
[no photograph]
Born Kirkcudbright
Interviewed in Whithorn
12 September 2013

EDITORIAL NOTE

Jack Niblock
Born Isle of Whithorn
Interviewed in Isle of Whithorn
15 June 2012

Aldo Petrucci
Born Whithorn
Interviewed in Whithorn 17 May 2013

Hugh Ramsay
Born Garlieston
Interviewed in Garlieston
2 September 2013

Alastair Reid
Born Whithorn, 1926
Interviewed in Whithorn
18 June 2012

Jean Rennie
Interviewed in Kirkinner
15 October 2012

John Scoular
Born Glasserton 1932
Interviewed in Isle of Whithorn
13 June 2012

Paul Soriani
[no photograph]
Born Whithorn
Interviewed in Whithorn
23 April 2013

Tina Soriani
Born Whithorn
Interviewed in Whithorn 17 May 2013

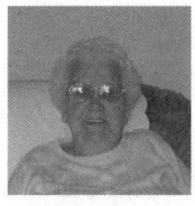

Betty Stuart
Born Whithorn, 1924
Interviewed in Whithorn 28 June 2012

Marion Sunderland
Born Isle of Whithorn
Interviewed in Isle of Whithorn
24 April 2013

John Wilson
Born Monreith village, 1938
Interviewed in Whithorn
2 July 2012

XIII

LIST OF ILLUSTRATIONS

1. Whithorn main street before the war memorial was built.
2. A view through George Street showing the Top of the Town in the distance, Whithorn.
3. No. 2 George Street, Whithorn, with gigs.
4. Miss Bie's Shop, Whithorn.
5. Drape's ironmongery and Whithorn Town House, Whithorn.
6. McKnaught's ironmongery and The Pend, Whithorn.
7. G.B. Drape's and apprentices.
8. G.B. Drape's with Billy Hawthorn.
9. Grapes Hotel with Denton's worker in foreground.
10. Miss McKelvie's Shop, Whithorn, 1890.
11. Pig killing, Green Lane, Whithorn.
12. The Windmill stump, Whithorn, c.1900.
13. George Street, with shops and carts.
14. Horse-drawn milk delivery cart, Whithorn, 1930s.
15. Wiffy Keith and the scavvy cart.
16. Kirvennie farm, near Wigtown.
17. Portyerrock Mill, near Whithorn, 1890s.
18. Three horse binder, harvesting oats, Low Clone farm, Port William, 1936/37.
19. James Milhench, smith at Clachan of Myrton.
20. Tam Buchanan
21. Groom with stallion, Sorbie, 1900s.
22. Annual Foal Show, Port William.
23. Tractor at Millisle, near Garlieston.
24. Building a hay stack, Felyennan, Mochrum, 1930s.
25. Nicholson family at Kidsdale, Whithorn, c.1875.
26. Hughan family, tenant farmers at Barledziew.
27. Hand milkers at Garlieston, 1900.
28. Stevensons at Broom Park.
29. Tattie howkers at Low Clone, Port William.

30 Hand shearing sheep, Glasserton, 1934.
31 Oat harvest tea at Torhousemuir, Wigtown, 1935.
32 Fox hunter with hounds, Whithorn, 1902.
33 The Meet, Craiglemine, 1902.
34 Dodds's cart, Whithorn, Castlehill, *c.*1900.
35 Willie McGinn's cart, Whithorn, *c.*1900.
36 Snib Scott.
37 Johnny Logie at the Hermit's Cave, Monreith.
38 English Gypsy children, encamped near Newton Stewart
39 Messenger the horse.
40 St John Street United Free Church, Whithorn.
41 Whithorn Roman Catholic Pilgrimage, 1932.
42 Brass band, outside the Free Kirk, Whithorn.

INTRODUCTION

The long strip of houses which makes up the core of Whithorn, the residence of 900 souls or so, sits towards the southernmost end of the low-lying Machars peninsula. The Gaelic word Machair, meaning 'coastal plain', hints precisely at the unremarkableness of the landscape: neither hilly nor flat, rocky yet largely without spectacular cliffs; remote in many respects, both physical and cultural, and yet without the separateness which marks off the Highlands from the rest of Scotland. Yet, even at a superficial glance, it is a place of marked contrasts: in the midst of a green sea of pasture and now intensive animal husbandry, the main street of Whithorn stands proudly Georgian and oddly urban in its intensely rural setting. Local people will swiftly correct the unwary who refer to it as a 'village', a mistake which is diagnostic of the incomer, who judges the town merely by its size and not by its pride and its history. That swift defence against outside attack is embodied by the town's internal space, firmly closed against interference or raids from elsewhere by the existence of the medieval ports at either end, which once protected the townspeople and their animals from the

1. Whithorn main street before the war memorial was built.

depredations of their neighbours. To this day, the flanking terraces of the east and west sides of the street force intimacy, even where it is not desired: there is no one who will not pass through the eye of its centre, see and be seen, at some point in the day. And largely, this intimacy is valued, desired and promoted, interwoven with the warp and weft of close family ties in a community which has not undergone the shocks of rapid change and, despite some emigration and modest immigration, remains, remarkably – and now exceptionally – slow-developing and closely interrelated.

Economic exchanges based entirely on retail, with virtually no manufacturing, are possible only because the rest of the economy begins on its outskirts: until very recently, Whithorn operated as the service centre for an intensive dairying district, an urban island in the midst of the sea of pasture, and, formerly, until recent times, impinged only on its northernmost point, where the churns were loaded onto the trains which vanished to Glasgow and the world beyond. At the period spoken of by the interviewees in this book – before the Second World War – within the town, craftworkers – blacksmiths, saddlemakers, agricultural joiners – served the agricultural economy. Farmers and farmworkers visited as part of a set pattern of time and season: ironmongery took up a disproportionate part of the windows on Whithorn's wide main street, and Saturday paydays were among the most profitable days of the week. Time certainly dominated the town, as it must, but in a circular manner, as the seasonality of ploughing, planting, snedding, shawing, harvest, and mill days imposed their specific vocabularies and technical demands on the town's rhythms, its services and people. Even today, the seasons of silaging and harvest are unavoidable in main street, as fast young men drive colossally expensive machines blazoned with such names as 'Dominator', on behalf of contractors who now serve all farms. Even today, farms are known and mentally mapped, but then the farm and person of the farmer were fused in the same name: Balnab, Bishopton (the same name, by the by, in two of the different languages of Whithorn), the Skeogs, Ersock ...

On the western side, pre-Second World War, the town doffed its cap to the Estate – not any estate, but the estate of the Laird (who is still known as such) of Glasserton and Physgill, and which provided employment for those who, as gardeners, maids and other staff might have to live out of town during the week and return for an all-too-brief visit on Saturday afternoons. The accounts by interviewees who were lady's maids and cooks in the big houses are the only hints of the heights of a social pyramid which in the town itself remained, and remain, relatively gentle.

Despite a complex topography and a hierarchy of places within the town, despite the keenly felt differences between local and incomer, and between marginal and key players, and despite and allowing for the possibility of disputes and arguments which rage with a unique intensity within the confines of its streets, Whithorn natives and even mere residents continue to acknowledge a common bond from their simply living there, which elevates its citizenship beyond a mere geographical residency to a sense of identity and belonging. When encountering each other outside in the wider world, burgesses – even those at odds with each other – will recognise each other as such, with a joyful acknowledgement of a common origin and bond of knowledge or at least with a sense of obligation that they ought so to do. As in a large family, all its members are acknowledged simply for that membership. Whithorn is more than a point on a map, a commuter base, or a mathematically calculable and infinitesimal part of the national economy; it is an identity and a badge of origin.

It is that sense of belonging, of being centred on itself, which underpins a deeper contrast: the way Whithorn perceives itself and the way the world perceives it, or indeed in large part rather fails to, an omission which simply convicts it of that otherness which, in the Whithorn view of things, is its main defect. As Alastair Reid says in his interview, 'It is not an ambitious place, but a place which is quite happy just being itself'. One has, however, to pay attention to which world one is referring to: in the annals of history and archaeology, and in the appreciation of connoisseurs, Whithorn has a high status, entirely justifying, but not surprising, its own people. As the place where, on the shores of Scotland, Christian ideas and practices first gave birth to literacy, bilingualism, trade in goods and ideas from the eastern Mediterranean, it is the place which gave a taste of, and for, the exotic in fifth-century North Britain. It is also a place which, showing early evidence of social hierarchy and ruling elites, and the consumption of luxury goods, kick-started the process of urbanisation, which has now so completely suffered an amnesia of its origins. Yet, ask a neighbouring resident of less privileged settlements at Wigtown or Newton Stewart, and you will find that Whithorn is a place beyond the pale, a place of ruffians and feuds, entirely undeserving of that historical reputation which has somehow been misplaced and ascribed to Whithorn.

The Whithorn described in the interviews, then, can be viewed as a space and a time made possible by a particular set of events; a socio-economic climate inherited from the pioneering urbanisers of its earliest history, and the later, gentler history of Whithorn as an agricultural centre. The combination of the two has made it both urban and extremely rural, protected within and yet open to the countryside and its seasons, intensely aware of its status and yet largely forgotten except by its aficionados. Yet, as the interviews progressed, it was clear that locating Whithorn in a socio-economic context was far too simple a way of accounting for the existence of its world.

As the contrasts between the exceptional and the unexceptional, the urban and the rural, the outside view and the inside, between the cognoscenti and the ignoranti deepen and conflict as they are probed further, this becomes a place which piques further enquiry. In particular, what seems worthy of investigation is that a generation of writers, more or less contemporary, who were born in the

Machars post-First World War, coincide – despite their differences – in understanding that they 'belonged', were part of that inside world, appreciating it most keenly when they were forced to leave it. Alastair Reid, John McNeillie (Ian Niall) and Gavin Maxwell all spent their early childhood in the Machars and all left it more or less traumatically – following their parents' careers or going to school. All three writers homed obsessively and ultimately creatively, in and through works which become more or less explicitly autobiographies of childhood. These were autobiographies set in a particular time and space and in which time and space, absence and return, belonging and not being at home, become conscious themes – meditations on and of locality, of localness and its possibility and its loss.

It was, fittingly, on one of his annual homecomings to Whithorn, that I was able to interview Alastair Reid, whose own work revolves around questions of foreign and native, outside-in and inside-out, near and far and whereabouts, and whose poem about his home at the Whithorn Manse is written from and about the view from outside in. His poem names the 'Eden' of his Whithorn childhood, and in his interview he speaks of the sense of loss as he moved, inevitably, away. Two other homes of the Machars (the House of Elrig and North Clutag), not far away, are celebrated, respectively, by Gavin Maxwell and John McNeillie, as the home which they never recover and always aspire to; to which they are, in the words of Andrew McNeillie, son of John McNeillie in his interview, 'always homing and increasingly reluctant to return'. Was this Machars literature of childhood, homecoming, and the parallel and uneasy reflections about not being at home, a chance coalescence, or did the time and space of the Machars, of Whithorn, pre-Second World War, offer a particular timeliness and place for dwelling, for being at home, which stimulated, or liberated, that poetry and writing once it was lost? And is the expression of loss simply a nostalgia, a longing for return, by romantics alienated by the march of progress?

The interview with Alastair Reid, and another with Andrew McNeillie about his father, explore the linked themes of speed, money, communication, and particularly the way in which their intensification – the speeding up of transport, the monetisation of labour, the instantaneous connection with others – mark the advent of modernity and define what we now call popularly globalisation and the digital world. Underlying this speed – its possibility and its dominance – is the infinite reach of calculation and enumeration which permits us to extend and dominate our world, but also, the writers argue, fundamentally changes our way of being in it. The question is then, how can an apparently merely quantitative increase – a mere speeding up – result in a qualitative change? How can, for instance, the speed with which we pass through a place change what we are able to see within it and, more fundamentally, our way of being in place at all? Further, were the meditations of the writers about the gains and losses represented by the advent of technology borne out by those who spoke in the interviews, who worked in that economy, lived in and thereby created that social space?

As the interviews progressed, they revealed how Whithorn had – at a certain time – preserved a small horizon, on which apparently insignificant things (the world of Whithorn itself) become visible and significant, and how its locality resisted and delayed (for a time) full exposure to the reach of vast horizons on which it becomes invisible. That resistance made possible the self-contained nature of Whithorn's world, a centredness which is alluded to by Alastair Reid and Ian Niall – and which made the Machars a centre of gravity which drew them back, which was sought and not found elsewhere. It was one which, both concluded, was being lost in the Machars too, as these small worlds were destabilised and effaced by the reach of remote systems.

For the purposes of investigating these themes, Whithorn seemed, physically and historically, especially to embody themes of enclosure and protection against outside forces: while other areas felt the full impact of industrialisation, Galloway, beneath the folds of the Southern Uplands, failed to develop. Brave efforts at a cotton manufactury on Whithorn's Ket Burn in the eighteenth century failed to replace the activity and the bustle which medieval King's Road had felt in quite different times, with quite different priorities. The fifth-century carver of the enormously important Latinus stone, I reflected, had described it, or perhaps predicted it, well: Barrovados, their kinsman, here [in Whithorn] made this 'sinum', which is variously translated in the *First Whithorn Lecture by Charles Thomas: Whithorn's Christian Beginnings*, published by The Friends of the Whithorn Trust 1992 as 'fold', or 'bight' or even 'sanctuary'. The word 'fold' describes both a protected space and a fold which causes a deviation from a straight line, like a fold in fabric. Whithorn's lack of industrial development does indeed seem something like a sanctuary, an exception or a respite from the forward march of industrialisation which affected other areas of the country from the late eighteenth century onwards; yet its particular conditions created something unique, which we should no longer describe in negative terms as a "lack" of development. The sparse population, while insufficient to drive those mills, actually permitted a gain in terms of proximity and human contact; the lack of a pure money economy permitted a different exchange, which was carried out through personal credit and a balance of favours, which still – exceptionally – continues today. The agricultural economy, supplying the liquid milk for those faraway cities, permitted a sort of timeless or rather an extraordinarily slow pace in those years before the Second World War. That circular and seasonal world was not, and could not be, immune to technological reach forever – which has now expanded our horizons to give us the modern world – but, for a time, it delayed its complete dominance, held it at bay. It created a haven or a fold, which is the small world described in the following interviews.

The positive possibility of a self-contained world like Whithorn, the space and time in which it was able to flourish, seemed to rest on a series of linked absences: people and places were not instantly connected, time and speed were not calculated in nanoseconds, and the economy had not emerged in its naked cash form. As compared with the world of virtual reality, Whithorn's world and economy is solidly weighted down by physicality, and the contrasts between being here or there, up or down, in or out are clearly differentiated and patiently spaced by that solid and obstinate physicality. What the interviews reveal is that the world of Whithorn existed within a mapping of differences and distances between here and there, inside and outside, and up and down, as measured by foot, eye and horse, and which permit a certain logic of contrasts to flourish. These paired contrasts have therefore dictated the organisation of material in this book.

As I probed the interviewees, who came from a variety of backgrounds and origins, both within the town and just outside its borders, they added detail which supported the views of the writers on what contributed to the stability, the apparent unchangingness, the intimacy, which was lost outside the town's defensive walls. I asked them what processes of attrition or faster and more traumatic change impinged on that unique world to alter it over time. By contrast with the limitless horizon which defines our modern globalised world – a horizon so vast that the individual is reduced to the infinitesimal – the world of the interviewees, whose memories extended from the 1920s to the present, is one where the slowness of pace, the resistance to the intrusion of the external, both allows and respects a solid presence of the physical and individual. This resistance being evident in communications, in travel, in the sheer cheek-by-jowl existence of people with each other and with the pace of their animals. The result is a face-to-face economy, which also shapes language – where names are good for credit, and landmarks identified through people who occupy, or occupied them. Both Alastair Reid and Andrew McNeillie recognise that access to this privileged world is through a language of individuality, which is not universally available and therefore which can be used as a password, denied to others from that wider world (as when Alastair Reid comments on the use of local names impenetrable to users of the world wide web) or as a key to gain access (as when Andrew McNeillie claims the power of using a familiar and recognisable name) to that local world. Whithorn's world resists, for a time, a process of anonymisation which deprives us of the local and the locality.

The interviewees not only describe their world, but speculate about it from a position of reflection where, even to them, it is no longer present. They are also themselves – by this time – outsiders, and I was intrigued that the interviewees echoed the strange dialectic expressed by the writers, who explore (both in interview and across an entire corpus of writing), the way in which as, though there is a gain through technological dominance, there is simultaneously a loss. In effect, the arrival of technology, inevitable though it may be, represents a qualititative change in the way we are. Yet it can only be a qualitative change because we are unable to reconcile this double entry of gain and loss. The writers, in their regrets, express a logic where gain is simultaneously countered by loss. Whereby the more progress, the more speed, the greater the gain, the overcoming of exteriority, then the less proximity, the less dwelling, and the more we are neither here nor there. Some might judge that the writers' meditations or the ethnologist's recordings – indeed the fundamental need to record at all – are merely a form of nostalgic romanticism, and yet throughout the interviews, this asymmetrical logic was in operation. A logic which accepts both the inevitability and desirability of technological progress with the simultaneous regret for the receding of (another) proximity. When questioned about the way in which the world they remembered has passed and how they assessed gain and loss, most interviewees were quick to agree the progress which came with, and as, the impact of a wider world – the huge gains in overcoming poverty, poor health, draughty housing conditions and sheer hard labour – '*and yet*' ...' There always came an '*and yet*' and a regret for the loss of a closeness which is not the same as instantaneous connectedness and which is inconsistent with that complete conquest: with all that immense gain, there seemed to come, at the very same time, a parallel and non-compensating loss, which, if we accept the logic of technology as it would have us do, should not have been possible. If progress proceeded in a simple overcoming of negatives, moving in a straight line towards its goal, there should have been no loss as technological mastery moves towards its end. Ian Niall's works, and his son Andrew's commentary on them, span this contradiction: on the one hand, the *Wigtownshire Ploughman* exposes the conditions of rural poverty, which can only be and must be overcome, and acts as impetus for change; *and yet*, the author in his later books gives utterance again and again to regret for the world which had been lost through the liberation of those forces for progress.

If we believed wholly in the march of technology and its definition of progress, there would be no room for regretting the effacement of worlds like Whithorn's. According to that logic, as we progress in our technological dominance, we should not be simultaneously losing something, measured on another and different scale. Regret and nostalgia should be illogical, written off in a final reconciliation in which the past has been merely an inferior version of the future. Yet, a place like Whithorn offers an obstinate counterexample to the logic of progress and our nostalgia for it cannot be written off as 'mere' romanticism. It is our sense of loss as such things and places vanish which opens up access to a world of other proximities and its different response to time. Technology (for instance, what Alastair Reid refers to as the improvement in domestic technology) exists as a particular response to time: it is always attempting to gain time, to economise, make economies or catch up on it. That that is not the only possible response to temporality is the inconvenient witness of Whithorn's patient economy. The increasing speed of technology – and technology is precisely increasing speed – is not merely quantitative increase or addition, which would permit it to gain in one direction only and would not allow us room for and justification for regret, reminiscence and recording. As the world of the physical – which implies the possibility of physical labour – retreats, it is possible and necessary to regret and mark its loss and its difference, which is the task and justification of recording and memory.

While the logic of our globalised world, with its infinite calculability and therefore its infinite possibilities of mastery, posits and predicts the overcoming of time and space, the small world of Whithorn exists only where limits are not denied but accepted, where time and space are overcome, but slowly, in a way which demands and permits the existence of the world of physical labour, the length of the day, the patience of the growing season and the distance of travel. This is a world where the requirement for the effort of the physical, locates and localises us in time and space. It is this reality which permits the emergence of an economy of people, an economy based on the talent and effort of hand, eye and foot, against the obstinacy of the land and the timing of the seasons. It is also the stimulus to an economy of economies, where the response to time and otherness is quite different: where labour weaves and stimulates strategems for deferring the arrival of that other economy which threatens it and will render it obsolete.

Economists and social scientists too study the themes of speed, time and money and may link particular phases of development (the world of physical labour and the agricultural economy) with the existence of a large population, intimately connected by proximity and family ties. Economists might describe this surplus of population, this populousness, as exerting downward pressure on wages and as holding back capitalisation of agriculture. However, that description of population and poverty as mere negatives does nothing to account for how, in the interval while technological mastery is delayed, there is, in its place, an economy based on family and familiarity – a different organisation of self and other, inside and outside. It was clear that some of that Edenic sense of security resulted from the face-to-face economy of Whithorn, in which personal acquaintance and a web of family relationships substituted for or overrode the raw arithmetic of retail, and in which money rarely, or at least slowly, changed hands. Alastair Reid's interview began with the moment of the Fall, when he asked his father what money was, simply because he had rarely seen it exchange hands, and he recollects how all shops extended credit and sent out bills once a month, or, as Robin Kinnear recalls in his account of the working of his father's drapery business, even less frequently. All this was possible because of the knownness of names.

As it emerged from the interviews, the delaying of the monetarised economy in its most naked form entailed the development of strategies of sparing and thrift, skills and perspectives which had their own timetable. This temporality of what we often call poverty operates on a completely different level from the folk wisdom which states that 'necessity is the mother of invention'.

Poverty and low wages are merely economic facts. The statistics which partially describe these aspects of being conceal and deny the creative act by which, for instance, the economy of poaching incorporates the countryside into the household budget and changes the relation between outside and in. How it transforms the use of the late nights and early mornings, the judgement of what is edible and what is not, the cuisine, the functionality of clothing, the understanding of animal life and habits, the sizing up of favourable and unfavourable weather, the skill with a gun and the charitable giving to neighbours who did not have such skill. The timeline of transforming objects in order to prolong their usefulness – which we would now call recycling, upcycling and repurposing – is a different one from the timeline of purchase and its skills and fabrics are entirely different. The timetable of poverty, or the non-monetarised economy, or rural life, transforms the margins of the day, the familial relations of old and young, the edges of the field and the gardens in the town, the patterns of work and leisure, the understanding of gifts and giving, and the proximity and distance of others.

Where benefits derived from technological mastery remain merely on a distant horizon, the economy necessarily requires the endeavours of those individuals who make up a community. This economy of people has its time of flourishing. The necessity of all pairs of hands, highly valuable and yet not valued, fills the farm cottages, the remote schoolhouses, the manifold churches, creates the anticipation of thronged picnic parties, and modulates the distance between life and death with a different understanding of dispensability and indispensability. This is an economy of people which works thanks to their being within a locality, within the call of a name, and which is what we would call, by abbreviation, 'rural society', or 'the countryside', which was once the pattern for

2. A view through George Street showing the Top of the Town in the distance, Whithorn.

social existence in general. These people make economies in a dual sense: they economise by using their own resources and talents, in order to defer the impact of the pure monetary economy. In so doing, they create an economy which is uniquely based on exchanges, familial obligation, neighbourliness, and the investment of their labour. Ultimately, as we know, the possibility of resisting the impact of new and wider worlds is only temporising. It is only a matter of time before places like Whithorn are absorbed, before people are fully absorbed into a wider economy. An economy which will ultimately render them and their obstinate locality dispensable. *And yet*, we can mark its refusal to be completely absorbed, the failure of its complete mastery and effacement, by responding to an obligation to remember, by respecting our nostalgia, by recording that other economy and marking the loss of its world as one which is not merely a defective forerunner of our own.

I

Leaving and Returning: Nostalgia of the Writers

The interviews with Alastair Reid and Andrew McNeillie, the latter describing his father's – John McNeillie (Ian Niall's) – relationship with the Machars, develop the complex interrelated themes of money, speed of communications, and time, and how the vast horizons which threaten to efface the worlds of Whithorn and the Machars, centred on themselves, were held at bay, at least for a while.

Time and Money I: Eden and the Fall

The defining moment in Alastair Reid's interview about the Eden of his childhood is the discovery of money, and the very fact that this had to be discovered demonstrated precisely that money was not all-pervasive: though he discovered it at an early age, it remained confined and curbed; its reach and therefore the reach of systems, of the outside world, was limited. His description is of a non-cash economy, only slightly threatened by his discovery of money through the display of a pound note, which is then carefully replaced, by his father, reassuringly, inside a book.

Alastair Reid

> Well, then we were only three children in the Manse, I was the third in our family and I always remember when we were, I think we had to take – we had to do church every third Sunday or something like that. We were given our pennies to put in the collection, which was the first time I had ever handled money in my life, and the extraordinary memory I have is about money in particular. My father never carried money and I remember that we had an account at the big Denton's, the bakers on the corner, and Charlie Coid in the butcher's shop which had the first elegant façade when he put these tiles above it.
>
> And that thing about money, for instance, I remember the first time I became conscious of money was when we, when I went to Whithorn School

and we had a lesson in money and I came home and I told my parents, 'We've had this exciting– do you know about money?' And they looked, and I remember going to my father once and saying to my father, 'What is a pound? We hear about a pound in school and it's 20 shillings and all the rest of it, but I've never seen a pound. What is a pound?' and he went to his library then, took down an 'Everyman' book, I remember it well, and he opened it and he had a crisp pound note in it and he showed me the pound note and I looked at it on both sides, and then he brought me a pencil and paper and I drew the pound and the figures in it and so on where it said 'a pound' and when I, and then I turned it over and drew the back and gave it back to him and he took it carefully and put it back in the book and back on the shelf.

And I remember that my father never carried money and I think that what happened was we would have an account with Denton's, the bakers, and the Martin's and the butcher and grocer and he would go to the bank and take out enough money once a month and pay the – my mother used to say to me, 'Go down to Denton's and ask them for a pan loaf' and I would go and I'd say, 'My mother wants a pan loaf' and he'd say, 'Oh yes' and he'd wrap it up and gave it to me and I took it home. And I thought that's how things worked and so on ... imagine a town like this functioning on just trust like that.

And that was a common currency then. It was very much a kind of a communal self-help in a sense and it ran like that on what we might call civic trust now, and to me the great difference between then and now is the fact that there was no domestic technology to speak of. The asset really was other people. And people helped one another and it survived like that, as indeed an agricultural community functions best in a, in conditions like that.

If you take milk, I remember always the creamery at the end of Whithorn there, and it was a delicious place to go. One of my jobs as a child when I was old enough, about four, five, was to go from the Manse across the fields, not coming through The Pend and down but go across the fields to the creamery with a little aluminium can and say, 'I've come for the milk' and they'd fill it for me and I'd walk back across and this was tremendous and of course the creameries were one by one closed down and then the milk is collected, not by the churns at the end of the road, as it was done in our day, to be collected by a great [unclear] what do you call it? A great siphon that sucks it up and beams it even across to Ireland. I remember just last week I was waiting outside Newton Stewart and truck after truck, milk-laden, was making for Stranraer and Ireland.

There was a film, there was a theatre down .... It was King's Road, that's right, and the theory was that when you, if you didn't have money you could take jam jars and pay them in jam jars. Anyway, I don't know if we ever did that but we believed it, certainly. But I don't think there were many attempts at opening new businesses here. I think they were more or less continuous and faithful.

The limits to the reach of the cash economy is linked, in Alastair Reid's interview, to the absence of fast transport, which gives us technological mastery of space, but also encloses us and cuts us off from social space where people greet each other. The limitation of this ubiquity is shown by the fact that the motorised transport was kept as an exception, sparingly, carefully conserved for future use by being stabled.

Alastair Reid

> So, and the other thing is that we had no, my father got a car, I think my mother's father was a doctor, as my mother was, died and left her some money and the first thing was that my father got a car and I do remember that vividly from my childhood when he had gone to Glasgow to get the car and he was coming back that evening and we were allowed to stay up and at a given time, long past our bedtime, the car drew up and we got, all went out and we sat in the car and looked at it; but it was one of three cars, the doctor, McWhirter, who brought us all into the world, he had a car and what was the other? There was another car that somebody had, probably Catyans the lawyer and my father's car and there were three cars in Whithorn and that was it, there weren't going to be any more.
>
> And so – but we were told – the car was something that was kept in the stable down from the Manse and we never, it never came out very, it only came out for a reason … . For a purpose.

Andrew McNeillie speaks about how an in-dwelling in space and time, permitted by the absence of technological mastery, allows for a focus and a sharpened perception. He ascribes his father's, John McNeillie's, increasing reluctance to return to the Machars, to which he yet 'homed obsessively' and believes it was due to the increasing speed which prevents such dwelling.

Andrew McNeillie

> I think that what he felt was that if human interest for him diminished as the people he loved were not there, then there was the consequent change that always comes to the countryside, and it's been coming ever since the Industrial Revolution at least, but he knew it would come but he didn't find that was particularly attractive. I don't think he was against it, I think

he was very realistic, I think he knew what farming was and that it was all hard work and, no matter what you do it's always going to be hard work, and no matter what machines you bring to bear it's always going to be hard work. So I'm not sure it was that change, that made him less inclined to come but I do think it– there's a letter he wrote to somebody, was it Jean McShane or somebody, that's been discovered where he talks about the speed with which we drive through a place. So we drive through Barrachan which people once idled through with a horse and cart, going to get peat or something, and the difference was massive for him in that sense and I think that he knew that speed and movement to which we're all attracted reduces the possibilities for attention, for seeing. And that's the thing, if you have to do the things by foot or by horseback or horse-drawn-ness you go at a pace where you actually see things, you dwell more, time passes more slowly and I still think, I'm sure that's what he was on about, that speed was something that drastically changed the nature of being. And not for the good in the sense of being and dwelling in the Heideggerian sense of knowing a place, I think he – or a Thoreauvian one, I think he knew that, I think that mattered to him and that's how he could spend so many hours fishing in the wildest places.

It didn't matter but that to him was a kind of gravitational settling of himself, again, and he knew that you just endure and the more you endure the more you register, the more attention you pay, inadvertently, to where you are and I think his writings show that inadvertently he showed extraordinary attention. It's quite breathtaking what he could remember, what he saw, how he could represent it, how in *The Resting Place*, for example, how extraordinary, extraordinary, his representation of travelling people and their culture and their way of life, I don't know if it's called a culture. Their way of life and their way of being, their way of speech. How did he know that, how did he pick that up? But he got it and I think it was a function of the fact that he lived in slower times and that he found faster times more alarming because they stop you dwelling. Now, he wasn't against speed, he nearly killed himself in a road accident once, he was always quite happy with fast cars and he was, he wasn't in any way precious or idealistic about all this but I think he knew the hard reality of change and in *To Speed the Plough*, at the end, I don't think he works hard enough to speak to how some things can be and should be resisted, but he was doing that for money, he did what he did.

Alastair Reid explains how not knowing the wider world was not an ignorance, but that it permitted a positive intimacy, which is not simply expanded on a wider scale when that contact does come, but lost – meaning in fact that the condition of a certain intimacy is that absence of connectedness, and that connectedness in its absolute, naked form, such as we now are approaching, with its absolute indifference to and mastery of time and space, is absence of connection.

Alastair Reid

> We knew a lot about the locality but we knew nothing about the outside world at all, nor were we, nor was there any curiosity about it at all, it was just the kind of– local society functioned as we understood it and it ran along these lines. I don't know what general gathering of information was then but it was fairly sparse. You knew your locality well and it didn't change, people didn't come in or didn't leave and of course all that was going to change with the mechanisation of agriculture, tremendously, which meant– the population was shrivelling and Whithorn now, I've no comprehension at all of what all the people in these houses do.
>
> And so it's a– to that extent it feels to me now, coming back, as a very left behind place that doesn't have the kind of intimacy that it had then. The fact that we used to know the names of all the people and when we, and people would greet you– because they knew you and so on. And of course there was no corresponding development within the locality in terms of employment or prosperity or anything like that and it must have become more isolated as time passed whereas it had tremendous functionality then, in these days. And that's why you wonder about. I think that it feels like a place that's been left behind in time, to me, very much. And the cars don't make a difference, the cars mean that we're more connected but mainly they're more connected for reasons of shopping and getting to other places but we counted then very much on buses and bus services. When we went to Newton Stewart we always got the bus and the buses were very efficient then. And so that was my first– and what I realise now, looking back on it, was that on leaving Whithorn was my first experience of loss in life. And in a sense it was my first experience of time because the time here seemed eternal; it was just seasonal, we knew that things would change, the food would change with the seasons, so would everything else but change was calculated in expecting and well known and then to suddenly to, that was a continuum that didn't vary and of course we were not subject to the outside world very much.

In the cases of all three Machars writers, Alastair Reid, John McNeillie and Gavin Maxwell, the sense of loss was precipitated by a traumatic and unexpected departure – respectively, to the Borders, to Glasgow and parents, and to boarding school and away from Elrig.

According to Reid, to Andrew McNeillie commenting on his sense of being at home in the Machars, and to Maxwell in *The House of Elrig*, the sense of loss is

3. No.2 George Street, Whithorn, with gigs.

connected with the intrusion of the outside, the wider world and with its anonymisation. For McNeillie and his father too, the gravitational pull of the Machars and its sense of belonging is associated with naming.

Alastair Reid

And I had a very staunch relationship with a wonderful woman called Mrs Muir, Mrs James Muir, who lived in 26 George Street, across the street, next to Alves who had the jeweller's shop. And she looked after us and I was very devoted to her because she told us endless stories and I loved her and I, when my father came and told us, when I was six, that we were leaving Whithorn, I was heartbroken.

And I pleaded with him not to go and he said, 'No, but it's not like that'. And I couldn't be comforted and he said, 'Well, you know, you can always come back here' and I held him to that, constantly, and so they allowed me to come back in summer when we were out of school and I would stay with Mrs Muir. And she told me all these extraordinary stories, she used to get a newspaper from Christie's, up there, and she would read me the newspaper and tell me – and her version of the stories in the paper. And she was an endless source of – she remains one of the most vivid people from my childhood altogether. And she had an extraordinary house there that had one of these long backs and the garden going right, quite a way back and she had, in the outhouses, she had a hayloft and a stable which must have been very useful before that generation. And it was a magical playground for me then, so I came back alone, I was allowed–

this was my deal, my part of the deal, that I could come back and I would spend a month with Mrs Muir in the summer and we'd go to the beach, to Monreith occasionally and I loved that house and I have the fondest memories of that time. I went back once to the house and it was all there. I haven't dared to go this time but I don't know who lives in it now but.

I'm trying to think what number 26 is.

26, it's just two doors down from what used to be the Alves, the jeweller, and he was an optician, I think, at the same time. And so that was my, I think my memories came from these returns more than from my beginnings.

…

That's why I find very offensive here, when we come back now and we get the newspaper every day, it's terrifying to read *The Guardian* in the morning now. And it intrudes in a way in which it never previously intruded. But going on from there, I came back in– it must have been in the '30s in '32, '33, '34 when I was about eight, nine and ten when I would spend the month with Mrs Muir and go back into this world that I knew much better. I didn't like, at all, the move. My father had moved to a charge in Selkirk, in the Borders, and I didn't take to Selkirk. I instinctively disliked it from the beginning because it wasn't like Whithorn. And people were very grumbly and the Borders are really a nasty part of Scotland where all the Border towns hate one another. And this entirely put me off so I longed to get back to Whithorn then and did.

…

If you can remember the shops, a lot comes back through that because they're common currency. Everybody knows who ran them and so on. I remember John J. Colquhoun very well, who signed my birth certificate, the father of Marjie Colquhoun, and he was quite a figure but he had an extraordinary face, he looked like a hawk and it was Mrs Muir who said she was a cousin of his for some reason and she thought he was so pompous and she mocked him all the time and she said, 'He looks – have you ever thought of it, he looks like a bald eagle' and he was known as 'the bald eagle' for, because of that. And people had nicknames too, which was a very common local fondness because the nickname was a kind of endearing characterisation of them.

Alistair Reid's description of the Whithorn system of naming seems to go back to the very origins of naming in descriptions and identifiable individuals, just as in the past, the Gaelic speakers of the Machars defined place names with reference to topographical features ('ridge of the pigs', 'fair fields' 'pool of the oaks') and personal names. Houses in Whithorn remain attached to their occupants long after they have died, and married women are often still known by their maiden names, so that the family pedigree remains visible.

Alastair Reid

> And I can remember washing day was boiling water and doing the sheets in a big thing, stirring it with a paddle. We had a Mrs Jones who came to do the washing and she used to have wrinkled fingers from … and they were known as 'Mrs Jones' fingers' and everything had a kind of local, the vocabulary was entirely local and what did we think of the outside world? Well, we knew Newton Stewart because I had great friendships with, well, we knew– the farmers were always known by their farm. I remember the– not the names of the farmers but they were referred to by their farms. 'Oh, Broughton Mains is coming for supper' and things like that.
> …
> The farms really were the essence of the Machars because they had, the people were the farmers, for instance Harry McCreath was known as 'Broughton Mains', and 'Arbrack', I can't remember the farmer's name now, but he was know as Arbrack. And, as a matter of fact, one thing I do to, I always give thanks to this day because whenever I have to do a password on the computer I always use the names of the farms in Galloway (laughs), which means my record on the computer is impenetrable to other people. […] is one of my favourite passwords.

The Whithorn accent was also domestic in nature.

Alastair Reid

> … it was very, it had a good part of the Ulster accent in it and. But it was a very, it had, it had a lot of diminutives in it and it was a very kind of endearing accent, very much a domestic accent, the kind of accent used to talk to children and small animals with and so on. It was a lovely voice he had. I doubt, I don't think I've encountered anybody, latterly, that still has it in that pure.

Andrew McNeillie describes the break with childhood and the pain of leaving, when his father was taken away from North Clutag and his grandparents to London and his real parents. The return to the Machars was eventually made obsessively and, at length, exclusively, in writing.

Andrew McNeillie

> And I think it's proven and well established in human psychology that these kinds of strange disturbance reach much further than we assume they do and that children are not resilient, that they do register damage by

change and adjustment and I do think my father was, in lots of ways, a deeply damaged man.

By the time I was ten she [John McNeillie's mother] had died, and she was a strong and sort of vulnerable woman who had many, quite a few children, one at least of whom died. That was my father's immediate young sister who died of– well it's said that she had sleeping sickness, they said that she had something called sleeping sickness and one never knows quite what that would have been. Anyway, there was an anxiety about it and that was what led my grandparents to decide to send my father down to the Machars to be brought up, initially, by his grandparents at North Clutag where he went at about the age of three. He always said that he was there really, really earlier but I think the facts show that he went there about the age of three and that by the age of eight he was back in Dalmuir so he had this five-year-period and there were family visits down, but there was some confusion, for him, as to who were his parents and he assumed as he moved down at that age, that his grandparents were his parents and that his grandfather was his father and there's a famous story within the family that my grandfather went down to see him and my father said to his grandfather, 'Why is this man down here, who is this person?' which so upset my grandfather that he made arrangements for him to come back to Glasgow.

He was taken up, without much understanding, back home by his grandfather who he thought was his father and he stood there in the flat, in Dalmuir, and was said to have said, 'When are we going home?' and he was told then that this was home whereof his father, his assumed surrogate father, went leaving him there in a family that had grown in his absence and a family he knew nothing about, anyway, and I think that psychologically this was the great trigger in affecting him. He was a difficult human being, amazingly complicated anxieties about territoriality within himself and otherwise and I think this, I'm sure he might have been a writer anyway, but I think that this drove him and made him the kind of very unusual person he was.

But I think there was a sense, perhaps, certainly, I think, in the family that there was somebody before my father, otherwise there was no one before my father who ever thought of writing. There were before him people who told stories and this was the world of his great-grandfather who was in many ways an old style storyteller who would sit up late over a dram by the fire at North Clutag and talk, tell stories that my father listened to avidly and consumed and he was conditioned, not perhaps not by the contents of the stories as much as by the fact of telling, the fact of the oral way of being and he was to live with, you see, the thing about him was he talked endlessly all the time, it's hard to understand how a highly intelligent man could do this, all the time, obsessively about his childhood. And he would begin many an account and we would be sitting anywhere we might be, saying, 'Grandfather used to say' and off he'd go on one of these things that would be some version of his childhood or some version of what old John McNeillie said– so we grew up, I grew up, although I was born in North Wales and spent the first 20 years of my life there, in a huge dimension, some other order, I lived in the Machars of Wigtownshire. And I lived there with the passion and a longing and when I went there. I remember at the age of eight being very cross with my father for not arranging for me to be born there. And knowing that there was something wrong in this, that I wasn't born there and it always – strangely now I'm, I still feel the wound of [unclear], when I come here, of it being my country, but I don't really. I don't belong here, it's still a wound, that is absurd but the absurdity is part of the strange intensity of the way my father spoke about that world to us continuously. It was never far from what he would speak about.

As with Alastair Reid, the recognition which comes with being named is part of what Andrew McNeillie associates with homecoming and being at home.

Andrew McNeillie

I think somebody asked me, it wasn't you, and it was Sally Harrod[?] from the National Library of Scotland said, do I feel particularly Scottish now that I'm up here? And I said, 'No, I don't'. I used to and I used to feel very worried about it but actually what I feel is particularly Machars. I feel because I simply know people here. I have more relations here, living, than anywhere else, and when I come they treat me so warmly, they welcome me, they're very pleased to see me and they're also proud of me.

So I feel that I belong significantly here in a way that in Wales, apart from my brother who was born and who lives ... we were both and my sister were born in North Wales, he lives there still, apart from going there, I don't know people in Wales in the way people here know me. And people in Wales don't know me, apart from the fact that I have some small reputation, a writer of Welsh-related poems, so if I consider where I belong, I belong here, though I wasn't born here, and though I cannot claim to have those things that you need on order to say you belong somewhere, in terms of factual information as to where you were born, birth certificates and the like, but it still a horrible wound for me, this place.

I think I would get away with it because my name, my name covers a lot of ground and I know that if I book up to go and stay with Alastair, in The Steam Packet, I know that I'm going to be alright. The name McNeillie works if that matters, well, it does matter to somebody like me. And it's strange, I keep wanting to re-examine it and I do re-examine it, what does this mean psychologically, what did it mean for my father? It was a tremendous thing for him— as you see a beautiful day today, beautiful day and the Machars are just magical, that was what he saw as a child and it was sort of like in a Wordsworthian way written across him, it was written into him. And he did find it disturbing as change took over, and there was a galloping kind of speed to things that I think there wasn't then, you see, there was no communications, talk about our age of global networks and information, our informational age, in those days there was only one information system and that was word of mouth and telling stories and asking, 'What's the news?' and the news would be very small, very little news. And he knew that world, he used to say to me, I remember one of— when he was very, very old and he was more or less out of it, he used to sometimes rouse himself and say to me, 'I belonged' and I always used to feel, and he used to say things like that often, what he meant was that he believed, for a time in his life, he belonged somewhere where there was a network of people that wherever you went and whoever you were and whatever you did they knew who you were, and you were of it and for some reason that mattered and I think that's what. And also I think he used to do it to hurt us, too, because we didn't. Because he was quite a cruel man, he was quite a hard man, could be cruel in a way that intellectual people can be cruel, hard on something.

So somehow he wrote me into him or him into me and I'm very pleased that he did. It made, it's very interesting that he did and it's very interesting that that was the way I was cast because my brother, very sensibly, very fed up with this kind of stuff, especially the fishing trips which sometimes were extremely hard to bear physically because we fished in the remotest places that took ages to get to on foot and ages to get back from and it would often be very bad weather and that didn't count, cold bitter rain in north eastern Snowdonia. My father seemed impervious to weather.

For all three writers, the trauma of the break with the Machars was a creative one – resulted in a life of creativity, which drew obsessively on an inner Wordsworthian reserve of themes of and from childhood, triggering a meditation on the theme of being at home and the unease of not at home.

Andrew McNeillie

I think what showed that he was weirdly wired and this writing thing that he had, literally he never— there was almost no material supporting what he tried to write, no manuscripts, he just wrote on the typewriter like this, so a thing like *Poacher's Handbook* which is a minor classic, he never changed anything in it and he never altered between his head and the typewriter, he just did it.

And endlessly homing back here and increasingly reluctant to come here which I now find hard to accept, I find lots of things hard to accept and I do wish he could have just come back. But he couldn't and he found that things that mattered to him in the end were his great-aunts, my, his aunts, my great-aunts, Mary and Ellen ... and Mary and Ellen were like, they were like mothers to him because he had two mothers and he had his granny, Grandmother McNeillie, so he had, he had a world that really was deeply important to him and when they – those two old aunts – eventually died he didn't feel that he needed to come any more. He went to their funerals, at the one of them, at the last of them, I think, he went off the North Clutag and took a little sample in an envelope, of soil, which I have, from North Clutag which I have got in a glass phial and he wrote the date of it on the envelope so just going back to get the feel of the place, to get the earth of the place, was very important to him.

...

And what he could do was very exceptional at its best and he could do it, turning a tap on in his head, the words came out and that was that and then he switched the tap off. And the next day he got up and was ready again to turn the tap on. And he would say, 'I don't know what I've written' he would get in a trance of invention and then he would say, 'Well, I have to read it to know what I've written' and that would sound like an affectation but it wasn't, it was actually the way it was with him, he was weirdly wired, he just: the words sorted themselves out.

He had no interest, very little interest in social life, in other people, couldn't be bothered. He was obsessed by what he was obsessed by.

John McNeillie's early returns to the Machars were fraught, having exposed that intimacy which he most valued to the world in his first and controversial novel, *Wigtown Ploughman*. The book was both revered for its stark portrait of rural life and brutality, and reviled for having betrayed the Machars to the wider world.

Andrew McNeillie

He was not like a Zola or a Steinbeck, campaigning, he didn't research to write his novel, he just happened to hit upon something that he knew about. And he also thought that he would tell it as it is, that is that he could identify the place, in very precise terms, and so I think he was shocked, probably, as well as delighted and amazed by the success of the book. People used to say here that he never dared to come back again in the wake of the novel, it's not true, he did come back and he met people, hard on its publication and was largely hugely admired by and revered by individuals. So he did come back but I think it shook him and I think he was surprised at what he had done. I don't think he really understood what he was doing in that way. And I think then he produced the novel about Glasgow, *Keelie*, the sort of gangs in Glasgow. And then *Morryharn Farm*, which I think doesn't really work and then the War really took over, there was no possibility of him writing anything. So, it's very interesting that his first novel, *No Resting Place*, afterwards, which appeared after a squabble with Putnam's who wanted him to change it and he refused to and sent it somewhere else under a pseudonym, it came out from Heinemann as by Ian Niall. It's interesting that that novel is as deeply a Machars novel as anything but you wouldn't know, unless you know, from its pages except canny people who know local names and farming practices and so on might begin to think. There's no indication in the novel. I think that's an extreme reaction to what he'd experienced and had troubled him in writing *Wigtown Ploughman* so explicitly. And my mother used to tell me that when *Poacher's Handbook*, which also gets quite, well, it does name people who were living, my mother says when that … on the eve of its coming out my father got very ill with psychosomatic troubles in his tummy and went to the doctor and had to be calmed down because he was fretful that he was going to get sued about identifying people so I just think that he wasn't a, he wasn't in the public sphere, an aggressive campaigner on this or that, he wasn't writing that kind of book, it was accidental, he did something and he didn't realise what he'd done. The beauty of it is, is that he didn't realise what he had done, or what he was doing, when he did it because I think it's probably the most interesting and the most lasting thing he's ever done, the first book, in many, many ways because of its social relevance but he didn't know what he was doing and so you could say that it was a kind of genius moment of a young, young man. That he just sold this story, had to tell it, knew what he had to tell, couldn't help himself because he just kept writing and then discovered what he'd done. So we never saw it, it is locked, it wasn't locked away, it wasn't that we weren't allowed to look at it or anything, but those books were, there were not many books in our house but they were all interesting ones. Those books, in particular, were put in a cupboard and if we had asked and persisted to look at them we could do but he just [would say], 'They're terrible'. In his view it wasn't that they were terrible because they caused an uproar, or didn't, or because the *Wigtown Ploughman* caused an uproar, I mean. They were just badly done – he thought they were badly executed.

Jean Rennie [related to the McNeillie family on her mother's side, her mother was John McNeillie's aunt] recounts the McNeillie's family's feeling when the book was published.

Jean Rennie

So tell me how the family felt about Wigtown Ploughman*?*
Oh well, some o them didn't like it.
Even in your own family?
They didn't like it. My mother was disgusted. And my auntie at Whithorn, she threw it in the fire. Very disgusted. But it was very true to life. Very true to life story, I must admit.
Is that why they were irritated, because it was kind of showing the area up?
I would think so. I would think so. But it really was a very true to life story.
And what did his grandpa think of the novel?
Not a lot, I don't think.
No?
No, I don't think so!
Did the whole family feel he'd kind of taken them by surprise?
Well, Mary and Ellen never said very much about it. No. So it was just one o those things. He wrote the book, and that was it. But he wasn't popular, you know. If they had got him they would have ham-strung him, I think! In Wigtown. They didn't like it. But it was very true to life.
So, did it take a while for the scandal surrounding Wigtown Ploughman *to die down?*
Well, it did, because it was in the *Sunday Mail*. I think it was the *Sunday Mail* it was in. And they were grasping to get the *Sunday Mail* every Sunday tae get reading it. So it kept it going on for a while. And he didnae come back for a long time after it. Didnae mix, he did come back, but he didnae mix. He never would mix an awful lot, but he mixed enough to get his gen.

Andrew McNeillie

Well, I think it did have a huge impact on the family that were here and it's a book that's a hugely intimate – in terms of place and locations and people, places where people could identify farms, dwellings and hopefully say, 'Well, actually we live here'. And characters haunt that area so intensely that you'd think this involves us, this implicates us in this story, this is our world, so there were issues and there's John McNeillie, my cousin at High Balcraig, has told me that his mother, Jean, who was a McNeillie by marriage to Jimmy McNeillie, threw the book on the fire in front of her children. So it caused a lot of it, it upset a lot of people and I have to say it still is a shocking book, the force, it is quite unbelievable really, it's quite hard to take.

There are lots and lots of examples in literary history, of books that have power from their ability to disturb the status quo or assumptions that people have. In its way, James Joyce's *Dubliners* but also *Ulysses* did with a massively disturbing piece of work and in its other, smaller way, *Wigtown*

Ploughman is a disturbing, deeply disturbing piece of work and had a kind of savagery to it that you still feel, but I think, which time will adjust. But yes, the family had to face it, and there were people who didn't know who he was, they would say, 'Who is this John McNeillie?' and they had to work that out because he wasn't living here and that was another interest, who was this person called John McNeillie who wrote about the *Wigtown Ploughman*. So my great-grandfather was immensely proud of him and constantly wanted, when it was in the heat of its moment, to be out there at the market and he would sort of talk to them and listen to them, finding out what they thought about it and feeling very proud and believing that though at first he was upset by the swearing that by the third reading he got used to it and thought it was okay and appropriate. And was constantly, in this short period, writing to his grandson saying what he'd heard about it and what people were saying about it and how the kirk was responding and how a committee had been set up to introduce reforms and how the newspapers were responding to it. So, yes, the family were deeply affected by the novel and I'm not aware of any of them disowning him, I think they were rather proud. My– I call her my cousin, she is a McNeillie, but Madge Vance, she can remember being at school and trying to write in school and being told by her teacher, 'You'll never, you'll never be like your cousin. You can't do it, you can't write' and she was very proud of that.

Ian Niall's (John McNeillie's) *A Galloway Childhood* was a second return to the Machars, in a completely different key. While the first novel, *Wigtown Ploughman*, exposes the brutality of rural life and proves to be one of the forces behind its improvement, the autobiographical novel celebrates all that will be altered by exposing it to these forces.

Andrew McNeillie

Was it attempting to redress the hurt created by his earliest novel?
It might be, I think it would be a very reasonable thing to think that might be the case but I don't think my father was like that, I don't think he was troubled unduly about *Wigtown Ploughman* apart from that, you know, that it was badly written. And I don't think he had a conscious or conscious conscience of that kind, I don't think he really was that way troubled knowingly and insofar as he had been he got through that quite early and he obviously was troubled by the extraordinary reaction because it, it was, if you imagine it today, it would be tweeted all over the world, it would be here, there and everywhere, it was a major thing. It was bad enough, I think it shook him but no, I don't think he was a compensatory writer in that way, I didn't think that he felt he had to make amends for anything but I

think he was always concerned to tell the story of that time of his childhood, which *Wigtown Ploughman* never set out to be the account of his childhood, as it seemed to him, as it pleased him, in a celebratory way rather than a critical way and so the *Galloway Childhood* is, I don't think is any kind of reflex or delayed reflex action to *Wigtown Ploughman* at all. I think it is part of the way— it certainly is an expression of the way he changed in himself and how always late in his association with that time and the place and then the giant mood of his sense of loss, which he came to the point when he could do it.

Alastair Reid recounts his return during the Second World War, to a place which still resisted the outside world and the exposure to a temporality which is calculable without reference to seasons and familiar routines of the farming year.

Alastair Reid

I remember once I went into the, into the Navy and I was on a, stationed on a frigate in Liverpool and, in '43, and I had a leave of about four days and, instead of wending my way home, I came up and stayed in, and got to Whithorn and I remember having a meal at The Grapes Hotel which was still open then, where I ate a meal that I'll never forget in my life, all the things we couldn't get outside, they were there. And Whithorn really came to life in the War in a curious way like that and it's never left my memory as a kind of idealised landscape and the mode of setting the year according to the agricultural round. You— summer was glorious, the harvest, you looked at the sky a lot and calculated the harvest and thanksgivings and so on and … there was always a— the time here was agricultural time which is entirely set by the progression of seasons, which is a way of life that has never left me and I've always sought out places that still l live by the agricultural round because it gives a far greater sense of reality to the passing of time if it has a substantial realisation in what's happening at your feet and around you all the time. Just as it is this spring, like today, for instance, it's an extraordinary day and the weather has a great effect on you all the time, you're aware of what's happening and you look at the sky a great deal, we still do.
…
So it was all very, very much, it was a town that, without any fears to it, childhood had no ghosts or fearful events or evil manifestations. It was almost an ideal society and it still remains, in a curious way, the ideal kind of equilibrium with work and survival and so on.
…
So these are the things that lodged deeply in me. They're really rhythms of life more than anything and I never lost these rhythms and even today

when I have— I divide my life between being in New York sometimes and being in centres of civilisation— and looking out from villages which are at the opposite end of that, which still go by the agricultural round. And the more, this summer has been, this spring has been very alarming because of the way of the world is falling apart and has become so global and I find that the life that's enshrined or incarnate in this part of the world is disappearing. And so Whithorn is a place where people go to escape from that. And I tend to go back to that simpler rhythm and it's pretty well doomed, I think. In fact it's so alarming now I think the fact that we've globalised human life to the degree that we have now means that we're subjected to the outside world. We know far more about— the outside world has nothing to do with the realities of life here and yet it intrudes by way of the news and there's a, there's such a contradiction between these two things.

Like John McNeillie (Ian Niall), Alastair Reid saw, and regretted, the vast reach of systems which made local dwelling – and locality itself – insignificant and makes a return to that protected Edenic space impossible.

Alastair Reid

… when you compare Galloway in general with the rest of Scotland it's far less afflicted by that intrusion but nevertheless that intrusion is present here now. And there's no way of stopping the onset of this incredible domestic technology on the one hand and knowledge of the outside world, like it or not, on the other that means that the isolation or the kind of self-perpetuating life here is ever going to survive that, it's going to be intruded on all the time. And the idea that the realisation now that we're all plugged into the same wavelengths and so on, there's no way of avoiding that. It's a kind of, it's kind of sad in a sense to see this world disintegrating. But I think that this makes Galloway, in itself, a kind of museum, in a sense, of a way of life that we'd lost and had. Because I don't see any way of that coming back.

2

Outside-In: The Rural Town

The interviews, conducted largely with residents of Whithorn, were designed to probe further the themes of connectedness, speed, time and money – and their absence or delay as a condition of possibility of dwelling and of a language of locality. How did the distinctions, the distances, between 'here' and 'there', 'up' and 'down', 'inside' and 'outside' measure a space and time which are not those of technological mastery?

Time and Money II: The Patient Economy

Distinctions between high and low, sacred and profane, outside and in, inner and outer, are at Whithorn's origins and serve to map the town. By definition, a Royal Burgh is a place of protectionism and protection, even its streetscape created by strictures, within which a free space is created and allowed to flourish, liberated by its enclosure. The notion of a free space created only on condition of constraint and protection was understood by its medieval founders: the closely guarded privileges of the burgh are known as 'freedoms'.

Spatial divisions, dictated by function, have mapped out Whithorn for the last 1500 years: the monastic precinct (the very word meaning what is drawn tightly round, bounded and defensively enclosed against and outside and an other) was clearly and deliberately distinguished from the outer, profane world, which met it, through a strictly controlled entry, a stricture, at the gates of The Pend. That profane world itself, where medieval burgesses are licensed (or not) to build their houses on defined burgess plots, and above all are permitted trading rights, is in turn protected from the unlicensed world outside, by its gates, or ports.

The medieval town, as recent studies have shown, had a hierarchy of spaces, from the wide ceremonial approach to the Priory in the middle of what is now George Street, to the industrial areas to the west as the Ket leaves the town, where smiddies, slaughterhouses, and grazings belonging to the burgesses were separated from the residential and trading area.

The centre of Whithorn is therefore a protected space, clearly referring both to the inner precinct and to the outer world with which trade is conducted; its long line of houses punctuated – in the memory of the interviewees – by shops, the naming of which, as Alastair Reid says, provides a test and proof of localness. Beyond the south port, the 'top of the town' developed as Whithorn's other reality: a mirror image, with its own economy, shops, schools and even poetry. the significance attributed to the distinction between top and bottom, outside and in, remains as obstinately present in the twenty-first century as it must have been in the nineteenth.

Time, too, is structured, dictated by the rotation of the agricultural world and economy outside, just beyond the verges of the town. The flow of trade and people was dictated by the timing of payments on the farms outside, and the commercial world within slowed by the absence of cash.

John Scoular

If you take Whithorn, for example, it was still, then, the farmers came in on a Saturday morning and their wives did the shopping and the men would have a drink in The Grapes. And in many cases the men, the men that worked for them, weren't paid until midday on a Saturday and it was then their turn to come in in the afternoon and do the shopping and enjoy what delights Whithorn had to offer in the way of social entertainment.

Betty Stuart

That's when they did their shoppin, on a Saturday. And if ye went doon, some o them, at a certain time ye got something off. Like Garrick's at the bottom there, right away doon the bottom o the road, it was a grocers, Billy Garrick. And if ye went in before a, before nine o' clock, Ah think, there was something off.

Greta Hawthorn

They worked Saturday, they didnae get their pay tae Saturday lunchtime, the workers in those days, and then you saw the wives gaun away intae the toon to git the shoppin.

So, it would be a busy day?

Yes, Saturday was a busy day, the shops didnae close tae nine o'clock at night on a Saturday. Because the second hoose o the pictures went in then and then the first hoose was comin out, you see, so they had to do that.

The Language of Locality: Shops

There is a distinct local language in Whithorn, or a language of locality, consisting entirely of localities, made up of the recitation of shop names, farm names and the names of residents of houses, sometimes a generation or more after the person has ceased to live in the house; it makes up a web of recognition and familiarity. The names map the town, told through mental perambulation, enumerated and recounted up and down, east and west, so that significant points are picked out: Drape's, Kinnear's, Cathy Hughes' house, Petrucci's, Denton's, so that space is not neutral or measurable but personalised. Naming survives the mere span of a lifetime; those fluent in the language will occasionally drop into the vernacular, and the old name will resurface, long after the business itself has ceased or the original inhabitant passed away – the sign of a native – just as old shop signs are only partly effaced on the frontages of buildings – such as Coid's or Gibson's feed store.

Names outlive their time in relation to people too: nicknames, in which Whithorn is perhaps uniquely rich, are inherited, even though the reference to the profession which gave the name in the first place has ceased to be relevant. Names persist too because the businesses were inherited – many of those interviewed were second or third generation in their businesses and some of the most iconic of Whithorn businesses survived for at least 100 years in the same hands. In the countryside, on the other hand, place names substitute themselves for people, as farmers are known, as Alastair Reid remembered, by their orthographically-challenging farm names. Andrew McNeillie, son of John McNeillie, writes about 'Airriequhillart', the difficulty of the word itself defying and defining the stranger, differentiating the insider and the outsider.

Several of the interviews included, in relation to shops, a Homeric feat of recitation, recollection and connection, in which new names are bound with the old, becoming part of the hereditary chain and softening the shock of the new. The endless fascination of these invisible maps, which subsist through recitation and memory, can spark a conversation at any moment in Whithorn, in which those with the longest memories vie with one another in recollecting ancestry and precedence.

Greta Hawthorn

> Shops?! Yes, there was one at the top of the town, about four doors, well it would be south o The Calcutta, that was Miss McKelvie's and she sold everything. You could get a bottle of paraffin tae a loaf or whatever else ye wanted, it was a good wee shop. Mrs Stuart made up a poem about it. And where the Williams girl lives, across the road near enough, her mother and her granny had the front room, that was a wee shop. And that big store as

ye went up to go to the Windmill Stump, that was Mrs Jolly's store and she had a cart and a wee horse and she used to go round the country selling dishes or pots and pans or clothes pegs or reels. And then down below that was, well, there was The Calcutta and The Kelvingrove and the Miss Torrances were in The Calcutta and Mrs Clenaghan was in The Kelvingrove Bar and the Miss Torrances were spinster sisters and had the, the barrel o beer just sat through in the hallway, the lobby, and they could gae in wi a jam jar and get a jam jar full wi this beer, it jist trickled oot, it wis jist like water and then it was frothy stuff at the top. Across the road fae that was Mrs, a wee sweetie shop, I'll maybe remember her name, and across the road from that again, there was one, where Bill Jolly lives and Winifred, that was Miss Bie's and then it was Mrs McGuffie's and then it shut down after Miss McGuffie died. Miss Bie was a relation to the McWilliams on the Isle that had the shop on the Isle. And then there wis what they called The Lodging House and it, you know where the brick wall is? Well, there was steps up to that house up there, that's where Mrs Chapman was born, in that house, but they called it The Lodging House. What they called it that name for I don't know. And farther down there was a wee lady before you go through the Port's Mouth that Mrs Jones, she made paper roses and she used to sit at the door and sing, 'Paper roses, paper roses' and she'd always them in a basket and the house where Sonny Marshall was, the one that's painted, that was a pub, that was The Star Inn.

And down the street a wee bit was Mr John Dodds and his brother and they had a market garden and they did wreaths and bridal bouquets

4. Miss Bie's shop, Whithorn.

and things like that. There was a, we called it the Honeymoon Villa, was
before that, there was four flats in there, they were only a room and
kitchen, but they called it Honeymoon Villa and Mrs McGeoch used to
take the rent for that and it was a shilling a week. She got hers free because
she collected the money, it belonged to the Alves that used to have a
jeweller's shop here and Mrs McGeoch used to work there. Down a wee
bit where the ironmonger's shop was, that was an electrician's business and
then Alec McGhie came into that, he used to have it there. Across the road
where the Carnochans, Mrs Carnochan lives, that was a grocer's shop, the
Miss Ross' had that shop. Coming back down the street again, just before
you come to the chapel, Miss Milligan used to sell paint in that house and
then it was Camlay: Campbell was the head teacher at the school here and
Mrs Findlay was the doctor's wife and they had– they started it off as a
wool shop, that's how there's that big window and that was Camlay's wool
shop, Ethel Murray used to work in there. Then there was what's the
charity shop now, the Miss Ross' moved down in there and they had a
nephew that repaired watches, through the back, you went through the
entry to get that. But before that, where the chapel's built now was J. B.
Little's workshop and store and it was just corrugated iron that was on the
front and they had a wee side door that ye went in there and that's where
they did quite a lot of the work there and kept their stuff for the
plumbing. The post office and school house, well you used to could go to
the dentist there, there wis two dentist came there, Mr Reid and Mr Kerr
and they came on a Wednesday, one, one Wednesday and one the other, so
it depended. I went, used to go to the– and they came to The Grapes and
had their lunch. The Clydesdale Bank and then, where Mrs Hall lives, that
used to be a hairdressers, Mr McAlister's that's how there's a big window
there and then, through the side entrance, there used to be a bookies
which is Mrs Hall's wee scullery place now, that was a bookies at one time.
And there was a Costley's, the grocers shop, and what's the Galloway Store
now used to be the hairdressers and when we were wee we used look in the
windows to see because the ladies were sitting in this great big– we
thought they were gaun away tae the moon and there were great things
that come hangin down, I don't know what, but it was a hairdressers. And
then there was the garage and it was Mr Coid that had the butchers shop
there, Charlie Coid and he had it there for years. And where Galloway
Store is that was Mr Drape's great-grandfather's first shop, for ironmongery. Then there was your [Julia Muir Watt's] bookshop, that was the
butchers, Frank Jolly had that.

  Then it was a hairdressers an a hairdressers an a hairdressers and it was
the Oratory for the children to go in, in the mornings, and if it was very bad
to go up to the Mains because they'd only the church at the Mains, it was a

5. Drape's ironmongery and Whithorn Town House, Whithorn.

brick building and they had that at the Mains, there was quite a lot o weddings up there. Paul Soriani's mother and father's were there. Mrs Muir, Mrs Murray's father and mother were in the shop where, next door tae the butchers.

Where the Dig is?

No, after they left the Dig they were up here, and then Mrs Vance from Common Park had the wee shoe shop where the hairdressers was at one time, where Dolly had her hairdressers, Mrs Vance had that as a shoe shop. And then the Montgomery's fae Wigtown, they had a bakery, and they came in with the bakery every morning, and it was the bakery and then Dolly got it when it was sold to Ruby. Your first house, it used tae be a pub, and the wee one next door was Mrs Potts and then Mr Whiteford bought it when he sold the big shop tae the Dig and bought the stuff in there and it was a wee shop at one time, your second house. And then the Dig was Mr Little's, J. B. Little's shop and workshop and then Joe Whiteford bought it and they lived up the stairs and then Cameron bought the house and it was a paper shop. David Doughty had the fish shop, very popular fish shop. Across the street again and there wis, where the two flats are opposite nearly the war memorial, that wis another ironmongers, Douglas Gibson and Willie Gibson were in there, two brothers, but the brother lived further up the street where the plants are on the outside and trees on the outside that was where the other brother stayed. That was– and they had a saddlers shop through the back and Molly Heron's father used to be the saddler through there and they mended horse, whatever you needed for horses or for the farms or that. Mr Alexander's was the rent office and the solicitors office and where Mr Lowe, that was Mr Davidson's house and they sold paint from the house in there. And where Mrs Watson stays, that was Martin's the shoe shop, and through the back, what'll be her kitchen, I think, now or her bedroom, that was where they repaired shoes and if you ordered a pair of shoes, you needed a pair of shoes today, you would get them in the morning, they were really very good and they had a band that they used to have together. They played wi, in the Douglas Orchestra, that was another butcher. Then, where Mrs McLean lives, there was a lady there used tae have a wee tea room, in that front room, it was a wee tea room and where Margerie is, that was another wee shoe repair shop, that was, she was Italian and she had one finger getting like mine, it always stuck up but she could sew the shoes and everything, it was a great wee place. Then there was Kinnear's shop and next door to Kinnear's was where Ketview House is, that was Willie, well ye used to take bones to him, if you were making soup, you brought the bones intae him and they crushed them down and you got a peanut, a salted peanut, that was what yer pay was, a salted peanut for thur bones, Wullie Farrell was his name and his wife used to make clove toffee, that was Sarah McGuire's mother and Nurse Maguire's granny.

Then there was Mr Alexander's house, he was the solicitor, and where Dave Brown has his house and shop, that was Miss Hughes' shop, Cathy Hughes, and you always got lovely Kunzel cakes and Fyffe bananas and ye can hardly get a Fyffe banana nowadays. You could get anything in Miss Hughes', it was a lovely wee shop but it was piled up wi boxes, she never put boxes oot, she kept them for somebody flittin. Then there was Miss Muir, where Elizabeth Anderson is, and her bed was at the window and

6. McKnaught's ironmongery and The Pend, Whithorn.

the hens were sittin on the bed and they used tae lay in the bed and she used to come to The Grapes for her lunch, so we had to get her to come for her lunch at half past eleven in the morning so that we could get the perfume away. Then there was Mr Hannay's the chemists and then it was a florists shop that didn't really work either, the folks at Castlewigg had it but it didnae work. And then there was Jack Kilpatrick, the electricians, which he could have got ye a house tae a motor car tae anything, that was my brother-in-law.

And then Miss Hughes was next door, that used to be a pub as well, and Miss Hughes had that big house there and she had the whole of the garden right down tae the school and there was byres at the end o it and her father had cows and that, and his daughter-in-law used tae go down tae the fields wi the cans and milk the cows, even in the fields, and ye could see her coming up wi two luggies and she would just lay it in the grund and her man didnae bother. Where the Priory Antiques is, well that was just, there was three ladies in there, three Miss Kerrs, they were old ladies, they yist tae have a farm out at Palmallet. One of them was a nurse and one of them had been the housekeeper at home and I cannae remember what the other yin did, but when they fell oot o bed they used to phone me and there was one night she had fell oot the bed and they were in that wee room that's jist, it's jist really for a single bed in it, but the two o them slept in there and she'd fell oot in behind the door and the other one said, 'Well, she's behind the door and I don't know how you're…' so I was coming oot at Drape's door, wi ma nightie and ma slippers and ma dressin goon, when big Willie Adams which was the local policeman then, 'An where are ye going?' Ah says, 'I'm gaun away to the Miss Kerrs, and they've fell oot o bed and one o them's behind the door'. So he came in and he was big and strong that he could push the door and then he tried tae get her, so we got her intae bed eventually. Ah says, 'Ye're an arm o the law tonight' (laughter). An then where Mrs Stuffit [upholstery] is, that was a drapers shop, it was Brown and Charters at one time but it's changed that many names and then the wee shop, the wee place where her mother lives now, that was, Mrs Potts had that as a wee tea room, it was a wee tea room but ye could go in and get a cup o tea and then it was hairdresser's, Mrs Mitchell had it and Dorothy Wilmot had it and then we had the bank, Petrucci's café, then where the new place is that Mrs Stuffit [upholstery] now is, that was the British Legion Hall at one time.

Then it wis a draper's shop as well at one time. And Mrs Cain was the folk that were the other shoe repair in Margerie's place, Bobby and Mary Cain. Where Gill has got her wee house, that was the hairdressers, Johnny Stewart's hairdressers and then it was Miss Christie had the paper shop and then Mrs Huxtable had it and Dorothy Wilmot had it for a boutique

and then I don't know wha bought it after Dorothy, I couldnae tall ye.
The Davidsons had it at one point. I think there was, was there a gun shop in there, very briefly, Eric Baird had a gun shop or something?

Yes, aye. And then Willie Templeton had it for a wee while. Then we had The Grapes, of course, and next door was Auntie Mary Cook and she kept lodgers, boarders, anybody that was working and all the girls fae the shop went across to her house every, eleven o'clock and three o'clock for their three o'clock tea and she had a great big black range and she always had the kettle sitting on the hob and they could come in and make their own tea if they wanted. And then we had Mr Carson who had the coal yard, he lived at number four, I think it would be or maybe it was six. And then we had Denton's the bakers, well it was a great bakery, they made everything that you could, and their fruit loaves were about this size and about that high and they were one and ninepence and ma sister and I used to come in on a Saturday and they were queued up nearly to The Grapes to get them. We were at different parts o the queue so we got two. Then round the corner there, where the Gibsons live, that was Mr Douglas the butchers, Willie Douglas and he played the drums in the band and his wife played the piano and they were sometime in wi the Martins as well, the Douglas Orchestra they called it, and Margaret Herron use tae sing wi them.

And we've been tae next door, well next door was Betty McDowall's mother, which was Mrs Broll and she used to keep boarders, she kept policemen or bank people, tellers or bank managers that hadnae got houses, she kept them, that was where they stayed, in there. And her big dining room and then Dr Brown used tae come over from Port William and he had his couch there and he used to consult in there.

Dr Brown's, Dr. Brown now's father, he used to come in there and she had a big long kitchen and there was a jewellers in there, in where the chemist is now, that was a jewellers shop and Mr Drape's has always been an ironmongers as long as I can remember and where Sonny Keith is that was Miss Hannah's shop, wee sweetie shop, and she had books and she'd had them in a glass case and ye paid twopence for tae have them a week and you just signed yer name in a book but whatever book ye had and when ye'd got it and she used tae make paper pokes like ice cream cones. Then there were two sisters there and there was a wee room through the back that she used to give the troops their tea on a Saturday.

Betty Stuart used tae work there wi her for a wee while. Then across the road, well there was the nurses' station was there and the health clinic and they used tae gaun in and weigh the babies where Isobel Dodds is, that would be 61 St John Street, that was the Health Clinic and ye went in and got yer dried milk there and had a cup o' tea and ye met aw the mothers or expectant mothers. And then there was Mrs Baxter's house, well Mr Baxter had his chemist shop there to begin wi and then he bought which is the chemist now when Betty sold it to them and Mrs Baxter used tae have a dentist that came there, every Thursday he came, Mr Morton, that was where I got ma first lot o teeth out, the top ones, and then ye sat, it was, she called it the surgery, it was where the shop was and ye just sat in her sittin room until he came tae get ye. Well, there was the library but where Joe Whiteford used tae stay there wis a girl had a hairdressers business in the room and then there's the library and Miss Henderson's house, well it wis Miss Henderson's father that built the library, she was a school teacher, ye'll have heard about her probably. Well, that was her house. Then where Costcutters is Mr Drape used tae hiv that as a showroom for furniture but before that it wis a hairdressers. Is there no a photograph o the hairdressers pole doon there? Aye, I think there should be. And then the Miss, that wis doon below, where Jamieson lives, the Miss Birchman she used tae live there and Mr Birchman and he did a lot o research in the graveyards and he gave me a copy of one of them and he did Glasserton, he did a lot of the graveyards. Where Pat Harman is that wis Jimmy Whannell's shop, there wis a wee shop there, and there wis The Railway an aw wis there, but there wis Willie Garroch used tae dae repairs, dressmaking and that where that

7. G. B. Drape's with apprentices.

8. G. B. Drape's with Billy Hawthorn.

old gentleman stays, there's two doors, doon below Stevie Kennedy. That was Billy Garroch's an he used tae do repairs there. Then there was St John's Gar–, well St John's Garage was the church, the Wee Free, and then it was Hutchison McCreath and Mr and Mrs – don't know, used to be there. I see their son just died last week, they're no Plymouth Brethren but they dae preachin as well. Well, Allerton was a hairdressers where Billy Lyons stays, that was a hairdressers. And then there's The Black Hawk.

Some shops became particularly famous, established themselves as icons, especially when several generations inherited the business, such as G. B. Drape's, Doughty's game dealers, Kinnear's, The Grapes Hotel and the Central Café. Greta Hawthorn lived above G. B. Drape's ironmongery shop after marrying Billy Hawthorn who was employed there.

Greta Hawthorn

Oh, yes, he used to mend some of the binder canvasses because there was no big machinery in those days. I've still got his wee hammer that he used for – and it's a great wee hammer, it's no a very big hammer but it's jist a great wee thing – that used to sort the binders. They had to put the wood on the canvasses and he used to work late at nights tae get them done.

There would be quite a few employed at Drape's, would there?
   Well, there was the Grandpa Drape, Mr Drape, Billy, Molly. Mrs Greenhorn wis there and did the books but before that it was Miss, she was an elderly lady and when she died, she really hadnae anything, and when she died it was the funeral that was the big worry because she hadnae had insurances so the Drapes seen tae everything and got it away. So he said, 'It's a shame that ye dinnae get insurances' so he insured Billy, later in life, for when onything ever did happen tae him.
And do you remember a saddler working at Drapes?
   Aye, Mr Bendall was the old saddler that was there. His son used to be the postman, Jimmy Bendall. Ay he had a saddler there and Robert, Molly Heron's father was the saddler at Gibson's.

Doughty's Game Dealers were in existence for three generations in the same shop.

Cathy Doughty

Oh well, they used to deliver the fish in the morning fae Aberdeen, and then they got, they had to go and dumped it off, cause they were going to Stranraer to get the ferry, and ye had to go to Newton Stewart and pick up your fish, bring it, and then ye had it all tae sort before ye started in the morning, ready for sale. It's a bit o work with the fish in the morning first thing. David did most of it. I just mair or less went and did the housework and then went in and did the shop, made up orders to take out and that sort of thing. There was plenty to do.
And what about the game? Did you have to do any of the preparation?
   Oh aye, plucking and cleaning. No so much as his father's time as far as I know, then I wasnae here then. But plenty of cleaning and working.
And what did you do with all the feathers?
   Well, they usually just bagged them and put them out, sometimes when they'd a lot before I came here they used tae put them out tae different folk and they cleaned and plucked and some o them kept the feathers and made pillowcases and things like that. As far as I know that's what happened. That wis before I came here. Mrs McLean used to tell us about her folks all doing the feathers and putting them into a big boiler and washing them and drying them off and making pillows. That's the way they did– oh, it wis busy, it's always busy. But busier in his father's time because there was rabbits and different things, a lot of stuff went away tae Sheffield to get …
Was that the meat that went away?
   That was the rabbits. They went away. And whatever, I don't know what else, and then the blackberries came in and they had blackberries, David did a lot of blackberries for Robertson's jam factory.

In the centre of the town, a grand new emporium was built in 1901, housing A. K. Muir's delicatessen, whose name survived in a mosaic at the front door until the late 1980s. Popularly known as the 'big shop', as it replaced a row of small houses, it was taken over by the parents of Betty Murray (née McEwan) in 1934. She recalls the grocer's shop, prior to pre-packaged goods.

Betty Murray

> Well, my father took over the shop that is now the Dig shop, and it was a licensed grocer, and I was about eight and a half.
>
> *Okay, right. So tell me about the shop, tell me what kind of things it sold?*
>
> All sorts of groceries, everything; wines, spirits, fruit, vegetables. There was a warehouse at the back and they sold treacle and syrup in big pails, because I think they were used on farms, I think farmers used them. Soap was stored in big long bars, I think people bought a big long bar and sliced it up. But there were other soaps as well – but still bars of long soap – I think they called it 'XXX' or something.
>
> *Because it's a very large building, isn't it, I think it must have been the biggest shop–*
>
> Yes, and I think also they sold flour by the five stone bags, and oatmeal – huge quantities. People bought a five stone bag of flour, most of the farmers bought that way.
>
> …
>
> I remember my father boning hams in the back. The cheese of course was cut with a wire. The butter too was a big round – not very good!
>
> …
>
> There were three counters; there was one for all the dairy products, then there was a middle one for all sorts of tins of fruits and all sorts of things, and then another counter for things like wines and spirits – snuff. This thing called snuff! Tiny quantities. And lentils, things like that came loose, nothing, there weren't so many things packaged then; sugar, lentils. All that was loose in those days.
>
> *To the rear, there was bulk storage, since goods were weighed at the counter.*
>
> That's right – I think it was before our time, that was used for wheeling out the flour, and large quantities of feeding stuff they sold to farmers. You'll see there's a kind of ramp goes up, and I think that was where the large stuff was stored.

In the days before the seamless links between refrigerated lorry and delivery points, there was the dairy counter. Spoiling of goods was reduced by the natural cooling properties of marble.

Betty Murray

> Well, it was marble. And of course, there wasn't central heating. And they covered things in muslin cloths.
> …
> My father bought his cheese at Millisle farm from Mr Ramsay – Mr Ramsay made cheese, you know. And my father bought his cheese there. I don't know where he bought the butter (laughs) – it came from Glasgow, from a firm in Glasgow.
> …

Right. And how many people worked [in the shop]?
> Well, I look back to when I was at the school, and I can remember, maybe three women? And a message boy, and the van man.
> …

And [did] you do any deliveries?
> Yes, at the beginning, I remember there was a van, and a young man drove the van. And then for some reason, I don't know when, there wasn't a van. My father did odd deliveries just by car. Maybe more people had transport, I don't know.

So do you remember the names of the people who worked for you?
> Yes, there was Margaret Hawthorn, and she was Mrs Kirkpatrick. You wouldn't remember her. She was Margaret Hawthorn, and she would be related to Greta's husband, I think. And there was Maggie Little, who was one of the plumber's family. And there was David Koche, that drove the van. There was somebody called Archie McWilliam, who came from Kirkcowan I think, he drove the van too for a while. I can't remember any more.

And you mentioned a messenger boy?
> There were several. … People got their order delivered, a big basket on a bicycle.

Though we might view the advent of late night shopping as a contemporary phenomenon and one symptomatic of the pervasiveness and availability of cash, in the 1930s long hours in the shop were due to the scarcity of cash and shopkeepers' dependency on the long working week and the payment to farmworkers on Friday or Saturday.

Betty Murray

> And the hours were much longer. Saturday, nine o'clock. On Saturday we kept open til nine o'clock.

Was Saturday a major shopping day?

Saturday, yes, was the main shopping day, because the farm workers would probably get paid on Friday night, but I don't know. And I can remember my father, putting up a huge – the first time anyone had put up a huge Christmas tree – right in the front, where the middle counter came down, and it went nearly to the ceiling. It was a massive Christmas tree, and [there was] great excitement, he's all sort of lanterns, and lights and things. They weren't as good as they are now, but it was the children – they used to come up and stare at the Christmas tree.

The cross-house at the northern end of Whithorn, mirror image of what is officially known as The Cross House to the southern end, was Denton's bakery. Margerie Clark's mother worked there.

Margerie Clark

It was a very busy shop, cause of course the bakery was all done on the spot. And I do believe too, in his younger day, my grandfather, although he was a carter, worked for James Wyllie and Sons with a horse and cart. He also was a bit of a baker himself, so he– one of his jobs was in the early mornings, he would go down there and do baking there, at Denton's, in the bakehouse, before he would then go off with the horse and cart to do whatever was doing at Wyllie's, usually with the ships coming in, either at Garlieston or down at the Isle of Whithorn, they would be loading and unloading. But that was when he was a younger man, so that would be in the 20s and 30s, and a lot of that went on.
...
One of the things I always remember when we used to come up on holiday was I looked forward to going down, because you got the smell of the baking, which was going on there, and of course you went into the shop, which was always busy, it was always a hive, and everybody, all the local gossip was going on. And there was always something different about Denton's rolls, to anyone else's, there was a different taste to them. And of course quite often you brought them home, they were still warm, just out of the bakery as well.
...
They always talked, as well, about the 'Big Snow', as they talked about, in '47, that I think Mr Denton made arrangements for yeast, I think, to be flown in, by helicopter or whatever, so that he could carry on with the baking, keep going, yes.

Robin Kinnear was the third generation in the family draper business, beginning at Port William, but acquiring a Whithorn branch in the 1930s. As at Denton's, little was pre-made and delivered from distant supply chains and much of the skill was with the tailors on the premises.

Robin Kinnear

My grandfather was a traveller for a Glasgow drapery firm and called in this area and became very friendly with a Mr Goodwin in Port William who had a thriving tailor's business and my grandfather and he got on very well and in November 1898 he set up business in Mr Goodwin's shop, eventually leasing it in 1899 and starting business there. He lived in the flat above the shop and his main trade was suit manufacturing and I don't know, they had a large number of compartments and shelves for cloth, but I don't know what it was because all the suits were navy blue serge, no one ever had anything else (laughter) so they must just have had various shades of navy blue serge. In 1904 Mr Goodwin became rather jealous of my grandfather's success and he broke the lease and demanded more money which my grandfather was most annoyed about, but Sir Herbert Maxwell – my father had become a great friend with the factor, Mr Walker, H. H. Walker – and Sir Herbert Maxwell gifted the site opposite Goodwin's shop for my grandfather to build there.

In 1937 we purchased a shop in Whithorn and then later, in the '50s, we bought a furniture showroom in Whithorn which my father tended to favour, he was very much into the sale of furniture especially with term customers moving some distance away, perhaps to Kirkcudbrightshire and we would follow up with our vans with samples of drapery and settle their accounts, as I said, every six months.

In 1971 we bought a shop, another shop in Port William, which we would make into a furniture showroom but unfortunately in 1982 we had a fire in the drapery shop, the one that my grandfather had built, so it was not very suitable after the stink of burning, we swapped over, we put the drapery shop into the furniture store and the furniture store into the drapery and we carried on at that. And in 1998 we had our centenary celebrations in a restaurant which was converted from the original building of Mr Goodwin's so we had our 100th anniversary in the building where we actually started with my grandfather.

We had, in the new shop we had nearly 20 employees in the shop. You had about four or five downstairs serving on the counter because by that time we were in drapery and various other items and we had a separate outside stair up to the second floor where all the tailoring was done, where the tailors all sat cross-legged and we had lady seamstresses in and we did eventually get a sewing machine and we had a big oven where you had the goose irons placed in to heat and they were, the sleeves and the trousers, were pressed and ironed on a board sitting on your knee, they operated doing that and there were quite a lot of junior employees and it was quite surprising, you had a register of all those employees under 16 and then you had another one for 17 to 20.

Well, the early shop of Goodwin's never altered at all right through Brown and Co. and then latterly Miss Morrston but it was just two big long counters and the walls all sectioned off into shelves, nearly all 48-inch-wide to take the bolts of cloth .... And we subdivided them, again the ... our shop was made exactly the same and it had hatches on the ceiling, wooden ceiling, wooden lined walls and you had a hatch in the ceiling because the workmen went from an exterior stair, they didn't come into the shop, so the contact you had with them was through a hatch and you would put cloth, or reels, or thread, or whatever they needed, you just went up the steps and popped them in up through the hatch and you always had extended steps to go up to the higher shelves to get various things. The shop was altered and modified in several different ways but essentially was just exactly the same until we unfortunately had the fire which charred everything and made an awful smell and it was an awful job getting rid of the smell of it.

...

Indeed, yes. And the floors were wooden planks, were they?

Yes, wooden boards and behind– we eventually put linoleum in the main part of the shop but behind the counter it was wooden floorboards and they were getting very well worn and they were wearing down and the knots were very strong so you had wee lumps in them as well and my job as a young boy coming in, last thing at night was to go around with a lemonade bottle with the cork in it sprinkling water on the wooden floor because of all the dust and things that was on it and then you had to sweep that up and this stopped the stoor flying up in the air but latterly we had it, it was linoleum but a lot of the old shops still just had plain floors.

And what about lighting in the early days?

It was gas lighting. That was in the early days, there was one shop opposite, the grocer's, they had gas, acetylene lighting, and my grandfather moved, he lived above the shop, he bought Ormeau which is– his father was a sea skipper and as a young boy he had gone over in the ferry from Saltcoats to– from Ardrossan to Belfast and always went into Belfast and played in Ormeau Park and when he bought the house it was the Free Kirk manse. He called it Ormeau after his youth, as a wee boy, because as they were changing over the ship, docking and reloading he would play in the park and then always came back. So when I went to Ireland the first time I really felt quite at home when I saw the name 'Ormeau'.

OUTSIDE-IN: THE RURAL TOWN

And the shop in Whithorn, was that an existing business that you bought out in the '30s?

Yes, it was, I think it was, the name was Johnny Jibb – because he had a sale, sale notice in the window saying 'Johnny Jibb's trousers are still coming down' (laughter). He was having a sale, a cheap sale but he had this 'Johnny Jibb's trousers are still coming down' and that was a joke, held on to it for quite a long time. But that was where the kitchen shop is, what do you call it? Ketburn Kitchens, that was our shop and had a house alongside with a common stair but it was a rather nice old building as well.

Yes, yes, it's got the Ket going underneath it.

Yes, the Ket Burn, in below it, yes.

I take it it never flooded?

No, no it never ever flooded but we were always frightened of rats because there was always plenty of rats but they never came up, they never came into the shop. And there was actually just the wooden floor of the shop and when you lifted up the planks the burn was down below you. … It was quite interesting and then the furniture showroom which we purchased, I can't remember now, oh yes, in the '50s, it was the drill hall during the War, the Army drill hall, they had one there and they had one up where John Wilson lived. There was another hall up there as well.

The Whithorn shop was also organised on two floors, with a more exclusive mantle room on the first floor.

Robin Kinnear

Well, the same as Port William, the tailoring part in Port William was turned into what we called 'the mantle room' where all the ladies' dresses were on hangers and all the gent's sports jackets and trousers, all the better wear was on the second floor, so this was the same thing. Any ladies wanting dresses, they went up to the room above and there was a fitting room there for them to try dresses on and very – now and then, just very rarely, during a sale you would have a rail with ladies' dresses downstairs on the shop floor but it was so packed, everything was so compressed, on the ground floor that you had to keep the ladies' dresses upstairs. And we had a storeroom up there for bedding and things like that.

The trade of 'Draper' appeared on the fascia boards of several Whithorn businesses and implied a specialist training.

Robin Kinnear

Yes, that was the draper. That would be his name then and I've always used it because it's much easier than being a shopkeeper, when you're busy writing things out, to put shopkeeper or company director or, I just put draper, it's much easier. But he was very much a draper and my father and myself because we were clothiers and outfitters and dressmakers, it was everything in the drapery trade and then into furniture and then I developed the carpet side of it where it was nearly 75 per cent carpet trade that we finished up with.

...

I was lucky that I was able to step into the business, although I wasn't terribly keen to begin with. I'd thought about staying on at school but, and then realised that it was a shame to let this business go so once I got stuck into it I really found it very interesting and there was a lot of scope and a lot of ways of changing the business and improving it. So I was very fortunate, really, that I was the runt of the litter but managed to get the business (laughter).

...

And was there a sort of formal apprenticeship that you had to go through when you joined the business?

Well, my father had served, worked in a warehouse in Glasgow, the one that my grandfather had come from, and I was sent off to do the same thing with I. & R. Morley in London. And then I worked in their factories in Heanor in Derbyshire, various places, Nottingham, just learning how the various things were manufactured, how gloves were made and how many different parts there were in gloves. ... And came back with quite a few ideas on how these other businesses were run, how their invoices were handled and completely differently to what we had at home. I usually had to suggest it to my father often enough that he eventually thought it was his idea. You couldn't come in and state that, 'We're going to do this'. You had to suggest it to him and eventually he thought that was a very good idea of his, to change the invoicing, to change this and change that. You had to do it very diplomatically.

...

Then I came back to Port William and just travelled back and forward to Whithorn and Garlieston but my main business from then– but I actually, my grandfather, he would do about 20 years or so, and then my father started in 1927 but he would retire in, very early, his 60s, so I actually did the longest share of the business, I did about 44 years; longer than my father and grandfather. But it's very funny how quickly time passes and all of a sudden you've got a centenary on your hands.

OUTSIDE-IN: THE RURAL TOWN

9. Grapes Hotel with Denton's worker in foreground.

Though the hotel trade, like the retail trade, has changed out of all recognition, as the notion of travel incorporates vaster and vaster horizons, and as the phenomenon of travelling salespeople ceased with the advent of our constant and instantaneous connection with the world of commerce, the reputation of the Grapes Hotel has survived its owners. Greta Hawthorn worked there in its heyday.

Greta Hawthorn

> Well, Ah started, ma first job wis washin the breakfast dishes and then getting the vegetables ready for the soup and helpin tae make beds, doin washing, well we had a big washing machine and ye had lines o washin because we had travellers fae Monday night tae Friday morning and maybe they were only in one night and ye had the iron on the table and then Mr Kirk got a rotary iron and ye could do the sheets better that way. Then I got promotion, I was up the stairs and down the stairs and well, ye'd always three fires tae light in the morning and fill the Aga cookers, and the big kettle was always sitting on the side that it was near enough warm and then ye put the big pan on and started tae get the breakfast ready and serve in the dining room and did the hooverin and cleanin and cleanin the bars and things like that. But Mr and Mrs Kirk were the best people ever ye could work tae and he could dae anything, he could have did any– baking or anything at all and then if there was somebody comin intae another room that needed an extra bed in it, he would shout at me for to go up and help him. ... But they were really great tae work tae.

47

And how long did they have The Grapes?
> They had it about twelve years, I would be the eight years there, it was sold … we had wur weddin there and it was the new owners took over on the Monday after we got married on the Friday but Ah wis stayin on wi them. … But they had lots o weddings, we had the Maguire double wedding and we had Elsie Muir's two sisters married, they married folk fae the [Burrowhead] Camp.

The Central Café, introduced in the place of one of Whithorn's many inns, established itself as part of the weekly routine of leisure, paydays and cinema.

Aldo Petrucci and Tina Sorianni (brother and sister)

> **AP**: [In the 1950s, fish and chips cost] I think that was about elevenpence.
> **TS**: I know chips were thruppence and sixpence for a long time.
> **AP**: Thruppence and sixpence, yeah.
> **TS**: And ice creams were a penny and a hapenny.
> *Would fish and chips have been quite an affordable meal for most people in Whithorn?*
> **AP**: We used to sell a lot.
> **TS**: Yes. And our fish used to come from Aberdeen.
> **AP**: By train.
> **TS**: By train, packed with ice. And there were no fridges at that time, no freezers. And it's the same with making the ice cream, there was a lorry delivered ice, Miln. I remember the name, M - I - L - N. And the fish at that time, I can remember, for at the very beginning, they had to be beheaded and filleted. I can remember that.

Up and Down: Top and Bottom of the Town

In the topography – indeed the iconography – of Whithorn, the most significant feature is the narrowing of the road at either end, the old medieval ports, which was once gated and defined the entrance to the burgh and its privileges. Yet, only the south port, the entrance to the Top of the Town assumes a particular significance: not a mere physical narrowing this, but the entrance to a place which was either forbidden or superior, depending on whether you were 'top' or 'bottom'. The ban on visiting, playing or shopping in the 'other' part of the town was equally and obstinately held on both sides. In the early part of the twentieth century, indeed, when the Top of the Town had its own set of shops and its own identity as a semi-industrial suburb with crofts, its Windmill Stump, smiddy and its own schools, the division was even clearer than it remains today. Some interviewees mention religion – the distinction between Catholic and Protestant – or economic conditions or the separateness of the schools which once existed as reasons for this most obstinate of demarcations. It is certain that the Marquess of Bute created the first permanent Catholic church at the Top of the Town, beyond the burgh boundaries, at Mains farm, but what seems more likely is the development of businesses outside the privileged space of the burgh created a virtually separate community.

Betty Stuart describes her life, lived entirely at the Top of the Town.

Betty Stuart

> Well, Ah wis born in 15 High Street, Whithorn, ma mother's name was Henrietta McGinn. Ma parents, ma mother's parents were Mary Huxable and Hugh McGinn. Ma grandfather died before Ah was born but Ah was nine years old when ma granny died. Ah remember ma granny very well, she was a tall lady with white hair, quietly spoken.
> …
> Well, two shops at the Top of the Town at the beginning, the end of Glasserton Street, was Miss McKelvie's and across the street was Mrs Murray's, now that's a granny o Davie Briggs that lives down. They had that, they had that pub. And then there was Miss Bie's, these were all before you came to the Port Mouth and then the Port Mouth. I think there was eleven or twelve altogether, between shoe shops and cobblers and things.

10. Miss McKelvie's shop, Whithorn, 1890.

So if you lived up here did you do most of your shopping up here?
> Aye we did oor shoppin, we run a weekly bill in Miss Bie's. I think everybody, in these days, run weekly bills and paid yer messages on a Saturday when you got your money.
>
> And then we also went to a shop at the very end of St John Street, it was called Garrick's, just across from where the vets is. We had tae shop there because we were related. We went there on a Saturday, I think, for the shoppin. And Miss Bie's was the most popular, it was more popular than the other one, Miss McKelvie's.

Betty Stuart further explains how some friends were forbidden to visit her part of the town.

Betty Stuart

> Cathie, was a wee girl aboot four, and she was— Ah was very fond oh her, Ah was good tae her and Ah gien her a sweetie when she shouldnae have a sweetie and she says, 'Can Ah come into Whithorn?' Ah says, 'Ye'll need tae ask yer mum and daddy'. So Ah leeved, as ye ken, at the tap o the toon and Ah said tae [her mum], Ah says, 'Cathie would like tae come into the town. Is it all right?' And she thought, 'Yes' she said, 'If ye avoid the tap o the toon'. Well Ah lived at it, Ah mean Ah couldnae get past my door, Ah couldnae, Ah lived at the top of the High Street, and an ye come up Glasserton Street and then it was High Street and Ah says, 'Ah cannae, Ah live in High Street'. She says, 'She's no gaun' so she didnae get. But Ah often wondered how Ah was to avoid High Street cause … Ah dinnae ken how Ah wis tae dae it.

So do you think the Top of the Town and the bottom of the town have always been kind of separate like that?
> They were, they were more so in years ago but noo everybody mixes don' they but no, they used tae hae kinna fights an wee battles, the Top of the Toon and the bottom of the toon …

But we don't know why particularly the bottom and the top couldn't get on? It was just, were they physically divided, the Port's Mouth, is that why?
> Ah think, Ah don't know why, it has been for years. Ah think it's different now, right enough, but then it wasnae, it wasnae up fae the Port Mooth it was further doon seemingly, fae aboot where Mr Kelly used tae leeve, fae aboot the Cameronian Entry there.
>
> …
>
> An, we had parties in the street on a Saturday night, an there was Pat Flannighan, big Pat, he had his melodeon, Johnny Johnston played the bagpipes, wee Johnny, Ah see him as ah'm talkin aboot, he was a comical

wee man, he drank, he was a really alcoholic an he danced, dressed as a
woman an danced. This wis wur entertainment on a Saturday night.
So where would that happen?
High Street. Right up tae the pump. Tae the turnins.

Jessie McLean, whose family was one of the institutions of the Top of the Town and worked in her parents' famous business there, comments on the separateness of the two parts.

Jessie McLean

Top of the Toon folk never mixed wi the bottom o the toon. Naw, we didnae mix.
It was like two different communities?
Yes, it was, Ah ma days the tap o the toon was different fae the bottom.
And yet you're down here now (laughter)!
But the tap o the toon folk never bocht off doon the street, they would rather shop at the tap o the toon.
Right, they never came down to shop?
No. They always, but Betty McKelvie's and Peter Bie's. Ah liked the school, liked the weans at the school, ye aye played wi the top o the toon weans, never the bottom of the toon weans.
Isn't that funny?
Aye the top o the toon.
So what was the name of some of your friends from the Top of the Town?
Peggy Murray, she'll be dead noo, Annie Crawley, they were ma best friends. Doughty, across the street, was in my class and he got me the strap often. He telt that Ah copied him.

Alex Haswell born at the bottom of the town, had a grandmother who lived at the Cross House, the fulcrum between top and bottom. His family moved to the house opposite the Cross House, once the Star Inn; yet even here, living on the dividing line or fault between the two, the difference between top and bottom was clearly felt.

Alex Haswell

My maternal grandfather I didn't know, I never met, but my maternal grandmother lived in Whithorn, and she lived in the Cross House; what we call the Cross House. Which is 137 George Street. The one that sticks out at the top. So born in St John's Street, I think my first real memory–was of Bell's garage, was still there, but it wisnae Lawrence Bell; it would be Sammy Bell, who was his grandfather, he ran it. Always went across to the garage, I was a wee boy, I was in and out of the garage.

Where the entrance to Kilncroft is, there was a market garden in there. I remember the market garden, I remember the Heid Pump, and the Windmill Stump, vaguely, and the big tank, very vaguely. I don't know if they're still there, but I remember that sort of layout. The Crudens [houses] were always there in my time; that's what Wigtown District did, we modernised the Crudens.

Describing his school days, when he graduated to the Douglas Ewart High School, Alex Haswell recollects the antagonism between the two parts of the town.

Alex Haswell

And was that because you went to the Douglas Ewart and they were at the Whithorn [School]?
It's a real. I never, I don't know why it was, it just was, and it had aye been. Because I was born in St John Street, I used to go around The Park. And I remember The Park when it was prefabricated houses; it was wee prefabs. Then the Dorans [houses] were built, I remember when the Dorans were built. But it was a strange thing. Until I moved to 2 High Street, I don't think I'd ever been through the Port's Mouth. Although, my granny lived in a Cruden house, at the very top – near where Betty Stuart now lives, at the tank. Granny lived there, but I was just a baby, and I would be pushed in the pram. But when she moved down to the Cross Hoose, I don't think I was ever through the Port's Mouth, until we moved to 2 High Street. And we moved to 2 High Street when I was a teenager, I was just going to Douglas Ewart.

There were various semi-industrial and commercial processes which were based at the Top of the Town, which may explain its separateness. Margerie Clark talks about her grandfather John Townsley Mills, who died in 1923, who was a well known master flesher.

Margerie Clark

I know he was based at, as they talk about, the tap o the toon, and we have – there was a photograph of him up there, I think possibly in what used to be Green Lane, up that way, and round the back, when he was still quite a young man, as a butcher, and he's got an animal he's obviously in the process of butchering, and he's standing there with another gentleman, a son, a Willie Mills from his first family, in that photograph. But I'm not

OUTSIDE-IN: THE RURAL TOWN

11. Pig killing, Green Lane, Whithorn.

actually sure where the shops were, it's just hearing my family talking about it when we were growing up, they would talk about it. My grandmother especially, she liked to reminisce.

Greta Hawthorn confirms there were industrial areas of the town on its periphery, and that there were in fact two schools at the Top of the Town, which initially separated the children from the two areas of Whithorn.

Greta Hawthorn

> Yes, there was one at the 'keep left', that was a school at one time. And there was a school in Glasserton Street and that was Kelly's Garage at one time, there was a garage up there. And where the waste ground is, it used to be the bus station in Glasserton Street. And then Henderson's took over, that sorted tractors and farm machinery and stuff, they were in Glasserton Street. And Ben bought the old school and that was at the 'keep left' and he had his first smiddy there and then he went to the one that's, where we still call it 'the smiddy' but it's no a smiddy any more. And there was gas works

53

down King's Road where Bertie Biagi stays and there was a carpet factory on the opposite side of where the old fire station is .... Because Beatrice Dunning's mother used tae work there, that was how her father and mother met, she was at the carpet factory. And the fire station used to be down King's Road and there used tae be a slaughterhouse doon there as if yer going to the burn, just doon past the side o the fire station.

Famously, there was the Windmill Stump at the Top of the Town until the 1960s, when it was bulldozed. The windmill features in a local poem, *Tarry Glancer*, which indicates that even in the mid-nineteenth century, it had already ceased milling and become an unconventional house. Both the poem and Jenny Jolly's reminiscences of its occupants indicate that the unusual nature of the dwelling set the occupants apart.

Jenny Jolly

> But Ah mind o the Windmill Stump. Ah mind o it. ... Ah think Ah was mairrit afore it was pulled doon for auld Jimmy Maxwell was angry. It was a landmark. An he wis the only man come up that day to stop them fae pu'in it doon. And he was disappointed, for he thought the folk fae the tap o the toon would hae been all there for it was a landmark. An he wisnae a happy man aboot it, Ah can tell ye.
>
> *So it must have lain empty for some time? When you were a child it was empty?*
> It was, a cannae mind if ye mind her or no, she was a wee wuman, Ah think Ah hae kinna mind her, for she was a wee wuman and she wore boots, boots that came up to here.
>
> *Uh-huh, this is Mary Ann McKie?*
> Mm, an she was supposed tae turn intae a hare at night, you see, and whatnot. And the story was, which would be a lot o lees, Julia, of coorse, everything spreads in the telling and she was supposed tae be oot this night in the field and somebody shot this gun pellets and wounded a hare and when they went in, Mary Ann was pickin them oot o her leg.
>
> *So people thought she was a witch then?*
> Mm, but Ah think a lot o they stories was telt in the auld days for the bogey man, tae try their weans tae get tae bed. Ah widnae pit ma pension on that they were true (laughs). Some of them was gey far fetched, Ah can tell ye.

Time and Money III: Credits and Debits

Despite the plethora of shops and commercial enterprises, which sprang up in seemingly every front room in Whithorn, many of which still show signs of

12. The Windmill Stump, Whithorn c.1900.

the (often slight) conversion from domestic to commercial, this economy ran on the slenderest and slowest of cash exchanges. As Alastair Reid recalled, money exchanged hands comparatively rarely and at measured periods of time; where cash existed, it was hoarded, delayed by credit periods and eked out by a marginal economy which did not run on cash.

All shops ran accounts, some of which were paid weekly on paydays which fell on a Saturday, but others monthly, quarterly, on term days which marked the old hiring fairs, or even yearly. The result was an economy of trust and the exchange of favours, which bound together the givers and takers.

John Scoular recalls the pace of this seemingly endlessly patient economy.

John Scoular

Some of these businesses had hard times, the ironmongers, I remember, Drape saying to me it wasn't uncommon for them not to be paid by the farming community for more than once or twice a year. And it's very difficult to sustain a business in those terms, so change has been forced on the commercial side.

Nothing shows the physicality of the exchange of money, nor the slowing effect of this physicality, more clearly than the transport of banking facilities by bicycle, as Jack Niblock explains, speaking of his father's early career.

Jack Niblock

> But as far as I can make out he passed all this banking exams by the time he was 21. He started in Whithorn and funnily enough in ... John Scoular and I, we used to run lectures in the community centre in Whithorn, auspices of the campus at Dumfries, which in turn was Glasgow [University] and one of the things that came up, they were talking about Garlieston and the past and I told them, I said, 'Well my father, when he was in the bank just as a young man, used to cycle to Garlieston with the bank books, cash, etc., do his business there and cycle back' and he said, 'We assumed the bank came by train, which came in these days, so that's something new that we've picked up from that'. And from there he went as accountant to Wigtown and then Castle Douglas, he was accountant in Castle Douglas.

The agricultural calendar of the hiring fairs dictated the payments to Kinnear's, and when this was reformed by a young Robin Kinnear in the 1950s, the pace of charging was still dictated by the round of clients, which could only be made every three months. The fact that purchases were made at intervals, delayed by the round of the cart and the pace of the horse, or later, by the round of the van, also dictated the progress of fashion in clothing and fabrics. The absence of financial credit and the fact that physical money had to change hands, in the absence of cheque books and invisibly regulated credit cards, meant that personal credit had to be extended, regulated only by the trust between two parties.

Robin Kinnear

> Business thrived and being the old agricultural structure with a hiring fair in May and November people were paid then so their accounts were rendered six-monthly, which would be rather awkward to try and do business in this present day, but this is the way that it worked and they would come and they would buy six months' drapery and pay for it six months later.
>
> Now, once we got into the '50s, when I joined the staff, we managed to reduce the credit terms to three months and normal. That was the only

reason we had to be three months was that was the circuit, that you could only get round them every three months. We had so many customers from Ayrshire to Kirkcudbrightshire, Dumfriesshire, right round to the Mull of Galloway so we had a big area to cover and we had, at one time we had three vans, three travellers going out.

The exchange of cash was tallied by the satisfyingly mechanical of the wooden till and its servicing spaced by the rotation of a travelling agent; even the credit terms were painstakingly recorded by the manual writing of a ledger.

Robin Kinnear

Yes, in the early days, when I was a wee boy, I can remember it was a wooden drawer, you pulled out the drawer and it rang a bell which would hit this wee bell that was fixed to the inside of it and then on the top there was a, like a great big till roll and you wrote in the amount that you had sold and then at the end of the day that was counted up with what was in there. Then we got an NCR (National Cash Register) big till where you wound the handle, it was all purely mechanical, and it lasted until decimalisation and we used to have an NCR man came round once a year to clean it and oil it and service it and once we got the electronic till it was no problem at all, it never needed any, if it did go, well, it would either refuse or it was thrown out and you had to get another one. There was no servicing of these, although we did take it once or twice to Glasgow to get it sorted, a wee bit sorted on it but no, I can remember the old drawer till, it was really quite fascinating. And I had one of them I had my own wee shop when I was a schoolboy, I had it upstairs, and I used to sell things to my granny and my aunties and people like that, playing shops, but I had this wee till where I had my pennies in it and I was very proud when I could pull it and the bell rang.

And did you keep ledgers, day-books, that kind of thing – of every item that was sold?
Yea, well not every item that was sold, every item that was on credit. It was entered in the day-book and then if they came and paid it then it was marked out of the day-book, if it wasn't paid it was then posted to a ledger and the account went out at the end of the month because we could keep the shop accounts to one-monthly but the ones in the country you couldn't because your man didn't get round except every three months. But latterly they were beginning to pay by the month or just send it, post it off, but they weren't very, they didn't have cheque books and things in˙ those days, you had to go and collect the money actually, real money.

Even the doctors, prior to the foundation of the NHS, sent out bills as dictated, not by a infinitesimally calculated charging system, but according to personal need, as Dr Guy Brown recalls.

Guy Brown

> So, yes, he sent out bills once a quarter, when my mother needed some money, and even after the Heath Service came in he had a number of private patients that stayed private. And it was sometimes two or three years before the bills went out, when a carpet was needed or something, something along those lines.

Kennedy Donnan recalls the services of his mill being paid in kind.

Kennedy Donnan

> One farm Ah went, he wasnae payin an Ah went tae, we were takin corn in place o money and there were a hundred and half bags. An oh dear, he never looked near me, Ah had these to load maself, ah'm telling ye, he put me intae ma boots. Yes, some o them, maist o them when ye went, nae problem payin ye.

Giving and Taking

The extension of credit was given within a context of obligations and favours, which were extended well beyond what might now be recognised as family to an extended network of neighbours. The term 'daughter' used here by Betty Stuart is applied metaphorically to a web of acquaintance, who took on the responsibility of parenting

Betty Stuart

> 'Here dochter, come awa in' she says, 'Ah've a bowl of soup ready for ye, yer ma's awa tae the steam mill so come in and get a bowl o soup' (laughter). They were the kind o folk they were. They were different, actually so different tae what the folk are now they were different, there wis no sae much carrying on and things and ye had tae mind yer P's and Q's, if ye ken what Ah mean, and [if ye] did anything wrong.

Families were indeed literally larger, but also familial ties and obligations were recognised as extending to a wider range of relatives, and by transfer, to other residents of the street and the community. Where many hands were required, the capacity of families to survive and accomplish manual tasks was not extended by technological mastery, but by the recognition of extended family ties. Kennedy and Jim Donnan worked the mills, and lived with their niece, Cathy Miller's family at Cherry Valley: in exchange for their board and lodging, they supplied labour in kind.

Cathy Miller

> And if it was, had been rainin and they couldn't do anything they helped on the farm, they cut weeds and various things and did a bit o painting if the weather was suitable and things like that for ma dad. Because ma mum made them their dinner and everything so lots o things were in kind in these days.

Though the economy functioned on a web of gift and exchange, yet the more anonymous gift of a state pension, without a donor and unrelated to any particular transaction in labour or favour, was more difficult to accept. With her daughter Molly, Betty Stuart recounts her mother's reaction to the first dawning of the welfare state.

Betty Stuart

> *Molly Stuart: Tell Julia aboot yer mother no takin the pension.*
> Aye, well, ma mother, when she got older she wis a wee bit kina, her mind kinna went a wee bit confused like. Confused a wee bit and the pensions comes oot, Ah think it was three-and-six, it was either three-and-six or it was five or six shillings. Anyway, this comes to her. She say's, 'What's that for?' Ah says, 'That's your pension', 'What pension?' Ah says, 'You get that money noo cause yer over ye're age tae get it an ye're no working – [ye're] by working noo', an Ah had tae go and get the lawyer, old Lawrie, the old lawyer, maybe you've heard o him. Mr Lawrie, because he came up, behind wur hoose tae gaun tae Flannighan's every night. He didnae come up the front street (laughter) he went up the Back Raw there up the Green Lane and went tae the pub an Ah watched for him this night and asked him if he could come in. Ma mother paid the rent tae him, he took the rent and when he got it aw explained tae her she widnae tak it. She'd twa or three weeks o it, she widnae, because she hadnae worked for it. But he was very nice, we paid the rent tae him. He was always very nice with us.

Outside In: Working the Margins

If the infiltration of the cash economy was strictly limited, the symptom of that absence was a hardy independence of it – the use of the long plots behind houses (the backlands) to grow and produce, the use of the bounty of the surrounding countryside to create a marginal economy trading in blackberries and snowdrops, and the extraction of a surplus from the already-used, a cultivation of the leftover and an extension of its life, by making do and mending. The countryside therefore infiltrated the town, through the presence of animals, productive plots, and the gatherer economy. The onslaught of monetarisation was staved off and delayed by the setting to work of all available hands – the employment of children, of the early hours of the day, and the putting to use of the margins where ownership was uncertain and a little could be saved and clawed back.

The outside world intruded on the space contained within the town, as cattle were daily driven up and down the main street, the countryside impinged on the southern end of the town with Jessie McLean's family croft. Protected though the inner world of Whithorn may be, the smallness of its distinctions between here and there, here and hereafter, mean that it was closer to the processes of production, reproduction, and death – less mystified, less sanitised, – less sanitary perhaps – than our wider and more distant world.

Speaking of a period as late as the 1960s, John Wilson comments on the presence of animals.

John Wilson

> Our next door neighbour, when we were in George Street, our next door neighbour had kept two ponies in her garden and you would see people walkin up the street and the door would open, maybe people on holiday, and the door would open and out would come a horse out the front door. Aye, there was quite a few horses in the town at that time, yea, yea and people, some people kept pigs and things.

There was perhaps more of an agricultural feel to the town than there is now?
> Yes, yes. They used to drive, when we came here, they would drive animals through the town. They would drive animals right through the town.

With her daughter Molly, Betty Stuart speaks of the use of the hours after school to earn in the fields and also to grow in the exceptionally long gardens or backlands of the burgh, designed expressly in the Middle Ages to support the burgesses.

13. George Street, with shops and carts, Whithorn.

Betty Stuart

Molly Stuart: And then of coorse they would grow potatoes then in the fields and cabbage and turnips?

And cabbages and turnips, well that was what ye did when ye went home fae school. When ye went home from school ye went away oot tae meet them at the hoeing, they were at the hoeing at night, hoeing the turnips an that an efter that when they were big and that you got tae pick the [unclear] on them and ye yaist tae get them and bring them home and sell them.

And did people keep big gardens here, like kitchen gardens?

Yes, there was quite a lot of folk wi big gardens. … Aye, there was a lot o big gardens and they kept aw the vegetables and new potatoes and potatoes an aw the vegetables and cabbages an everything like that, aye they did. And then there was a man doon the road there, [unclear] he had a big garden jist next tae the Cameronian Entry, Jimmy Carr, his was a vegetable garden, ye went there paying yer twopence for, some vegetables.

…

Molly: He must have grown them purely for selling?

Aye he was always packed oot wi folk wantin them and then there was, further up there was Dodds, they sold too, they had a market garden. Just as ye went back up the road fae – just below the Port Mouth, aye. … They had a lovely garden too, they selt, that was their, they had nurseries up The Pend too along with their garden.

WHITHORN: AN ECONOMY OF PEOPLE, 1920–1960

The Jollys' croft was located at the Top of the Town, where the rural infringed upon the urban. With her daughter Mary, Jessie McLean recalls the movement of cattle and horses in and out of town.

Jessie McLean

> An wur horse was that, and wur coo, we had grass doon Isle Street at a farm ca'd The Mains and the horses kent that, there used tae, an auld milkin man, opened the gate and the horse followed, come oot o the gate an up, the coo did the same tae be milked. We didn't, aye, we didnae need tae gaun for them. In the morning that's what they did.
>
> *So which was your house on Isle Street?*
>
> The same hoose as yet, it was left tae ma Granny's and ma faither.
>
> An then she'd that big red hoose, that was it, and there were sheds an aw at it and we leeved there that was the Jollys' hoose. An ma mother got her horse, then the farmer selt the farm, and ma mother got her grass fae Mr Edgar, the vet, and what. We didnae get money for daen his garden or his path up tae his hoose, he gave us the grass for the horse for naething and the coo. And we walked them the whole road doon the street an the calves tae the field doon the Garlieston Road. Every morning and brought them up at night when we got oot o the school at three o'clock or fower o' clock, we went tae the field and got them for tae bring them up tae be milked.
>
> …
>
> And ma brother never learned it, but he was the best man at killin sheep and cattle that ever was. He got first prize in the unction mart in Glesga for killin cattle. Sheep were skinned and calves, ocht. He was a clever man and naebody learned him he learned hissel, he was clever. An he got a first prize.
>
> *Mary [Jessie's daughter]: An then ma Uncle Frank learnt tae butcher it. Yin was a killer an the other yin learnt the butchering theirselves. An they killed an butchered their ain meat. An up at the tap o the toon, up the close.*
>
> *So there was a place they did that?*
>
> Whaur Jessie Jolly leeves noo [unclear]. Ma granny before us leeved there.
>
> *Mary: There wis stables an byres an everything up there.*
>
> Aye, everything, we had everything. Aye, the auld man opened the gate and the horse and the coo come hame. The coo come tae be milked and the horse come to get fed and get yoked for gaun wherever we were gaun tae. Now there was a life.

Children were essential to eking out the margins of the economy and to staving off the need to pay cash and extending the value of adults' labour; the need for them to swell the workforce was both expected and accepted. Both town children and country children accepted the same regime of hard work from an early age.

Robert Galashan

And we had a lovely garden, my uncle was a great gardener. Oh, he grew wonderful stuff. Too much for me, when the rest were oot playin I wis made to go into the garden to weed it and help him, dig it, and oh. And that's how he made his money, my uncle grew acres o potatoes, up at the top o Cruggleton there was a bit maybe the width o the street there, fae the house to the street, and it wis sloe bushes. And he broke horses, and he pulled aa these bushes oot breaking in horses, and cultivated it. And he grew acres o potatoes in there. And when the Irish people come over tae the Portyerrock to dig their potatoes, he used to get them on a Sunday, a Saturday and Sunday, to come and dig them there. And he always had potatoes that passed as stock seed and ye could get whitever money ye could get for stock seed. And he used to send tonnes doon tae England. And that's how he made his money tae buy Brownhill. He rented a piece o ground at Palmallet that the RAF had where they did the bombing, the practice bombing, he had about maybe two acres there. And then he rented another four tae five acres fae The Kevans, fae Sammy Hanlon, and grew that in potatoes. I've seen me on a winter's night, sitting up behind a dyke wi two byre lamps and a great long pit o tatties maybe fae here to the middle o the road, walin' oot half a ton o potatoes for the Cafe, Monday morning. On a winter's night.

The most labour-intensive jobs of the agricultural economy rested on the backs of children and women who could perform the most mundane of tasks, to save the labour of the adult male workers for more skilled tasks.

Robin Kinnear

In fact we used to work with the Kays, they had a dairy farm and, to lead in the horses from the harvest field, it was always called 'the leading in' and so you got a job as a wee boy just leading the horse in, it saved the men, they could start and get their stooks and things brought down and loaded onto another cart. So we used to do that and at The Clone, we used to get an endless job of picking stones in a very stony field which was beach at one time and this old horse was trained so well it just walked along at a very slow speed, just two or three steps and it would stop and two or three more steps and you had to load in all the stones, into the back of the cart, and you'd go to the other end and turn and come back down and you had maybe a whole cart full of stones and you couldn't see where you had picked them, you couldn't see any difference between the bit that had been picked to the that bit you were about to pick. But it was a soul-destroying job, but they were very well trained old horses that went along and then you led them in and they tipped them up and you'll see them in quite a lot of fields up by Elrig, great mounds of stone, where they've been lifted off the field and just dumped. But no, there was a lot of horses and then the coalman in Port William was Phillip McKenzie and he worked for Wyllie's and kept, they had two horses down the harbour, the back of the store, and they had their coal store there so he used to take a slip doormat from my mother's front hall and put it in the front of the cart and I would sit there so that I didn't get my backside all covered in coal dust and I'd go round with, delivering his coal. And then another funny delivery we had was the baker, Jimmy Little, in Port William. Emily Kevin rode this tricycle which was a big box on the front and the lid, she lifted it up and inside were lovely cream cookies and iced cakes and things so she did her bakery round and I used to go along with her sitting on the top of this as well, getting the odd wee bun that went the wrong way (laughter).

Grandparents extended the capacity of the family and saved the labour of parents, who, sometimes a lone mother, went out to work, whether on the cart like Mary Jolly, or in the fields, leaving the older generation to bring up the children. Jessie McLean confirms that the domestic economy leaned heavily on the labour of grandparents, who in turn inculcated skills and the work ethic into their grandchildren. With her daughter Mary, Jessie McLean recalls being required to 'hawk' from a young age.

Jessie McLean

Mary: Yer young life was hard when ma granny was— had tae hack— an yer brithers an that, thay aw had tae work.

An they aw workit and ma sisters aw workit. We're a family that nane o us haud back, we aw stuck in, the whole lot o us. We're a family, no yin shirked their job, we aw workit, boys and lassies, an ma brothers were clever, guid scholars an aw, just came in.

…

Ma Granny gien ye sair slappins, ah've had mony a sair slappin for gien a body an extra clothespin. We, lang ago folk worked hard for work, an ye didnae get much money. That's hoo we're aw [learnt] tae cook for ye learnt fae ye were ony age tae cook, tae make soup and stew and bake an aw that. Before ye were ony age ye were learnt tae— ye werenae even fit tae reach the table, ye had tae staund on a stool to reach the table tae bake. Weans disnae ken their leevin (laughs) no they dinnae. Mony a lickin a got fae ma granny, mony a lickin, aye.

…

>Ma sisters, ma elder sisters, were aw learnt tae cook, they were aw guid cooks, every yin o them. And they were good dressmakers so we aw guid sewers ... we were a really handy family, we were aw clever at daen things even the boys. We were that.

So what did your brothers so to make a living?

>They were dealers tae– And then Frank bocht [unclear] the farmin. They were aw in the War, the four of them.

That must have been difficult for your mother?

>We were kinnae grew up then. I had three brothers awa.
>...
>But ma sister was maid tae a woman that kept the schoolmaster, Mr Brown, an Ah got a shilling a week from Mr Brown for tae clean his shoes every night, a shillin a week.

The family was unusually entrepreneurial, and Jessie, at a young age, took to the trade in rabbit skins, turning to account, quite literally, the slimmest by-product from a food source which was free of charge.

Jessie McLean

>In the morning Ah got up early, before I went tae school, and knocked at the door jist asked had they any rabbit skins for sale and ye always got rabbit skins, they always kept the skins for us. Sometimes they had half a dozen skins and that's what they were, a penny each, and the hares were two pence.

And how old were you when you were doing that?

>Well, Ah widnae be very old because I wasnae a good clever lass so Ah had tae be old enough to ken ma money, what tae pay the skins, so I would say ah'd be ten or eleven wouldn't ah? For I was able to pay them for their skins and look after ma money.

So how did you carry the skins?

>Over ma, Ah strung them through a string and Ah hung them roon ma neck an ower ma back. Roon ma neck and doon ma back and Ah was loaded wi skins. In the winter time Ah was loaded and hoo Ah managed [unclear] hame and Ah [unclear] if it was rainin and then the whole of the summer holidays Ah went wi ma mother wi the cart, there was no cars then, tae gaun tae the hooses for skins.

And what did you do with them afterwards?

>We sent them away, we packed them aw, strung them aw up and we sent them aw on the station wagon tae Glasgow.

And then they were used for clothing or–?

>Or whatever they were used for and we made a lot of wur skins. We made a lot of money.

What did the other children think of you gathering the rabbit skins?
'Here's Jessie Jolly, she gathers aw the rabbit skins.'
Do you think they were a bit jealous of the money you got?
Mary: They cawd ye 'Ragbag Jolly'.
Aye, they cawd me 'Ragbag Jolly' (laughs).
That wasn't very nice (laughter)!
Aye no, it didnae worry me, Ah kend as Ah was makin the money, it didnae. That's what they cawd me at the school, 'Ragbag Jolly'. And oh, ma granny used tae get that angry when Ah went hame and telt her. She would 'Ah'll be doon the school the morn an find oot mair aboot it' but she never did.

...

We had tae sleep wi ma granny tae see tae her, there was naebody but me an ma sister ... ma sister couldnae dae it herself for we had tae get ma granny oot o her bed, an we had tae help her oot o her bed, an pit her clothes on and light the fire and dae aw that afore we went tae the skil. And then Ah had tae [unclear] ma skins for she wouldnae gaither the skins and what I didnae get in the morning, I got at nicht.

And were you late for school?
Late nearly every morning and some of the teachers wis nice wi me, they didnae gie me the strap, they jist gied me a row. But I was ca'd for yin of the teachers, Jessie Morton Jolly's on ma birth certificate. She asked ma mother before I was born, if I was a girl, if I would be ca'd for her. And she liked me but she teached, she was the teacher, so that's whae ah'm ca'd for.

[Speaking of Doughty's game dealer's shop] They were aye game-keepers, bocht pheasants and rabbits an aw that an selt fish. Ah can mind Davie's faither, his mother died awfy young.

Did he mind that you collected the rabbit skins because it was kind of his business too?
No he didnae, he didnae like tae get rabbit skins. But Ah used tae ask him wha bocht rabbits. And sometimes he widnae tell me, he twisted his finger, aye some days he wouldnae tell me wha bocht them. Ah said, 'What bocht the rabbits the day, Mr Doughty?' 'I'm not tellin you' an he widnae tell me. But if Ah went intae the shop an onybody in, Ah kinna aye edged maesel in and stood tae be the last served tae make shair I seen whae bocht a rabbit. Ah was cunning (laughs). Ah can mind o it fine.

Because you needed to know to know which doors to go to?
An then Ah kent tae gaun.

But most people wouldn't mind if you knocked on their door because they would be getting paid?
They used to, 'The rabbit skins [unclear]'. O ma mother used tae hae tae send them awa twa or three times a week. Maybe aboot twice a week. Aw that money. Oh, I was a good skin gatherer. I was guid at ma job.

Though few would be involved in as extensive an enterprise as the rabbit skin trade, most children participated in gathering of various kinds of bounty which could be put to use, freely available in the surrounding countryside.

Greta Hawthorn

> We thinned turnips, what was it? Nine pence for 100 yards or something? They were a big 100 yards I can tell ye and nae wunner ma knees are bad, ye went on a stone and ye went the wrong waiy. Well, it wis yer pocket money. And then we gathered brambles and brought them intae Davie Doughty, I think it was sixpence or something you got for them, for a pound or something. But that was a lot o' money and then we went for snowdrops in the winter time and we put them in a wee shoe box and ye maybe got a cheque back for ten shillings, that was a lot o' money.

And they went off by train?

> Train, they went in the train down tae London. And ye could put them on the train at night and they would be there in the morning. We used to gather them so that they were fresh and oh, they had to be perfect. And ye had tae put tissue paper in between them, damp, so that it would keep them fresh an a' the rest o' it.

Jenny Jolly speaks of gathering sticks at a distance of several miles from Brighouse, near Whithorn.

Jenny Jolly

> Ah just liked the fresh air, jist liked oot. Ah wis aye an ootside body, onyway, wis aye running tae Black's Plantin' and bringing sticks hame for ma mother an Ah fair loved daen that, bagged ower ma shoulder.

By the age of 14 or 15, children were fully fledged members of the workforce. Before that age, the hours children had in the margins of the day, before and after school, were also put to use. Catherine Miller explains her chores at the start of her working life.

Cathy Miller

> Yes. I was one week off Christmas when I was 15 and I was brought from the school for the last week to start ma job, ma chores on the farm. I was able to help with the milking, to go and get the big horse, Belle, from Longhill and when Ah was walking along a road with him he was that

tall he used to clip ma heels. And Ah would put him into the cart and take dung out to the field and put it in lumps and bring a load of turnips back with me, which I had to shaw first. And on a wet day it was hittin ye everywhere and then when ye come home ye had it tae empty intae a pile and then put it in a machine that ye used by hand to cut it all up for cows that couldn't eat the whole turnips, do things like that. And one thing I hated most of all was the kail because it was about four feet tall and every time that ye hit it, ye got a shower, so it was a pretty messy job.

And before you started full-time did you do chores when you were still at school, did you work on the farm a bit?

Yes, ma dad had the milk run for ten years, and Ah used to do ma share at the Top of the Town before Ah went to school. And ma chores were, on a Friday night, for tae get the kindling, the coal, that was really every night, the kindling and the coal, and the sticks in and go and feed the hens, collect the eggs, and in these days we had a big water tank up beside the wash house and it had a handle on the side and ye had tae pump 100 gallons every might for water for use o the farm. That was my chores.

So, how young were you when you started doing chores like that?

About eleven year old. And there [at Barrachan Home farm] Ah did the same sort o things, sticks, kindling and coal.

And so you helped on the milk round?

Well, just gettin cans or jugs or whatever, just at the top, the Wards and down Isle Street and then Ah went tae school.

And so what time was that before school?

Just the back of eight o'clock we were in the town and then ye hared it down the street to be there on time.

And did you get any pocket money for that or was it just?

Yes, Ah got a sixpence on a Saturday and there was two ladies, ma brother helped when he went to school as well, and some people got eggs and potatoes for ma dad did vegetables in these days, a turnip or a bunch o carrots or a bag o potatoes, things like that. And there was a lady called Mrs [Fennian?] and she always gave David, no, Ian, a shilling and that was a lot o money and across the street there was a lady called Mrs Maxwell, her husband worked at the creamery, and Ah got a shilling from her and we were in heaven. That got us a lot of sweets.

…

There was, when ye had a thrashing mill and were doing the bales there was all the chaff, they called it, and that was my job, and I hated it, because you were throwing it into the baler and wi the wind it was all over me, more on me than was in the baler, Ah wasn't tall enough. And Ah also had to shout on Jock Nicholson, when the bags were full o the corn, cause he couldn't hear very well.

OUTSIDE-IN: THE RURAL TOWN

14. Horse-drawn milk delivery cart, Whithorn 1930s.

Tina Soriani and Aldo Petrucci, whose parents came from Italy to found a dynasty at Whithorn's Central Café, recall that their childhood too was fully taken up with working in the family business.

Aldo Petrucci and Tina Soriani

> **AP**: Yes, we were always in the shop.
> **TS**: I was the oldest. And I was the oldest of three– four children, because my sister was only two-year-old then, and I wasn't quite eleven. So my father was away eight month, in those eight month I became quite experienced. And at the weekend, I was in a school concert, and we practised on the Saturday, and I wasn't allowed to go to these concerts, these practises. There were things to do. But I made the excuse of taking my little brother, who was born then, out for a walk or something, and I would leave him outside the school and go to the practice! Because it was something I enjoyed. No, no, I was –
>
> *You were expected to do quite a bit?*
> **TS**: Yes.
> **AP**: And I remember my brother and I used tae prepare the potatoes for the shop every night, for very often. So we were all– But we did it willingly, and, you know, it was–
> **TS**: Oh no, maybe sometimes it was reluctant with me. But I did it!
>
> *Did you get any payment or was it just expected?*
> **TS**: No!
> **AP**: Just expected, we didn't look for payment, you know.

> **TS**: But they worked for their family, and when we needed it–
> **AP**: The funny thing is that when, they helped us all in our careers, whatever we were doing, and when they retired, they didn't have a house to go to!

Using family land, resources and inherited skills were among the strategems for resisting the impact of the cash economy. Garments and fabrics would survive through an extended life cycle in which they were made, handed down and transformed; there was an extendability and a margin for cultivation; there were leftovers and offcuts, an economy of economies which was, in terms of temporality, the reverse of built in obsolescence.

Greta Hawthorn

> And when the butcher or the grocer came we were aboot last in line, they had delivery vans round once or twice a week, and the grocer, it was Carson's the grocer and it was butcher was Charlie Coid, if he'd something left, extra, ye got it a wee bit cheaper suppose it was even a pound o sausages, ye always got that wee bit extra. And my mother used tae– Kinnear's had a man that came round wi his pack but he came fae Kinnear's shop and they had khaki wool and he asked ma mother if she would knit socks for the soldiers so ma sister and I, we knitted them up tae ye come tae the heel, and then ma mother would turn the heel and she would get it shaped, and then we would knit the rest and she got a shilling for a pair of socks but if we had ten pair that was ten shillings and it was a lot o money in these days. So he used to come every so often wi this wool and we would knit up the socks for the troops. Or wee comforters, they were just like a wee bib wi a bit roond the neck, cause we were taught tae knit. Aye, and sew and things like that and darn the stockings.

Were there a lot of things, presumably, would be mended at home which are now bought?

> Bought, whah. And we made rag mats and things like that, there was really never anything wasted because we had hens as well which we got the scraps for the hens and ye got the eggs and ma granny used tae milk a cow and ye got the milk for that and we used to love when it was jist fresh, new, and it was hot and ye had a moustache, ye had a mug tae drink it oot and ye had a moustache wi this cow's milk.

Jenny Jolly recounts her life as a teenager at 133 George Street. Soups designed to use and spread the value and usefulness of vegetables, grown in the rear garden plot, were what orchestrated Whithorn menus; even the flour bags themselves could be made into aprons by a sleight of transformation.

Jenny Jolly

It was vegetables and tatties, it was all for food. Leeks, carrots, cause she made a terrific soup, God, we got enough o soup (laughter). Guid soup, though, ye ken, broth an aw the best an veg, we'd aye hiv vegetables. She [Jenny's mother] was workin in Denton's the bakers.

So that was, what, six days a week or?

Gosh, I cannae mind, I think it was five days, I'm no shair. She was in the hoose, but onyway, when Ah started tae work I cycled up and doon tae Rigg Bay. In the winter time ye were aye shair o soup when ye come hame forby yer meat, tatties and veg. But she used tae watch me comin up on ma bicycle by the memorial and then she went ben and lifted ma soup so that it would just be nice for she'd had it very warm, ye ken.

She sounds like a good mother.

Uh-huh, and she had it just sittin ready for me tae sit doon tae, efter ah'd had tae wesh ma hands an face, of coorse, oh gosh aye. She did aw oor bakin tae, were fetched up on thae girdle scones, bread, soda bread, they werenae sweet.

Well, she would get some of that in Ireland, they're strong on—

Aye, but she could buy the flour, she used tae buy a big bag o flour. Ye used tae get big bags o flour, a hundredweight or something, they were right big bags onyway. Did away wi them and there's maybe a blackbird on some o them, there was always a pattern on them, these big bags, and what ma mother did, an auld people, they opened they bags that – ripped them – got them nicely opened up, the sides, the bottom an aw, an they joined maybe four o them thegither for sheets but there wisnae a mark on them, they were bleached and bleached and whatnot. An the farmers used tae get stuff in these great big bags that you don't see noo, different bags they were and the auld folk got an empy yin o them and they cut roond the bottom, they made aprons to keep them clean when they were working, tied them roon their waist and they were right doon tae there jist aboot. And they were washed tae, boiled white bit o ribbon they got, no fancy ribbon for yer hair, that tape? Roond the top an for tyin them on. Ye always could do … durin the War they could kinna make and mend, ye ken? And ma mother got aw the odd bits o wool she could lay her hands on and she knitted my socks for ma boots and they were aw colours, what a colours they were but they were warm, you were glad o them in the frosty weather. For ye had tae wear tackety boots, couldnae wear wellies or ocht wi using the big axes and the saws. So, she made sure ah'd guid socks, fancy socks. They were cosy an that's aw that mattered.

Self-Help and Helping Yourself

The poacher was in the very margins of this marginal economy, making the most of what was freely available. Betty Stuart recalls how surplus fowl and game were turned to account.

Betty Stuart

Do you remember much about poaching in the countryside?
>Aye, there used to be a lot o poaching, aye. There was quite a lot of poaching Ah think, if they wanted onything they just went.

Molly: Of course, Ah expect ye got a gun easy then?
>Ah but some o them didnae need a gun for it. If they were at a mill workin and they were ready to come awa an a hen went past they could have had it. 'And you'll walk home with me tonight, ma dearie' and intae their bag (laughter). Aye they did, they definitely did they kind o things. Aye, there was a lot o that, it was aw pheasants, they went for pheasants.

Was there a lot of rabbits still eaten, that you can remember?
>Yes, Ah certainly remember we ate rabbits. But we had it in the hoose, rabbit stew and that and things. No for me, but they had aw these things. The farmers knew they were pinchin things. They would let them dae it for so long and then they'd come and sack them. Ah can remember this wuman, right enough, the hen went past and she got a hawd o it, 'Heuch!' Jist like that and intae her bag and, 'Walk with me tonight, ma dear'. Aye they did, they helped theirselves.

Jenny Jolly

But lots of people would eat rabbit?
>We did, we aw did, because it was the cheapest thing ye could get. An folk that was poachin would threw in a couple tae folk that's no oot tae get them. But ... Bill yince had them tae but then he caught yin, yin day, and fetched it hame and he skinned it but neither him nor me could eat it. It was smelly, but Ah mind o ma mother, when she cooked a rabbit she always got a bit o mutton, a bone o mutton or something, ye ken, and she cooked it with the rabbit and it took the smell o the rabbit smell aways a bit. Ye got mair o the kinda, Ah cae it mutton but they ca' it lamb nooadays, but it was jist mutton. Ah yaist tae make a hotpot wi the neck o lamb tae but, ye ken, wi the fat off it, but it was a nice hotpot, it wis a recipe Ah got oot o a book.

Did you know people poaching salmon? I guess that would be further north towards Wigtown?

Oh no, they poaches salmon tae, some o them, cannae dae it sae much noo though, ye get permits noo, but they used tae poach them. … Oh, aye, they got, if they were caught, they got fined maybe ten shillings or something, a pound. But there wasnae mony o them caught (laughs) but if they were, they were fined if they were poachin and then they fetched this disease in [myxomatosis] tae kill aw the rabbits, it didnae make sense that, when folk could hae been eatin them. But no, ye wouldnae hae ate them ah'm tellin ye, they were lyin dead wi their eyes stickin oot o their head, puir wee things. Somebody said they never stopped eatin them but Ah don't know aboot that.

Oh aye, we, ma mother had a lot o rabbits, she used tae get them gived tae her and she used tae boil them and fry them and roast them and yin thing an another, make soup, for they werenae greasy they were mild. And then sometimes the pheasants, oor Molly never liked much the pheasant meat, Ah did, Ah wis used wi them, for Bill was aye shootin. … Ah mind Ah went ower for him yin time, Ah wis using the car for his work before he used the tanker and we were comin alang the back road fae the Port, ye ken, he spotted this pheasant away doon this big field at the other end; other times, he could hardly walk, but this time he spotted it, 'You drive slow, now dinnae jerk this car' he was shouting at me, 'Don't jerk it just slow, slow, slow, but keep moving' and he got the gun oot o the windae and he shot that through the windae and, other times he couldnae get by, but that night he was oot the car like a greyhound awa doon tae the field, picked it up. Ah used tae pluck them, cook them.

They would eat hare as well, I suppose?

No really, but Mrs Jolly used tae make hare soup because a hare was a different kinna cookin thing. It had tae be, the red, and it was the blood ye yaised oot o it, a bowl o blood oot o it for making soup and stuff. She used tae make tomato, mushroom, mushroom ketchup they used tae gaither wild mushrooms and she yaist tae make mushroom ketchup. Oh they made aw thae things in the auld days, noo it's easier jist tae buy. It's the same wi the tatties noo, it used tae be the farmers grew a lot o tatties but, and folk had them in their gairdens tae. Noo they come in fae abroad and awwheres.

Inside Out: Houses

The houses of the Machars in the early twentieth century were not, as today, private enclaves connected to services of water and power through links to vast networks connecting them to the rest of the country, endowing them with capabilities and afflicting them with disasters beyond their control and, indeed, well beyond their borders: the privatisation of domestic spaces and the internalisation of services had only just begun. Just as country and town invaded each other, outside and inside, outdoors and indoors were not separated by a great distance. Houses offered a far more fragile protective shield from the outdoors and from the intrusion of neighbours and the community, which, therefore, was less viewed as intrusion. The natural world was kept at bay by only the slightest of divisions and tamed only by a slender technological mastery. The origins of power, heat and services were not flows of forces down lines sketched across country, but were traceable and identifiable, individuated and lumpen: sticks and coal; pails and tin baths.

Yet, unconnected with the wider world, social connections and a burgeoning population filled the void; indeed the void left by the just detectable future of technology was the condition of the existence of the labouring and skilled populousness of the countryside. Privacy itself could find no hiding place in the sociableness of large families, of the bothy which existed in farmyards for farmhands, or the mingling of generations within one household. Spaces within were not as yet highly differentiated, with the communal central space of the kitchen serving for dining, eating, socialising and sleeping; symbolic of this is the box bed which had not as yet been banished to the bedroom but was built in the warm corner of the kitchen. The house, even within the town, was still a shelter, still cowed by the impinging outdoors, and dominated by the iron routine of days and seasons – of going out early to the fields and returning in the dark.

The minimal technology of washing was the opportunity for the sociability of the shared clothes line, described by Jessie McLean. Hints of the link between privatisation of the house and the growth in domestic technology comes in the account by Jessie of the exclusion of school friends from viewing the new electric light and flushing lavatory which her family were first to have at the Top of the Town.

With technology appearing only on a distant horizon, within the intimacy of the domestic which appears in its stead, there is the complementary presence of large families, their numerousness an asset and one which affected the social space.

Alex Haswell

And that's the other thing that's not the norm, it was not unusual for
families of ten, eleven, twelve kids. In fact, the family that, there was the

Brolls – I've forgotten the name of the other family – but the town council actually built them a special house up where Kelly's Garage was, a big house. And that was built specifically for that one particular family, because they were in The Park, and they just outgrew the house.

Services were located outside so that the trip to the pump, which were located at strategic points in the town, incorporated the outdoors into the domestic economy and diminished the privacy and the possessiveness of the private space.

Betty Stuart

> Well, it was– we had a livin room, we just cawed it the kitchen, the kitchen, an a bedroom, an it was quite a big bedroom which it would need to be because there was two, an we had what ye cawed a settle bed in the livin room, wi a lid on it. That was it and we had a range fire. Nae toilet. Just a widden [seat] thing, we hadnae anything like that, we had no water for any, we went to the pump. Went to the pump for all your water, we had no pump at all, nothing like that, no, and it was oil, paraffin oil lamps. … Yes, and ye did all your cookin on the fire … it was a coal fire, but we had a kinna oven beside, attached to the range thing, ye could put things intae. It was very, it was really nothing much. And ye were lyin on the floor.
>
> *Molly Stuart: On yer mattresses.*
>
> That's right and [unclear] if anybody come they just lay doon on a mattress. We hadnae much room at all, just the room and kitchen. Ma granny, while she was alive, she had the main bed in the living room, it was the kitchen we used tae call it then. While she was alive she had that.
> … We had nothing like, no hygiene, I would say there was nane at aw. Very, very little hygiene.
>
> *Molly: And a minimum of food and a minimum of heat.*
>
> Ye know, ye only had the, we only had a coal fire, we hadnae onything else. And then the toilet was, there was nae flush toilets, dry closets was they caad them. … there was the scavenger's cart in these days, a horse and cart and ye could, if it was properly in a bucket, an aw covered up an that, ye could put it intae the scavenger's cart. … It was Wiffy Keith, he was the scavenger. The cart.
>
> *He'd be employed by the town council?*
>
> He was employed, aye. Oh he would hae some mess but it was just everything, ye had nothing really, it would aw go into the scavenger's cart, likely. … Ah think it was roond a lot, it wisnae a once a week thing, it would need tae hae been oftener, the cart, wi the dry closets and things.

15. Wiffy Keith and the scavvy cart.

And did you have a tin bath, or anything that you could put in front of the fire?
Aye, it was a zinc bath, that's where ye were bathed.
Molly: Yin efter the other.
Sunday was the bath day, no it was Saturday for the sake o the Sunday School in the morning. It was jist yin o they, jist an ordinary bath we had, zinc bath, one at a time.

Jenny Jolly remembers the coming of water on tap, a water supply which began to be divorced from local supply and its exposure to the surplus or deficit of drought, and where the risk of the wells running dry in a hot summer began to be managed. Wash days too, just like the harvest, were dominated by the coming and going of good and bad weather.

Jenny Jolly

That's right, it [mains water] come late tae. Ah mind when it come because there was a lot of folk come tae Whithorn, women took in lodgers, although they hadnae a lot o room but they made a spare room for lodgers, it was extra money. And they aw got a room onyway.
The men who did the water would have to hire lodgings?
That's when Jimmy O'Donnell, Jimmy come tae Whithorn but he married Annie Mills and he stayed on in Whithorn. It was work tae. Aye, there

was pumps so far in the street but sometimes the water went, they got the water fae a bit doon the row and it was really hot weather the water went scarce but the one doon below oor hoose, wi it being in the slope o the hill, ye were aye sure o getting a drop.

So you had to go out with a bucket every day or more than once?

Oh aye, as much water– what we did– ma mother still had the auld bath Ah telt ye aboot oot there, Ah aye mean tae let ye see it. We took the bath tae the pump and filled it wi water an then she'd a big steel, iron pot for washing the clothes in, don't know how she aye lifted it off fu o claiths. She boiled the water for hot water and then it was filled again, the clothes intae it and it was covered again wi water and the clothes was boiled in it. Ken, there wisnae the weshing stuff there was nowadays but they still got, and they had tae be nice and white, you know. And then the blankets, ye had tae stand and get the blankets outside and Ah stood at yin end and ma Ma at the other. She turned this way and ah'd tae turn that way, to get them on tae the line. I always mind getting them dry tae, nice and dry, ye had tae get a guid dry day onyway for them. They wouldnae hae been washed if it hadnae been a guid day.

And was that once a week, you did that?

The blankets, no, because there was big sheets, poly, no polyester sheets, other sheets and bedspreads, bedspreads wis aye weshed and the sheets was aye washed but they were washed regular the blankets, dependent on the weather.

Yes, and you did your clothes, what? Once a week?

Oh aye, well, sometimes ye washed, was washed at night what ye took off gaun tae bed, they were strung up.

And she would boil using what?

There was coal and sticks.

We used tae gaun tae Blacks Wood and get the bags o sticks that was awfy guid for kindling up the fire, ye got a quick fire wi them, ye ken.

And then for ironing she used what?

Aye, the old fashioned ... Ah had that auld iron till Ah come doon here and Ah don't know where it went.

Cathy Doughty describes an agricultural worker's cottage at the Cults, where even the very inside of the mattresses were supplied with filling from a byproduct of the milling process and comfort came and went with the approach of the harvest.

Cathy Doughty

We lived in a cottage, two rooms and a kitchen, there was nine of us altogether, that's counting my father and mother, there was seven of a family.

How did you all fit in?
> Well, ye just had what they called a settle bed, if you know what a settle bed is. Ye bring it down and ye put it into, and ye fill it with chaff at the mill, when the mill come in, and you fillt it and ye were away up here, then by the time the mill come back again ye were doon on the bare boards!

And did any of you have to share a bed?
> Oh aye, we did, we had two beds in one room for the boys, and the younger ones, well, the younger ones would sleep in my mother's room and I would sleep in this settle bed.

By the 1960s, the simplest of systems conjoining houses was in place, as John Wilson describes.

John Wilson

> Well, ma father retired in 1964 and Ah got married in '64 and Ah bought a house in George Street, in Whithorn, an Ah come in there and again, the house Ah got was just a shell. It had just stone slabs on the floor and it had a toilet, it had electricity of sorts, basically light, and Ah can't remember, aye, it had runnin water obviously, it had runnin water, but it came from the house next door. And the toilet was, there was a wee outhouse attached to the back of the house and in this outhouse was a cubicle about the size of a telephone box and in that cubicle was a toilet and that was it. There was one little window about 18 inches square in the room and this cubicle was at the side of it but the people next door had built a shed right up against it so there was basically no light in the place. At the other side from where the toilet was was a set pot and there would be a tap in there somewhere, Ah can't quite remember where the tap, there would be a tap near the set pot so that was basically the house. So we had to set to and get the drainage sorted out and get our own drainage in and get water, etc. intae it. As far as the town itself's concerned Ah can remember we used to hear the town crier going up, occasionally going up saying aboot warrant sales, that was still, the bell, ring the bell, warrant sale at such and such a house, at that time. Whithorn wis— one o the other things Ah remember was there was dogs all over the place.

The origins and destination of food and goods were linked by a short supply chain, still connecting those who knew each other by name. Those who were living in the countryside cottages and cothouses were dependent on the circulating timetable of deliveries from local shops, as Cathy Doughty recounts.

Cathy Doughty

So what would a typical day's food have been, what did you have for breakfast?
   Well, there was porridge, or my mother always had fry in the morning, the boys were going out and they werenae coming back, some o them, til night, but she'd sandwiches to make up for their midday meal. My father liked a scone wi an egg in it. She always baked every day, fresh scones and there's always plenty to eat, she'd always a good oven to bake in.
Was it a coal-fired oven then?
   It was a coal-fire oven. The old fashioned swee, you know, for the pans, put them on the kind o, hang them up. Big pans.
And what would you have had at lunch time?
   Soup, and potatoes, and whatever, and then there was always a meal at night. Always plenty to eat, the fish man came round, and the butchers came round, we had plenty of [fish], we had bakers. Ye had to buy your things, they came aboot twice or three times a week, but ye got your groceries, and ye got your butchers and your bakers and there's aye plenty coming round. There was aye plenty to eat in the house.
So she didn't really have to go out to the shops, she just had the shops come to her?
   The shops came to her mainly. … It was handy. They used to come in wi different bakers, different grocers. It was MacCaulay's, Garrocks, and there was Costley's, and different ones came round. Some were the Cooperate, some were the [caught?] folk like the Cooperatey. They used tae come. And there was plenty of grocers, plenty of bakers. Bakers came from Newton Stewart. And he come round twice a week, so ye'd to buy your bread, and coorse it lastit. And then Denton's startit and ye could go to Denton's, he came on a Monday night, and ye could buy your bread there if ye wantit. There was plenty o shops and plenty o grocers coming, plenty vans. … came to Whithorn for the better shops, really. Went tae … we liked Garlieston, Cults is halfway, ken, between Sorbie, Garlieston and Whithorn.

Sources of food were not only closer to home – or grown at home – but the processing intruded directly into the home: Cathy Miller and John Wilson speak about the preparations for butchering a pig, whose very extremities were put to use. The deferral of the impact of money, an economy of the economy, allowed the space and time for skill and industry of the home producer, unmediated by cash.

Cathy Miller and John Wilson

   CM: Mr Coid, he was the butcher in Whithorn. And the dairy was along the far end, the dairy was all washed and hosed down and used salt and water as well tae clean all the corners and everything, it had to be, and then left for a couple of days till it– and before he came it was washed down again and he used to hang them from up the rafter bit. Nothing was wasted, the ears, everything, tongue. Ma mum made potted meat, she had stone jars and Ah did not like it (laughter).

So, did Mr Coid take it all away or did your father's–?

CM: No, he would take half of it away, ma dad couldn't but ma dad rolled all the hams, wi [salt] then rolled it all around and then put a muslin on it and it hung from the ceiling, maybe about six, seven, hams hanging from the ceiling, did us through the winter.

JW: One of the highlights for us when we worked at Catherine's mother's house, she always got the, she did some baking and it was the most wonderful place to go and work, couldn't get there quick enough because the baking was just something else, wasn't it, Catherine? … She was the most wonderful baker. …you'd gaun in there and the next thing you would see this big bake board being produced and she had a white apron on, she was always absolutely immaculate and this baking was produced and it was to die for, it really was, absolutely wonderful. Apple pies.

CM: Yes, treacle scones, pancakes, soda scones.

JW: And with very basic equipment. Really.

CM: Well that was all, a knife and a rolling pin. And a bowl.

JW: And just an ordinary standard oven?

CM: Yes, yes.

And was it every day that she baked or just–?

CM: [Everyday] Yes, and if she couldn't sleep she would have a baking done at three o'clock in the morning and when ye came down, it would be all sitting, all covered wi lovely white towels, she'd been up for a couple of hours. She worked hard ma mum. … Homemade strawberry jam, ma mum made all her own preserves, rasps, blackcurrants, strawberries, gooseberries.

So, in many ways you must have been fairly self-sufficient. You had milk, you had pig products and you had all your own baking and you had your preserves?

CM: Yes, and we also had carrots, which we sold by the bunch, turnips, beetroot, ma dad always had his own onions and things and leeks, these were never, ever bought, there was always, there was a strip in the bottom of the Mill Hill it was kept solely for the produce of the carrots and things like that. The only thing Ah hated about it is ye had to go down on yer hands and knees and weed it, get big bags round your knees and ye couldn't do it with gloves or anything on cause ye would pull the whole lot out, ye had tae just, bare hands.

JW: And then he had, had bees as well, hadn't he?

CM: Yes, a lot o bees. About twelve boxes o bees. And they all had to be looked after, fed in the wintertime with water and sugar and it was put intae a jar and then a piece of muslin over the top of it and just set at the front of the box.

So, really, what you had to buy in a town would have been what? Tea and sugar and–?

CM: No, she didn't even buy that in the town, there was a wee man came round for years and years and he brought bakin soda, cream o tartar, tea and coffee, not very much coffee. It was jars about this size and it was black, black, black (laughs) but she definitely got her tea from him.

Houses were the simplest of porous envelopes, not hermetically sealed against the outside. Tom McCreath describes how the earth and its damp, intruding within the house, could be tamed, but was not excluded, by simple means.

Tom McCreath

I remember the cottages on the farm and all ours had either concrete or wooden floors but some were damp, I know, or maybe the odd room in a house was damp but an essential part of that, even with an earth floor, and there were one or two even after, just after, the War, that had earth floors was a roll of linoleum and it's amazing what a comfortable home could be created despite that problem. Yes, dampness was the biggest problem.

Yes. And presumably, I think, running water, I mean water inside the houses only came to Whithorn in the '30s, am I right?

Oh, absolutely. The only cottage of ours that had running water inside was the dairy house, the others had a pump outside and of course all cooking was done on the sort of open fire in the living room, although it was a semi-grate as it were and pots could be hung over it. Yes, it was very primitive.

And probably that had implications for the diet: it would be completely different because it's determined by what you could do with what you had? The fire would not be very controllable?

Well, that is so and on the farms the wages were very low but they had milk, potatoes, sometimes oatmeal. I'm trying to think of the other things but oatmeal provided a large part of their diet but of course the countryside was hotching with rabbits .... And you know, a rabbit made a very good meal.

So that would have been more common than beef or lamb, presumably?

Oh, I don't think many of the cottagers could afford beef or lamb. In the farmhouse you would get it because the butchers bought in the local market in Newton Stewart so my father always insisted that he would buy the meat, wouldn't let mother do it, because he wanted to keep up his relations with Charlie Coid and others (laughter).

The least calculable and measurable of fuels was peat, still rich with the roots of prehistoric plants, and much in relation to its efficiency depending on how much it had been exposed to the rain or well dried on the peat moor; Kennedy Donnan remembers how it was used at Faldarroch, near Barrachan, for cooking and heating. The controllability of the fuel had, as its substitute, the deft skill, alert eye and calculation of the cook, who would also calculate that the range also heated the bed in the kitchen.

Kennedy Donnan

I suppose it was quite warm at least, if you had your bed in the kitchen.
　　Yes, aye and the fire was aye on. There was aye peats cut every year tae, there's a peat stack just outside there.
Right, so where was the peat cut from?
　　… Where the water trough is, in the Moss, first gate on your left going up the road.
　　[On cooking with peat] Aye, Maggie, aye, it was a big hearth, put peat on and when she put shortbread or that on she had a – what de ye ye caw it – tongs and nipped oot a red peat, or a couple and put them on top o the lid … it would cook that much quicker. And then the swee tray, when she was cooking onything wi pots or ocht she hung it on the swee tray and then swung it roond on tae the fire.
So, who cut the peat because that's a heavy job?
　　Wullie [Aitken]. Ah yaist tae gie him a hand because Ah wisnae busy.
And was there a special tool that you used?
　　Yes, yes. It cuts it aboot that length. Ye push it in the breast and then break it off and take it away, put it intae a barrow, maybe put twelve or that onto it, took it intae the Moss a bit and tipped it intae a lump to let them dry. After a bit ye set them up against each other so as they'd dry better, then ye went on horse and cart and built them intae a horse and cart and then brung them into the stackyaird. It was quite a bit of work.

When the mystery of systems and the miracle of their instantaneous supply reached Whithorn, Jessie McLean and her daughter Mary tell how they elicited curiosity, and a certain possessiveness. Yet, the sociability of the shared clothes line and use of a mangle continued; where domestic technology was in short supply, it seemed, it was not wholly privatised.

Jessie McLean

Yes, we were the first people at the top o the toon tae hae electricity. The Jollys wis the first house to have electricity and we were the first people to have a flush toilet, the Jollys. There ye are.

You were ahead of your time.

That was us, we were the first folk at the top o the toon, the twa pubs had nane, the shops had nane, we had it. First folk at the top o the toon tae hae electricity an a flush toilet.

And was that in the 1930s?

Ah cannae mind. I mind that for we were the first folk and we weren't allowed tae bring our friends into the house to the toilet. Ma granny, we werenae allowed tae dae that and we werenae allowed tae bring them in tae see oor lights. No, because it would hae got too common and we weren't allowed tae.

So people wanted to see?

People want– we telt them at the school that we had this licht that ye jist switched an we had a flush toilet. But we never were allowed tae bring them intae the house tae see it. Ma granny never let ye bring a wean in. Never, ever, did a bring a pal intae the hoose in ma life, never were allowed (laughs).

But you were allowed to play out in the street? Or not?

Aye ye were allowed tae dae that, but no bring them intae the hoose.

Did you wash once a week? Did you have to wash once a week or more?

More.

Mary: They had a hoose though, hadn't ye? Ye had a boiler hoose, ye had a wee hoose up the tap wi a boiler in it that they pit a fire, a wash hoose wi a big boiler an they pit a fire doon below it didn't yaes and you had tae stand on a stool because you were so wee ... . To dae her, when it was her turn.

Ma sisters were aw tall, like you, all tall and well built, but me, an Ah was a wee tottie lass.

Mary: But ye had tae tak yer turn in the hoose an dae the work.

But Ah had tae tak ma turn. It took me longer for Ah was wee compared tae them. Ye had tae work, an yer size didnae make ony difference, ye still had tae dae it.

Did you have a mangle?

Aye we had a big mangle, an ye ken what we done, we were the only yin at the top o the toon tae have a mangle an as mony folk come for tae pit their claithes through the mangle.

Mary: An they had claithes lines the whole width o the field up at the Top of the Toon hadn't ye?

The claithes lines, we didnae hae lines in wur gairden, we hung wur claithes on the fence, right fae the yin end o the toon, the fence, tae the top end. Naebody ever stole fae onybody, ye aye got yer ain things. That shows ye how freendly folk were then.

Jock McMaster recalls how the advent of a minimal supply of electricity in its early beginnings continued to allow opportunities for socialisation. Jock remembers the coming of electricity, a slender line stretched just far enough to reach the farm cottage, at the extremity of the electrical supply system.

Jock McMaster

> Yea, there was cottages on the farm, traditional Wigtownshire cottages, just a long line with a lean-to kitchen behind and traditionally just a room and kitchen. They're now all one house but you can see where the one door's been blocked up. And they've a door at each end and kitchen or a living room and a bedroom and that was it. And Ah can remember them, no running water, in the '50s, no toilet, it was an outside toilet, but of course since then they've all been revamped. So we had one, two, three, four, five, yea we had five cottages in the '50s with people in them and most of the wives worked too.
> …
> Two rooms, mostly, yes. Aye, there was a main, living room and there was another, a bedroom and just stone, they were stone floors– they were tiles like quarry tiles and a black range for cooking. Oh Ah remember them well, Ah remember takin them out. And the water at the pump down the road, they had tae walk down the road tae get the water, carry it up in buckets and big families.
> …
> In ma dad's day there was Kevans from Port William, Ah think there was about eight or nine o them reared in a room and kitchen up there. How those women managed Ah don't know, Ah don't know at all.
> …
> That's right and children in those days, I think, were seen as a sort of asset, they could go out and work. As soon as the kids were big enough they'd be out earning some money. But in the late '50s the houses were gutted and made two into one which made them much more suitable. And kitchens and toilets and what not put in, but that's just the way they were.
> …
> Electricity obviously must have made a big difference to them, although the line we had going across the stack for the house over there, by the time the electricity got to him it was so low that he couldnae watch television and boil the kettle at the same time, that was just totally out and Bob

being a knacky kinna chap got in wi a screwdriver and he altered the television to take less electricity. Seemingly in those days you could turn them down, the voltage down, to keep the picture the full size, cause as soon as ye put lights on the picture shrunk away down into just a box. But Bob got a screwdriver and fixed that. But it was, they didn't know any better. Sorry, Ah don't mean to sound like that, it was just the way things were, then. … Everybody was the same. And he, Ah remember him buying an old motor car and he was over the moon wi this thing, he'd never had a car before, and a bicycle was their only means of transport.

Beyond the family circle, larger farms would often have extra hands coming in from the fields to feed in the farm kitchen; the surplus of population bulged into the farmhouses, into the attics above the kitchen, as 'live in' hands, or into bothies located on the farm.

Hugh Ramsay

Well, there was one man always stayed in a bothy up at the farm, so she [Hugh's mother] fed him. Night and morning, and weekends. He was usually a ploughman. The only other feedin she done was on mill days and thrashin days, she fed the millmen, and the workers on the mill days. Also harvest time, if they were workin a wee bit late at night, she fed them then.

On larger farms too, there was 'help' living in the house, supplementing the lack and predicting the coming of domestic technology. Households were essentially porous and their management was accomplished by the expandable labour of extra hands.

Judy Brown

Yes, we had a live-in housekeeper.
Somebody who stayed with you a long time?
Yes, I don't remember the ones, the first ones, but certainly Mrs Kirk, she must have been with us about nine or ten years.
And did she do, did she do all the cooking or help your mother do the cooking?
No, my mother did all the cooking. She would help prepare the vegetables and do the housework because there were no modern (laughs) things were just beginning to get washing machines and things. But we still had the copper boiler down in an outhouse which had, the fire had to be lit under it in a Monday morning, to get the washing done. So there was a lot, housework was a lot heavier too in those days.

Oh yes. And did she have her own room?
> Yes, yes she had.

So, how big was the farmhouse?
> Scullery, kitchen, dining room, office, sitting room, first floor there were four bedrooms and a bathroom, and then there were two attic bedrooms. So there were six bedrooms all told.

3

Outside: The Farms

The Rhythm of the Work

Thanks to the minimal impact of technology, the countryside was populous (and therefore possible): we have to reimagine not only the crowding of big families and the intrusion of spare 'hands', the filling of all cottages to bursting point, but – before the advent of the motor car and its internal space insulated against the outdoors – the fact that people were seen and heard on the roads, were exposed to each other as they walked, cycled or drove on carts. The fact that the pace of life and business was dictated by the speed of foot, bicycle or horse, and the sparseness of social events and contact magnified their impact and, oddly, brought them closer. The very small becomes visible and meaningful on a horizon whose breadth is measured by foot a nd horse.

Betty Stuart speaks of her mother's working (and walking) week.

Betty Stuart

> She just walked, she walked for miles and miles anyway, wherever she was going, she was always walking, walkin. She just walked, Ah don't think that she'd ever been in a car that Ah ken o.

Was there any particular job your mother didn't like doing on the farms?

> Well, Ah really don't know, no Ah don't. Ah think she did, Ah think ma mother could hae worked onywhere on a farm. For they were always wantin her tae go oot tae work, ye ken. But, Ah mean, she walked, she widnae take a lift, she walked in the morning and that, she walked tae Brownhill, Sheddock, and aw these places. … An Drury. Ersock, these were her main ones, Drury Lane, Ersock.

And was Sunday a day off? Did she get that?

> Aye, Sunday was off, she got her washing done then, the weekly washing. Aye, she didnae work aw day on a Saturday, twelve o'clock, Ah think. Ah think it was half day.

Tom McCreath

Well, I know today how difficult it is to drive through Whithorn (laughter). It's not all bad but yes, and of course people who didn't have cars would either cycle or walk unless they had a motorcycle and masses of people walked for very long distance on a Sunday, really well-dressed and turned out, to call on their friends or meet relations. Long, long distances.

Judy Brown

You weren't going running round in cars and things then, you walked and with the War and the end of the War there wasn't petrol, there wasn't the transport that we've got now. The farmer had a phone and the farmer had one car or one vehicle and the workers had nothing. They walked and we just walked and we played there. Because there was one bus went up the road past Cutreoch once a week, which was known as 'the picture bus' on a Saturday night (laughs).

Jessie McLean and her daughter, Mary, describe the working week for men building the Clatteringshaws Dam.

Jessie McLean

Mary: An the men used tae break stanes at the quarry.
   Aye, ma uncles.

16. Kirvennie farm, near Wigtown.

Mary: At the quarry.
   For the roads.
Mary: Oot for, whaur Ma, whaur wis the quarry?
   Prestrie.
Mary: Prestrie. An ma mother used tae, me an aw, she used tae tak their piece oot.
   Aye, they did. And their stanes were in great big raws and that's hoo the man, he measured the raws that way and that way, an that's hoo they were payed.
Mary: An you took the pieces oot at dinnertime and–
   Ah took the pieces oot an ma auntie would gie us pieces an a lang can an the tea in it an the sugar in it. An Ah got somebody at the farm tae fill it fu wi water and that was the men's lunch. Puir souls.
Mary: An then the men frae Whithorn built, a lot of them built Clatteringshaws Dam, ye ken.
   Aye, Ah mind o that.
Mary: They went on bikes and walked on Sunday. They walked aw week an just come hame on a Setterday. A lot o wur uncles done that.
   Ah mind o that tae.
It's a long way to Clatteringshaws from here.
   Aye, tae gaun tae work, for aw the pay they would get.
And did they have to stay there during the week in a camp?
   Aye, in an auld tent kinna thing that they made. No a right caravan, no, ye ken, it was just a kinna makeshift thing.
Right, and that was some of your brothers?
   Aye an cousins.
Mary: Cousins and uncles.
   There were cousins. Hard working men. Imagine, that was what they made the roads wi, the stanes, they men chopped. Noo they dinnae even get that for they get in the prison.

Jock McMaster tells how the advent and the speed of the new-fangled motor car was recognised as causing a loss of connection, and loss of sources of local information, between people.

Jock McMaster

And the old farmer along the road, he had a car but he preferred to cycle to Whithorn because he said if you went in the car, you never got speaking to anybody. You wouldn't stop and talk, but the bike, you're only doing seven, eight, nine miles an hour, you just stopped, 'There's Willie, so, I'll stop and have a blether' and he took– he went in on the bike more often than not for that reason.

Those in the professions too, even those we now know as 'emergency services', served wide areas on bicycles or horseback until the advent of the first cars in Wigtownshire. John Scoular's father, minister of Glasserton Church, was on call on a bicycle; the breadth of the parish and the smallness of his means for crossing it only serving to sharpen his readiness and his connection with it.

John Scoular

> All the years that my father was in Glasserton, he and my mother travelled the parish, it was a considerable parish stretching from Monreith almost to Isle of Whithorn and into Whithorn, bringing in Ravenstone, and all the period they were in that, in running that parish, all they had was two bicycles. There was no car for the parish minister and yet they and the doctor, really, were expected to provide a 24-hour service to anybody in need in the community
>
> I remember vividly my mother and my father going visiting people who were ill or in trouble and you're talking about, all they had was bikes and even before electric light on bicycles. I remember these carbide lamps that fizzed away at the front of the bike, a marvellous light but they were [unclear]. And you're talking about a considerable– Glasserton parish was a big parish, it stretched from Tonderghie right through to Monreith, inland to Ravenstone and back out here.

The local doctors were among the first to acquire cars, marking the onset of systems, both medical and motorised.

Dr Guy Brown

> And the [Dr]Selby Senior came in about 1870s and he had a pony and trap, I have several photographs. His son joined him later, about the end of the century and he had a car, I have a photograph of him in a car with no number plate, I think number plates came in in 1903 and one of him in a car with a number plate, OS3, which is the local registration. … Yes. So, from then on it was, they had cars, the District Nurse had a cycle, bicycle, the first District Nurse to have a car was a Nurse Robertson and it was her own car. She had been a sister in the Victoria, native of the village, but at the beginning of the War went back to Glasgow, back to the Victoria. And somewhere about then nurses were provided with a car. There had been talk for a wee, a number of years, that they maybe should have a car, the nurse, but they never managed to raise enough funds, the local nursing association.

OUTSIDE: THE FARMS

The rarity of cars in pre-war Whithorn was demonstrated by an early traffic accident in which Betty Stuart, ready for her first day at school, was injured; the lack of drama with which the whole incident was handled, both by her grandmother and by the driver, betrays the balance between the comparative rarity of the car with the surplus of children.

Betty Stuart

Aye, there wisnae many cars. Ah think Willie Rogers was the first car in. He was a motor hirer in Whithorn. Ah think his was the first one. There wasnae many cars in my day. Quite a lot o them wi the horses and traps, … That's how I went away to ma work, was on the milkcart.

Before Ah went to school. Ah wis knocked doon by a car an ma mother was away working, of course ma granny was there. Ah can hear ma granny yet sayin, 'Oh well' she says 'That finishes the porridge makin today' (laughter). I can hear her sayin it, she was a lovely lady, ma granny, she was really lovely. And Ah was knocked down by a car and, of course, Ah was ready to go to school, and then of course May Steele an aw them, ma friends, called in for me, well Ah couldnae go, I was that annoyed because– no because they had to go to school an Ah wisnae goin– so Ah wasnae at the school for quite a while. Because Ah had leg injuries and roond ma tummy and that. It was ma own fault, it wisnae the, but the two ladies, there were two ladies in a dark car, ye didnae see many cars in these days, to me it was a beautiful car and the next day there was a knock at the door an this was the two ladies and they give ma mum something, like money, an I got a doll an that was the first doll Ah ever had. So I lifted it. Ma granny says, 'Let me see it', she took it oot o the– sorted it a bit, got a chair and there it was, put up on the wall and Ah never got touchin it (laughter). Never got touchin ma doll. It's the only doll, I think, probably I ever had but it was put up on the wall.

But you never protested?

No, we couldnae protest to ma granny, no, no. In these days ye didnae refuse onything, ye had tae just do what ye were told, ye ken.

As Greta Hawthorn describes, the roads had as yet not been smoothed out into ribbons of tarmac, fit to facilitate the speed of the car.

Greta Hawthorn

Isobel and Margaret, they were born at The Dowies and they used tae have tae come up the road tae the school in the governess car, as they talked aboot, horse and cart. Of course it was, or come up on the top of the dykes because there was that much water. ... I was 14 when I left the school and we cycled in from Claymoddie an ye started at seven in the morning tae three and two tae ten at night but ye always needed a lamp on yer bike. And they were the carbide lamps in those days, that it was the water that tricked doon and kept the flame going. Sometimes Ah got it lit and sometimes Ah didnae, it was the owls that scared ye and the bats, going up the Glasserton road, there was always owls darting aboot someplace.

Cycles and the sheer effort of the cyclist were substituted for the expense of delivery vehicles, as John Wilson recalls of his father's joinery business.

John Wilson

Ah remember actually goin to one place wi a ladder tied to the bike and it was tied along the crossbar, so it chafed the inside o ma leg. I mean this was the way it was, we used tae get– the farmers used to come wi a horse and cart or a, this was early days, a tractor, they'd come with a trailer and take the timber down if there was a lot of timber. But I can remember also we'd go to change a pane o glass somewhere, say a pane o glass got broken, and it would be sandwiched between two bits o hardboard or two bits o plywood and you tied it in yer bike, on yer back, and off ye went. But then, eventually, he got a van and that made a big difference.

Trains had come to the Whithorn area in the 1870s and provided a visible, determinate and measurable connection to distant markets.

Hugh Ramsay

I remember the passenger trains, never mind the goods trains, aye. If you were going to Glasgow, you got the train at Millisle Station and that was you away, changed at Newton Stewart, and you're away to Glasgow.
So in your time, do you remember, there was an extension into Garlieston harbour, do you remember that?
Oh yes. I tell ye, I went down once a day intae Garlieston to the harbour, and when the new mill was made, they made it in such a way that the carriages would go right down under the mill – so the bags of malt, whatever they were, were nice and handy, right into the mill.
And was there somebody manning Millisle Station?
Yes, there was a station master, and there was also a station master at Garlieston. But they called him a station master, but he was mair just a porter. Then the train had to cross the road there – at what we call the Bridge, down there, Tunder's Bridge. And they came out wi a red flag and

OUTSIDE: THE FARMS

17. Portyerrock Mill, near Whithorn, 1890s.

a green flag, two of them, a red flag and a green flag to stop the traffic and let the train across. … but there was plenty of things comin in on the train. Plenty of feeding stuffs, animal feeds, coals, lye, manures. Aye I don't remember anything going away on the train. I think some of the boys that grew potatoes, they used to go on the train, it went away on the train. And you were talking earlier about Marshall fae Cruggleton, with horses, they were a big Shorthorn outfit. They used to bring horses in and send them away on the train, I remember that.

It must have been a big change when the train went; it comes right across your land, doesn't it?

Aye, cam right through the land, right through. Well, latterly, there wisnae so many trains goin. There was only goods trains latterly – and there'd only be, what, two trains a day or something like that; one in the morning; and one at night. That was what they did. But when the old passenger train was on the go, there was quite a few trains then.

Horse-power

The technology of the horse and of horse-drawn equipment, some of it thousands of years old, measured out the daily and weekly routine of feeding, caring for harness, repairs and made possible a specialist economy of feeding, repair, farriery, breeding, export and sometimes showing and racing. Harnessing the horse's ability sped farming and business to mitigate some exposure to risk, and there was a careful fostering of human skill to protect that gain: through breeding, breaking, and horsemanship. It also meant a careful management of the calendar and timeline of the horse which had to be tallied up against the arrival and departure of the seasons and their chances. Shoeing was carried out every six to eight weeks, which meant that the blacksmith became the hub of the working community, as well as a place to gather and exchange news. It was a technology which liberated a social space, and did not eliminate it. The horse was powered by the oat crop in the field – and its power assisted with and hastened the urgency of harvesting it – and shod by the skill of the blacksmith (whose smiddy had to be within walking distance), and harnessed by the skill of the saddlemaker.

Tom McCreath

> Well, that's right, [Saturday] was a day when the farmers had time to go in and in the course of talking would buy things, but I go back to the days when it was a six day week. I remember as a small boy the discussion when Saturday afternoon was to be an off holiday for the men and the farmers wondering how on earth they would get through the work. And one has to remember, that if you fell behind with work there's virtually no way of catching up because it was the speed of the horse and no way could you catch up. ... Yes, and it was tough going because the horsemen would get up at six, take their horses to the stable, feed them, go back and have their breakfast which was probably porridge and milk, and then be ready to start at seven. They would come home for lunch, well, it was dinner in those days, quite a big meal, and stop at five at night, groom their horse, feed it again and put it out for the night. These six days were long days and it's amazing how fit these ploughmen were.

Hugh Ramsay

> [On feeding] Well in time gone by, when the horses wis used in the barn, they got fed quite simply – they either got hay in the manger or a heck in front of them, or oats, raw. They got bruised oats, that's like rolled oats, and bran. And that was their complete diet; that's all they got, the work horses. Nowadays, wi gie them a bit something like, a bit of meat pulp, obviously wi give them some bran, a bit of maize, that type of thing nowadays. Because we don't grow oats on the farms; we don't have oats to give them. But the working horses, that's all they got, was oats and bran.

18. Three-horse binder, harvesting oats, Low Clone farm, Port William, 1936/37.

Tom McCreath

As a boy everything was hand work or drawn by horses.
And that again is a massive change isn't it? I mean the whole expertise of handling horses?
Yes, some men were not able to make the change efficiently, others were. But the younger men, after the War, grew up preferring tractor work.
So, did you have stables on the farm?
Yes, I'm trying to think how many. I think it held ten horses and I was thinking not so long ago, that if I was blindfolded, I could walk into the stable, take down the horses, I would feed the horse from the oats bunker and put the harness on a horse blindfolded. I think I could still do that.

Greta Hawthorn cared for the harness at Claymoddie, as part of the weekly routine.

Greta Hawthorn

> And on a Sunday night ye yist tae have tae bring the horse harness intae the back kitchen and ye out papers on the floor and ye had tae polish them and Brasso them and Silvo them for the Monday morning and that was done every weekend and there was maybe six horses, so we just did everybody's. Well, it was nice for them gaun oot in the morning.

Horse-power, in the literal sense of the words, was harnessed externally, not through the application of hydraulics or systems which require materials and science quite different from the talents of the local joiners and blacksmiths.

Hugh Ramsay

> *Can you tell me a bit about the machinery they worked in your father's day, or indeed, after you were operating them?*
> Aw, the machinery is pretty simple; it's no like today's machinery. Ye had cairts, obviously, for certin turnips. Putting out dung– box cairts, you call them. An then we had rails you pit on these cairts, for tae bring in the harvest, we called them harvest rails – different areas have different names for them. An we had a plough obviously: we had ploughs. An then we had harrowers, and that was just about the full thing. A roller, maybe. That was just about the full implements, there wisnae a lot o' implements.

As the machinery was either iron or wood, the trade of agricultural joiner was an integral part of the working of the economy, as much as saddlers, harness makers and smiths. John Wilson's family business dated to his grandfather's day, in the workshop at Glasserton village. The possibility of repair, and of extending the life of the implement, posits a timeline which is more continuous and a location which is more local than the time and space required by replaceable, disposable objects; these are created by and within systems, for which location and proximity are neither here nor there. A judgement of the quality of the wood and the season for repairs formed part of the skill of the agricultural joiner.

John Wilson

> We used to repair a lot o binders and we used to repair mills, threshin mills, the threshin mills used to come round. We used to repair binders

and reapers, if there was any … we used to use ash on the mills, there was what they called ash shakers which was a piece of ash about, it varied in length, aboot three feet long, half inch thick by about three inches wide. And ash was used because it was nice and flexible but occasionally they would break and we used to repair things like that. So, yes, Ah can remember them and Ah can remember being at one of the farms helping, doing stookin, as they talk about, and we used to repair, we used to have hayricks and they had a special thing for lifting the ricks and they would break occasionally we would have tae sort them, have to sort shafts, put in new shafts into these machines, originally. But as I say, by about 1960 that was all gone, '58 /'60, it was all gone.

I suppose sometimes when things broke it was a bit of an emergency, you'd have had to be on sort of standby all the time?

We always, yeah, we always had, we always had these things spare in the workshop but they had to be done straight away, yea, we'd always have a spare pair o shafts because they were basically the same shape, we'd have a spare pair of shafts, we always had trough legs and that sort of stuff, yeah. Shakers for the mills, we always had them sittin there.

The distance horses could travel for shoeing or repairs to equipment measured the distance to the nearest smiddy, each the centre of its small world. Whithorn had two saddlers and two or three smiddies to cope with demand.

Hugh Ramsay

So do you remember a saddler being at Drape's shop?

Oh yes, Bendall, we called him; that was his second name, I canny remember his first name. Then Gibson's too. He had two saddlers. One of the Gibson's was a saddler, and then there was a chap, Heron, and I think he was saddling at Drape's once upon a time too, but he was at Gibson's when I remember him.

And where did they work?

In Drape's, it was at the back of the shop, where Costcutters is now, at the back they had a tin shed. And Gibson's was the same, the wee alleyway up, and a couple of wee tin sheds they worked in. At this time of year, you'd hardly get in the door for binder canvasses, you know, canvasses for binders. They're a pair, them.

And did they actually do leatherwork for the horse harness?

Aww, they made everything; they made everything. They made complete sets of harness: Gibson never made collars, but Drape's made collars. Well, I'm maybe telling you wrong, maybe Gibson did make collars, but I'd never seen them making collars.

How much would a harness cost?
> Well, money, the harness I get now, the work harness I get now I get out of Canada. Aye, well, it's a lot cheaper, because Amish type people, they use all horses, so there's plenty of harness makers there. So I really don't know what price it would be here. Couldn't tell you.

So are there any Scottish harness makers, or has it more or less just died out?
> Pretty well died out – there's an odd one or two that's probably sort a wee bit of harness – but there's no real harness makers. And certainly no collar makers.

And so Drape's would get leather from somewhere and start from scratch?
> Oh yes, they were brought in [as] hides, oh aye, they made good harness.

One smiddy was at the Top of the Town in Whithorn, as Betty Stuart recalls.

Betty Stuart

So, who was the blacksmith that you remember at the Smiddy?
> His name was Hawkins, Mr Hawkins, he lived up at the very top of High Street and he turned roond tae Green Lane, we cawd it the Back Raw, where the pub was, where Flannighan's the pub was.

And he'd get a lot of agricultural work, I suppose?
> Oh, got it aw, all the horses were aw there, tae get shoed and that was, jist a line o horses waitin tae get their turn. He had Alec Steele worked with him, auld Alec Steele. Alec Steele's father, Alec Steele that died, his father, he worked wi him. They had leather aprons on, a kinna leather, they wore leather aprons.

Jock McMaster describes the Clachan of Myrton forge.

Jock McMaster

> Oh yes, we had a blacksmith over at the Clachan, the Clachan o Myrton, Jimmy Milhench. Up until, '80s, late '80s maybe, just a man on his own. And spent a lot of time wi him, yea, fixing things, shoeing – well Ah didn't shoe horses but he was shoeing horses and just generally doing repairs but by the time Ah came along his job had changed, electrical welders had appeared and he was sortin machinery, agricultural machinery, more so than making things but he could make horseshoes and he could make all these things. And the smiddy, actually, is exactly as it was. His son has just closed the door and if ye ever want tae have a look in it's just a throwback tae late-Victorian times. The bellows, the bellows are all made o leather and a big long wooden handle that ye put

19. James Milhench, smith at Clachan of Myrton.

up. He'd electricity right enough, latterly, jist for light and all his machinery was driven by a small Lister engine and a system of belts and pulleys that drove the grinder and a drill and whatnot. Aye, he was a craftsman. It always amazed me how he never seemed to measure anything, if he was making a band to go round something he just seemed to know how to cut it, that it fitted. Of course, he'd done it so long. And Ah can remember seeing him putting metal bands on a cartwheel when they warmed them up and then put them on a cartwheel and then when they cool they shrink and they pull the spokes in tight. Ah can remember seeing him doing that.

There was one at Clarksburn, that's just at Monreith here but that's before my time. But see, there was so many horses then and things had to be fixed locally and the blacksmith's shop, as far as Ah remember the old boys telling us, it was a social place, cause he worked at nights as well, the men went there at night, well it was warm for a start for there was fire on and the conversation would be good because plenty of the local worthies. And in those days the ploughs all had shares on them and the plough-share had to be re-metalled every so often after maybe every – Ah don't know – 20 acres or so. So they'd take them to the smiddy and the blacksmith would put some more metal on and ye may take them today and leave them and go back and get them tomorrow night, that sort of thing, that's the way it was done usually. And Milhench was quite funny, chalk was a favourite item because they would chalk out things on metal when they wanted tae cut it, where they wanted to cut it, and he chalked messages and he always wrote on the anvil there, the anvil was always shining like a shilling because it had been used sae much and every message always started wi 'Just': 'Just at the Port', 'Just at Troddie' – Troddie being Drumtroddan farm.

He always told ye where he was, maybe when he'd be back, maybe wouldnae know when he was comin back but 'Just' was always the start of the message, Ah remember (laughs). Trivia but some things ye remember about it.

So clearly it was never locked?

It was never locked and he had 'Open' painted on his door, there's not many tradesmen do that now. He was never shut, Ah would go over on a Sunday morning at ten o'clock tae get an emergency thing sorted and Jimmy was there, fixing something, doing something, jist the way those boys were.

At Cruggleton, where there was a specialist trade in Clydesdale horses, Tom Buchanan, Robert Galashan's uncle, had a smiddy on site.

Robert Galashan

And my uncle had a, he had a forge, a smiddy, and one part of the shed was the smiddy, and Tommy Woods, the blacksmith fae Sorbie, and Ben [Wilma], used to come tae Cruggleton tae shoe a lot o the horses. My

20. Tam Buchanan.

uncle did their feet, a lot o them, himself, but when it came tae shoeing them and that, Tommy made the shoes at Cruggleton, at the forge, on an anvil, and everything that he needed. And a big day maybe brought in aboot 20 or 30 horses. But Ben, he worked there with Tommy Woods.

21. Groom with stallion, Sorbie, 1900s.

The stud groom was a heroic figure, leading stallions from farm to farm, wearing tight-fitting breeches, sold by Kinnear's in Port William. The length of service and of his experience was written into the fabric he wore.

Robin Kinnear

> I can remember J. B. Hoyle from Hebden Bridge, they made Armourclad working trousers, very, very strong, you could actually get a suit made from them, they had waistcoats, jackets and trousers, but they also did britches and we'd only sell maybe a pair a year or a couple of pairs a year or just a special order for them but they were the great, they jodhpurs the great big ones and very heavy here for the leathers of the saddle not digging into your leg. But that was mainly just used by the– as walking gear for the stallion leaders, but they usually would buy Armourclad clothing, trousers, they were a wonderful thing, they wore and wore and wore, they used to fade before they would wear out, they never wore out on the knees or anywhere at all and of course you could see someone who'd had a pair of Armourclad trousers for a long time because they could have stood up on their own, the big bulges on the knees but they never, ever went through, they didn't hole.

At Cruggleton, horse breeding was a large-scale operation, extending the skill of the breeder through the length of the pedigree and, through trade via train and boat, across continents. The farms of A. J. Marshall bred both Clydesdales and Shorthorn bulls. Robert Galashan speaks about his uncle, stud groom at Cruggleton.

Robert Galashan

> And of coorse the horses, aa the Clydesdales, that wis a big business too. My uncle, he was the stud groom, and he worked them hisself, if he needed a hand he get an extra man. But the amount o employment that that one farmer gave in this area was colossal. … [my uncle] looked after aboot 80 head o Clydesdales. And he foaled, he must have foaled aboot 40 in a year. And, do you want to know all the farms that was involved?
>
> Well, the trading name was A. J. Marshall, Bridgebank. That was the main one, it would be Bridgebank such-and-such, or Bridgebank, the cattle, and the horses. But they also named them Cruggleton too. Well, Mr Marshall, A. J. Marshall, he was always called Bertie. And he lived in Stranraer, and he had a chauffeur, and he come down almost every day to Cruggleton, where he had an office in the farmhouse. And when the foreign buyers came he entertained them there, and usually if there was a meal involved he took them down to Abbot's Hoose in Garlieston, which is the Harbour Inn now. And he winet and dinet them there. But they came from all over, different parts of the world, to see theirn Shorthorns and the Clydesdale horses. Competed in a lot of the big shows, the Royal shows and that. And the cattleman hired from here, or from Carlisle by train.
>
> …
>
> My father and uncle would start off in the bothy, there was a bothy at Cruggleton and the cattlemen, there's maybe three or four cattlemen, stayed in that bothy, and eventually of course, my father got married, and he moved into the farmhouse at Palmallet. And Uncle Wullie, I think he went tae Bridgebank. He wis a kind o foreman at the finish up. So, oh, it wis a big, big concern. Really was.

So your uncle, he was the stud groom, and were all these horses for use on farms?

> Well, that was the original thing o the Clydesdale, you know. But he bred them and they went to all different parts of the country too, just the same, there was buyers came and bought the Clydesdale horses. And when he foaled them, he maybe had 30 mares tae foal. At that time he had loose boxes, dae ye know what I mean by the loose box? Well, he had two there, two there, two there, and he built a bed with sheafs fae the mill, maybe the height o the top o that clock. And he put a gate, he hung

> a gate across it. And he had a mare in the box with him. And the other mares that was in the other– he put a string on his wrist, and a mare'll only lie down if she's going tae foal, and when she lay doon, she pulled his wrist. And he used to get up and take her out intae the paddock and foal her, and bring her back in. But he slept up there for a month and a half, tae foal aa the mares and get the foals right. He used tae go up at night, he'd come home and have his dinner at night and then his supper and then away up, come back for his breakfast in the morning.
>
> ...
>
> It didnae matter which stallion came about, the first time he did, he was on its back. He put a helter round its mouth, and I seen him jumping the height o that fireplace and him on the back, no saddle or anything. And he used tae take the stallion right along, maybe to the Dinnans, or to Palmallet or roond tae Cults or wherever the mares were. And he used tae ride on its back

Robert's own career was indicative of what was on the horizon, as the smiddy was first accompanied, and then replaced, by the garage and its petrol pumps.

Robert Galashan

> Oh aye, there was more mechanisation. It gradually wis comin in. Davie Broon and Ally Chalmers owned a Fergusson tractor. But earlier on, the Brownhill work was aa done wi, ploughed wi a horse. In fact when we went tae Brownhill we hadnae a tractor for a good number o years. My uncle did aa the ploughing wi a horse, aa the work wi a horse. And I never took tae horses. And I was reared wi them. But I just never took to them. I went to the mechanical side. Served my time, I went to Universal Garage, then I finished my time doon here, in the garage doon there. ... There's a lot o new houses, there's the old part o the town if ye go oot by Glasserton, and when that finishes, there's new houses built, like, up and down houses. Well, the garage was there. And there's a big house, it's been all modernised, they tell me it's one o the most modern houses in Whithorn. That's where Mr Kelly lived, in the garage, and there wis petrol pumps there. And the garage, the garage wis an old school. And right at the point, that wis the smiddy, where Mr Ronnie and Ben worked. But the bus garage wis doon there too at one point.

Hugh Ramsay explains the timetable and the patience for breaking a horse.

Hugh Ramsay

It's a thing that has tae come pretty well naturally to ye, obviously you've a lot of homework to do, you've got horses to get broken properly. Get them working properly; it's a lot of homework to do. Continuous work, no just one day, it's every day.

So how do you break a horse?

How do you break em? Well we start off with just putting a bit in their mouth. Usually at two and a half year old, if possible at all, it's a good age to break them at. Put a bit in their mouth, just let them feel the bit in their mouth for a few days. Then after you have them bitted, you tie them back a wee bit to what they call a swingle, that's the bit you tie round their middle, tie them back a bit – no too tight – so that the horses don't pull against you. Then after that, you start driving them on the long reins. Do that for maybe a week or ten days, everyday. Then introduce them to a pully-stick or a sledge, or something else; then just gradually work them up until you get them up into a cart – a two-wheeled cart or a four-wheeled cart. It's time, it takes time.

As those who were aware of the coming change at the time knew, the replacement of the horse was one of generational breeding, whereas the tractor was one of purchase and disposal. Stallion shows allowed the selection of the best stock to carry on the next generation.

Robin Kinnear

… then you would have a stallion show in the square [at Port William] where you'd maybe get as many – I can remember as many as 14 or 15 stallions all beautifully groomed and tied up with tassels and bunches and their coat groomed to perfection, their feet all oiled, the hooves oiled and the feathering, the hair round the feet, all done with a talcum powder to make them look absolutely superb and they were brought into the square and all the farmers came down to see which stallion they would get to serve their mares because they would get a foal every year. And this is what they always said when the tractors came in, 'You cannae get a wee foal out o a tractor every year' (laughter), because you couldn't get a new tractor every year. … these stallions would, were nearly all led by a halter, they would walk from farm to farm and they would stay on the farm, they would get their accommodation until they had served the mare and then they would go on, on to the next farm or where the stud farm, wherever it was.

22. Annual Foal Show, Port William.

No family was closer to their horses than Jessie McLean's, nor depended on them more heavily for their peripatetic business as 'general dealers'. The skill and an instinctive understanding of the horseman resulted in a partnership between owner and horse which was so intense and internalised in the case of the Jollys' horse, 'Darkie', that the horse did not survive its owner long.

Jessie McLean

> We had the two [horses] aye. We had this black yin for donkey's years, tae ma father died and then we had tae get it shot. No wurselves, it wouldnae let oorselves work it, ony oh ma brothers harnessed him or ocht he' have jist killed them. We had tae get it shot. An ma faither hadnea tae yaise a whup he just had tae, 'Go, on Darkie' that's aa he had tae say. He never had tae yaise a whup or a stick. And Ah can mind o this [unclear] there was a big tall sodger, Ah was standin the day they were takin [horses], whaur ma dad had died and they couldnae tak the horse by the windae, couldnae go by the windae in the room where ma dad was lying in and they had tae turn the horse an tak it and pit it back in the stable, wouldnae gaun by the windae. Ah can mind o us aw greetin, that day an ma saying, 'Oh pit Darkie back in the stable'.
>
> *Mary: When ma granda died his horse couldnae be yaised, naebody could ride it.* Naebody could even put the harness on tae it, it would hae killed them. So, one man's horse, so they were wantin the horses for the War, an they took everybody's guid horses and they took oor Darkie and they had tae bring him back, he would have kilt everybody. Everybody that put their

hand on them he would hae kilt them. They had tae … and he was a young horse and the farmer at Arbrack said, 'Oh, bring the horse here and let him run' and at the very finish we had tae get the horse shot, naebody could work wi him, he would hae kilt them. An he's buried oot at Arbrack, Ah could tak ye tae the field, where he was buried.

Mary: *I'm sure the day they were gaun tae shoot him, the whole lot o yis went oot tae–*

We aw went oot on the Sunday, he was shot on the Monday, and every yin o us went oot tae say goodbye to the horse. … An Ah can mind as if it was yesterday he was away in a corner of the field an it was, 'Darkie, Darkie!'. But we had tae because he would have killed somebody, he wouldnae let anybody put harness on him or dae ocht wi him. But he [unclear] ma faither, an he was an awfy good wi horses an animals, that's a sense that a horse can hae. … And that was as true as ah'm sitting in this chair, we had tae get the horse shot by the vet for we couldnae let anybody shoot him. An it was because he wouldnae let anybody work him and he stood like a soldier tae get shot. We were aw greetin, every yin o us wis greetin at the horse being shot. An when he was shot we were aw lyin ower him, cuddlin him and kissin him. It was terrible. Folks didnae ken hoo a body leeves, that wis [unclear] ocht an we had tae, we were aw greetin.

So you'd had him for years, that horse?

We had him aw his life. He widnae hae any other owner, ma da would get him as a young foal an he was jist one man's horse. An ma da, when he had a drink in him, ma da wouldnae sleep in his bed, he went up an slept wi the horse. That was a horse for ye.

Mary: *Tell Julia aboot when the hawkers used tae come tae the heid o the toon wi their horses, tae sell horses and swap horses and buy horses and dogs. And youse tae tae gaun doon tae Maxwell's field at the heid o the toon.*

And ma dad used tae tak oor horse and race ony horse … it beat every horse it raced and some o us would run and tell ma ma, 'Ma, come quick, ma da's took Darkie off tae race such an a horse. An ma mither jist flew up the street an she would hit ma da and haen a fight. 'You're no racin a horse, Darkie, agin that horse' an Darkie won the money an Ah can mind o that as a–. Mony's the time Ah run doon masel tae tell her tae 'come on quick,' ma da was racing Darkie an ma ma says, 'No he's no racin the horse' an she would run. Oh bit she couldnae dae ocht, if ma da decided he was racing the horse, he raced the horse, an Ah can mind o that fine.

As horse-power multiplied by many times in proportion as horses themselves decreased and ultimately disappeared, the relationship between the horse and its master was replaced by ownership of tractors. These themselves underwent a process of internalisation, as Jock McMaster recalls the retreat of the horses and the arrival of the first tractors, at first unenclosed, with trailing equipment, and then with cabs and hydraulics.

Jock McMaster

Aye, Ah can remember horses ok, in the stable, and our last horse was kept for the turnip crop, for what we called 'scufflin' the turnips, that was when ye scraped away the soil from each side o the drill, to make it easy to hoe them, instead of having to push a huge amount of soil away ye were jist left wi a narrow ridge and the horse was still there in the '60s. Aye, '63/64 but that was the last one. Ah don't remember seeing any ploughing wi horses but Ah can remember horses carting in sheaves, a horse and a cart. Although Ah was born here we stayed in Monreith shore for two or three years and Ah moved up here and came up by horse and cart. And Ah can remember sitting on the horse and … on the cart coming up in 1952 or something like that, so that's how Ah moved here, or moved back here, anyway.

So, generally, across the Machars would you say the last of the horses went in the early '60s?

Aye, maybe even sooner, yea. Ah would say yes, the early '60s or late '50s, yea. Ah don't, the only ones that kept them after that were the enthusiasts, they probably still have them.

Hugh Ramsay for instance and Sheddock, these kinna boys who kept on their horses but there were no horses next door. Ah don't think Dourie next door or Monreith Estate next door would have horses, even then. Ah think they would be gone in the '50s, yea.

And did you, did you learn to manage horses at a young age?

No, not personally no. In fact Ah never really had much time wi horses at all, Ah once saw the horse, a horse biting a woman's shoulder and from then on Ah thought 'no'. I would rather have something with an engine Ah could control.

Yes. So when you were growing up you were already operating with tractors on this farm.

Yes, Ah was using tractors from an early age, yea.

And was that the sort of pre-hydraulic stuff or–?

Well, the very first one, yes, was, it just pulled the implement along, it didn't have any hydraulics at all, it had a belt pulley on the front which drove some machinery, like a threshing mill, a saw bench and a bailer. And then, but the tractor I drove when Ah started at 13 or 14 had hydraulics, it was a Fordson Major and they were introduced about 1952/53 and it had a diesel engine whereas the previous one was petrol paraffin. And this thing had hydraulics, yea, no cab, you sat out in the open. Very cold. Because the old petrol paraffin one, ye sat away down deep in the thing and the

OUTSIDE: THE FARMS

23. Tractor at Millisle, near Garlieston.

heat from the engine kept you warm but in these modern diesel ones ye sat up right on top and it was seriously cold. Jobs like harrowing or ploughing in the spring, ye were wrapped up like an Eskimo, fiendishly cold it got, ye sat there not doing anything just driving away hour after hour. And then cabs came along, they were rickety things too when ye think but at least they stopped the wind and kept the rain off.

The Circulation of Milk

While the horse may have dominated the working day and the speed of production and travel, agricultural time was dominated by the calendar and the crop rotation required to support the dairies. As Jock McMaster makes clear, the increased capacity of the machines and their ability to reduce the exposure to the risk of bad weather was nonetheless at a cost of the skill which was in the deft hands and keen eyes of the human harvesters and forced the abandonment of crops which required their finesse.

Jock McMaster

So, in terms of crops what's changed in your lifetime?
   Well, the main crop in my day was oats, we grew oats in a big scale for human food and for cattle food. And the straw was very important to feed the cows with. So now, oats are more difficult to harvest with the combine because they're later but in those days they were cut wi the

binder and put into stacks and then thrashed during the winter so now we've no oats at all, we just grow – we grow barley, it's easier to harvest. It's a heavier yield and that's the difference now, yea. All the farms round here grew oats. Oats and turnips, that was the staple crops. And stuck to rotation, the field would be grass for five or six years, and then ye would grow a crop of oats and then next year a crop of turnips, then the following year another crop of oats, with grass underneath and that was the traditional. And ma dad, and his father before him, stuck to that religiously, just went round all the fields so they were all re-seeded every five, six, seven years and occasionally potatoes, in the turnip field. Ye'd use part o the turnip field for potatoes. But we don't grow any potatoes now. Mainly because the ground's too stony and modern machinery, when it's gathering potatoes, cannae tell a potato from a stone whereas the human being could, didn't put any stones in the bag.

So, in a way, the capacity of the machines somewhat dictates what you're doing?
It does really, yes. Hay is a lovely crop to grow and a nice thing, a nice healthy crop to feed but it's so difficult to get with the weather. Whereas now, as I say, this guy can do 100 acres of silage in day, that's my whole winter feed, for the whole stock on the farm is made in one day. We normally cut in on a Monday and it lies and sunbathes on the Tuesday and we chop it up and put it in the silage pit on the Wednesday and that's it done. It is just so much easier. And I think the weather has changed so much too, I don't think we could ever make hay now, on the

24. Building a hay stack, Felyennan, Mochrum, 1930s.

scale that we used to. Especially this last three or four years, terrible, terrible wet summers.

Tom McCreath

Yes, yes, there was quite a bit of arable because pastures had to be renewed, there was some permanent pasture but in the renewal of the grassland it would be ploughed up and usually a crop of oats grown, then a crop of turnips, which were essential for the dairies because a lot of the dairies didn't have water bowls in front of the cows in the stalls, feeding them turnips they didn't need to do that because turnips, are they 90 per cent water or something? And then another crop of oats that had grass seeds sown under it so that it was in crop for three years and back to grass for four or five years.
…
I forgot to say, by the way, that all the grain crops in the '30s and mostly during the War were oats but that changed to largely barley because it was easier to harvest with the combine harvester and oats were more difficult. But in other parts of the country they're still grown, wheat is grown more now than it used to because we have the fertilisers to encourage good yields.

With the large-scale capitalisation of farms still in the future, the workforce was not imported, but by and large resident, cramming the farm cottages with a closely woven network of extended families.

Jock McMaster

Mm, well, when Ah left school in '63 Ah was number seven on the payroll. There was five full-time men and a woman, six, six people, aye. And now there's only one man and maself but we use contractors. Contractors provide us wi machinery to do all the heavy work, yea.
And presumably that's the sheer capital outlay it takes to buy these enormous machines?
That's right, that's right.

Tom McCreath

Oh yes, they were days when fewer people lived in the towns but many, many more on the farms and my mother told us that from the three farms up Reiffer Park Road from Sorbie, 43 children walked down to the school.
…
I'm trying to remember just the exact number on the farm, there would nearly be a dozen in total.

WHITHORN: AN ECONOMY OF PEOPLE, 1920–1960

Greta Hawthorn remembers the press of population on the Glasserton Estate. In exchange for the extra labour which was on hand through the range of age groups inhabiting the cottages, there was a range of non-cash benefits supplementing the cash wages.

Greta Hawthorn

> There was, we were in the big house and there wis the Dodds family, ye know Billy Dodds, PC Dodds' grandfather and grandmother. When Billy Dodds' father was born his mother died and that was just during– beginning o the War so the granny came out to look after the other two girls that were there and they were at the farm and there was Sally Martin's mother and father-in-law were there as well and Margaret Forlow's father and mother were there down in the road, halfway down the road, they were in a wee cottage there. But all the farm cottages were filled, it was the same at Kidsdale, all the farm cottages there were filled.
> ...
> And they had head gardeners and head gamekeepers and, for the sawmill, they had a sawmill, there was the head man for the sawmill.
> ...
> We were in half of the, we were in the farmhouse in those days. And the farmer was Mr John Nicholson which his grandson's in the farm still, at

25. Nicholson family at Kilsdale, Whithorn, c.1875.

the moment, and we used to get benefits, that was added on to their pay. Their pay was never very big but they added on benefits. Ye got a ton of coal, and we had a huge big coal shed that was through from the kitchen, you went up three steps intae it. And we had a great big range wi' two huge ovens, which didnae work, but never mind. We dried the kindlin' off in there, they were warm enough jist tae dae that.

So, were you living with the family?

We stayed with our grandparents.

And my mother stayed there as well. Then they got this benefit and you got coal, potatoes and every three months you got a sack with flour and oatmeal and the meal, that stayed in the kitchen.

Ploughing with horse and my grandmother worked out in the fields, backweeding turnips, shawing turnips, shawing mangel, they worked the whole year round.

Hugh Ramsay

We had three cottages on the farm, so there was always three who lived on the farm. The other workers usually come from the local village.

Do you remember how much workers were paid when your father was here?

When I remember first? Oh, about £4 tae £5 fir a ploughman. A just don't remember what the dairymen got, but it was so much a cow, from November to November. And then he paid his assistants accordingly. I just don't remember what they got per cow. Ploughman got between £4 and £5, if I remember …

In these margins of the cash economy, room was made for anyone who could form part of the body of the workforce.

Jock McMaster

In those days it was– and then of course in those days too, aye that's a subject I want to go onto too. There was always room for sort of semi-handicapped people on the farm in those days. We always had– Ah can always remember somebody– and one in particular who worked here who wasn't able to work on his own but he jist was swallowed up by the rest of the men who looked after him and he could do menial tasks, he couldn't drive, he couldn't count, this poor lad had trouble speaking but that's another story, but there was room for him and he had, he had a valuable input into society and sadly now there's none of them now because there are no big numbers of staff to keep, to help them and Ah can remember Johnny, he would just have been put in a home, I presume, if he hadn't been working here. And as long as you gave him cigarettes he was usually quite stoic, he got very cross if he had no cigarettes but as long as ye kept him plied with cigarettes. But it's amazing and that's something that's quite sad now, cause there'll be still the same proportion of people like him who need help that don't get it. This guy's nickname was Johnny Pey and as a child he was always asking for a penny but with his speech impediment he couldn't pronounce penny and he called it a pey.

With labour market taut, a circulation of the population of hired hands was created, with the possibility of moving from farm to farm at the November 'term', lured by the promise of better conditions elsewhere.

Jock McMaster

Oh, aye, oh yes, aye they did. Well, the shepherd, Ah remember old Tom was there 40 years and the tractor driver 30-odd and his wife was more, she came in 1935 and she just retired in, it would be in the sort of late '70s or something. She had her 40 years as well. Although, there were a lot moved on very quickly, a lot of them just stayed a year or so. Ma dad always said in the spring, if ye saw them putting their garden in, it was a good sign, because they were gonnae stay on that, another year but if they didnae get the garden in you could say, 'Ah ha, he's movin on'.

Ah think the ones who are maybe down the ladder a wee bit seemed to move on more often. The shepherds and the stockmen, I think, and the tractor drivers latterly, in those days, maybe had more responsible jobs and Ah think they tended to stay, to stay on the place longer. But some of the sort of second or third men down the line seemed to move a lot. The ones Ah remember too, it wisnae so much the men that wanted to move, the wives werenae happy, they were away from their mother or their own family, maybe from Ayrshire, Kirkcudbright or somewhere, they seemed to be ill at ease, wanting tae get back. Ah can remember that on two or three occasions, aye, so the poor man just had tae up sticks and go somewhere else.

Farmers themselves, however, were bound to the land, with a perspective which reached back through inheritance from generation to generation and remained the constant in the moving population of hired hands. There had been a slow migration from the outside, particularly with the late nineteenth-century movement of farmers from Ayrshire, who brought their milking herds and followed the introduction of railways, which gave farmers the capability of exporting the milk and reaching the markets in the cities.

26. Hugham family, tenant farmers at Barledziew.

Jock McMaster

> Well, Blairbuy and Stellock Farms are together and my great-great-great-grandfather came to Stellock farm aboot 1820-something. And he farmed there for a few years and then Blairbuy farm came up to let, Ah think aboot 1830, and we've been here ever since. And we were tenant farmers on Monreith Estate, until 1963, when ma father and I had the chance tae buy the place and we bought it then and ah've farmed here ever since.
>
> Well, those days it was mainly crops, they grew a lot of wheat, potatoes and barley and kept a few cattle and sheep but in my day it was a few crops but mostly cattle and sheep. And now it's just cattle.

Hugh Ramsay's father came to Millisle from Whitefield in 1931.

Hugh Ramsay

> Yes, we had a dairy, and made cheese on the farm. And we had a cheese loft, then we kept the cheese about six weeks – two months – and then it was sold.
>
> *How many people did you have working there in your father's time?*
> In the dairy side, about four workers; a dairyman an' three assistants. Milking the cows and making the cheese. And then outside there wiz three full-time ploughmen, and a pair'a– there was nine horses, there wiz three full-time ploughman, and three horses spare.

That's a pretty big farm isn't it, by local standards at the time?
   Aye, we broke aboot 158 a year.

At the heart of the Machars economy, then, was the milking of cows, a skill and a rigid routine which still dictated the rhythm of the day, but then the beginnings of mechanisation still required the aid and skill of the handmilker. Tom McCreath's father increased the herd at Broughton Mains.

Tom McCreath

> Yes, my grandfather increased the dairy substantially and he was most successful with breeding horses and had a big trade in horses, from south of the border to up in the Orkneys, but in father's time, he wasn't a horsey man, so dairying. But at that time it was the early days of milking machines and they weren't very efficient so that when cows were not milked out properly mastitis suddenly arrived and almost ruined him. … Whereas the Ramsay family knew that they had to follow the milking machines and draw out any improperly milked quarter and that made them very efficient without the huge losses that father had. From then on he increased his sheep to as many as the farm would carry, to see him through the depression.

Hugh Ramsay remembered the process of properly milking out cows.

Hugh Ramsay

> Aye, with stribbin. What we called stribbin; was goin behind the milkin machines and just milkin them out. Aye, I've been at that job, but my father did it all his days. Well, hand milked, in his earlier days, but then latterly after– the milkin machines werenae quite as good in those days, and they didnae get the cow completely emptied. We'd go round with a pail and stool and strib it. But I don't actually remember hand milkin, no. Before my time. That photograph you would be talkin about, must of been about 1920? I would think it was. Cacks, was the name of the people the dairy people.

Milking came with its own occupational costume.

Hugh Ramsay

> A milkin fecket. Oh yes, a wee fecket to keep you clean. An the menfolk, they wore a bunnet, they wore it back tae front, so that the peak wisnae stabbin the cow.

And when did people stop wearing the fecket?
>Well, in a sense, they still wear sort of feckets to protect themselves; no the same feckets, very often, they were stripped, they were like what a butcher would wear, that kinda colour anyway, But they still wear protective clothing yet. It's different now, it's oilskin type stuff.

Slowly, to ensure an economising of labour, the direct contact of hand and bucket was replaced by flow through a the suction pipe, the pipeline and the rotary parlour.

Hugh Ramsay

>Well, it's changed three times. It used to be that you milked them, you milked the cows, you went in-between them wi a bucket, an there was a suction pipe up above. And then you would put the tube on the suction pipe, and then to the cow. Then progressed from there; you just went in wi the tube, an there was a pipeline that took the milk to the dairy, right round the byres. Then it progressed from there into the milkin parlour, what they call the herringbone, the milkin parlour; and now it's progressed again intae a rotary type parlour. So, it's progressed a few times – in my time.

And what's the advantage of those?
>Well, the advantage is, you don't move – you just stand there – and the cows come to you. You pop the machine on, you pop it on tae one, you pop it on tae the next one. The carousel keeps movin round, whereas like the parlour we have, the herringbone parlour, you've a wee bit of milkin to do. But it's easy milkin, they're at eye level there, so its easy milkin.

The dairies were adjacent to the piggeries, where the by-product of cheese-making was fed to the pigs, both at Whithorn and Port William, as well as on individual farms. The trip to the creamery, described by Ian Niall, by horse and cart from each farm was replaced by the arrival of the bulk tanker and the movement of milk to more distant creameries. Although the ebb and flow of milk was triggered by demand in the cities, it was still open to seasonal flood and dearth, according to the availability of grass.

Tom McCreath

>Yes, it was run over a water cooler and put into, in my day, ten-gallon cans, as we called the milk cans, but they superseded the twelve-gallon cans although we had still some of those. And we had given up cheese making when I was a kid, but I still remember cheeses in the store there and the milk was taken to Sorbie creamery, there was an old chap with a horse and

four-wheeled cart and he took our milk and our neighbour's milk to Sorbie creamery. And our neighbour, Bob Allan, did pretty careful costings and he reckoned he could produce milk for threepence a gallon, I think, and he got threepence farthing at Sorbie creamery but, because it cost him a halfpenny a gallon to get it there, he was out by a farthing. Not very high mathematics involved there (laughter).

So, at Sorbie, it was actually processed at Sorbie, it wasn't shipped out by the train?
It could be shipped out by the train when milk supply was low in other parts of the country.

But when the flood of milk was on, in the spring and early summer, cheese making was a major factor, yes.

And do you actually remember cheese making at your farm or–?
Not the actual making but it had stopped just before I was aware of things and as I say, I remember the cheeses still in store but when they were sold there was no more.

Was there a dairy room at the farm?
Yes, with vats, I can remember the vats still there and it was spotlessly clean because it had to be and the piggery was still there but no longer pigs in it, in them, because the whey was fed to the pigs. All part of the dairyman's work.

Before milk processing was amalgamated at central creameries in Whithorn and Port William, cheesemaking was originally on individual farms, the curds stirred by hand before the arrival of the automatic stirrer.

Hugh Ramsay

Oh aye, I remember the cheesemaking, I made cheese for five years myself, after I left the school. We couldnae get a dairyman to make the cheese as well, so I made the cheese for five years. We stopped in, I think it was about 1970, the last cheese we made.

How the cheese was made? It was cheddar cheese we made, how it's done?! It's a wee while ago since I made it now, partly forgotten. But eh, well you started off with the raw milk, then you added a started-egg to spoil the milk to get the acidity started. And you added rennet, when it got to a certain acidity you added rennet, a certain heat, then it coagulated, then you cut it with what we call the crud knife intae small sections. And then, well, latterly, we had an automatic stirrer, and it'd stand for aboot two hours. Then we drained the whey off, and then what we called cheddared it, cut them into slabs and kept turnin them for another hour and a half. Then we put them through a curd mill, added salt to them, put em in mould, chissocks, we called them, and then put them in presses, and they were in the press for two days. Then they were bandaged and then put up on the cheese loft. And then turned every day in the cheese loft.

And how long were they in the cheese loft for?
> Roughly aboot – we coudnae keep them too long – aboot two months we kept them. And then they were sold on, cos we didnae have the room for keeping them any longer than that.

And before you had an automatic stirring machine, how was that done?
> It wiz done wi what we call raiks, wooden raiks, nothing like a raik you would raik the gravel with; wood. Two boys staundin in the back for two hours, just kept goin up and down, standin, keepin the curds movin all the time.

You've obviously tasted the cheese that your father and you used to make, compared to the cheese now, how is that different?
> It is different … because it was more mature when we made it. We made them in round moulds; latterly we made them in 45lb round moulds, but it used to be about 80lb in the round moulds. And they were bandaged. They were greased and bandaged, and that let them mature better. You maybe got a bit of mould on the outside, but the cheese matured better. You don't get that flavour now. Even the best of cheese, you just don't get that flavour.

Most milk, however was delivered to the creameries. These buildings, at the outskirts of Whithorn and Port William, were at the centre of the ebb and flow of traffic, and collections and deliveries dictated the working day, and the train connections to distant Glasgow.

27. Hand milkers at Garlieston, 1900.

Greta Hawthorn

We had a good railway station and the coal come in there and the food stuff, a lot there, the papers come in and the creamery, when the creamery shut and the railway closed that was when Whithorn finished because there was no work for anybody and ye used tae see the carts comin doon the street and the horses knew where they were goin, there wis a lot o work there.

And the creamery processed the milk and put it on the train or was there also butter and–?

No, they made cheese and butter. Aye, they made cheese there and the whey went oot tae the pigs at the piggery and they did quite well wi their cheeses.

Sort of how many people would have been working at the creamery?

There were loads, I just couldnae tell ye, but there must have been 40 or more.

Men and women?

Men and women, because they had rakes to rake the curd and things and they were just like rakes that ye would do in the field for the hay, they were wooden rakes.

And was that cheese sold in the town or was it shipped out, all of it?

Well, it went tae bigger creameries and they sold it on. But ye could get it, the men were allowed tae buy, well it widna be very much in those days but it would be plenty if ye were buying it and ye could get the whey if ye wanted it, folk that had pigs could get it and ye used to see the horses and carts going up and doon wi the milk butts. From the farms, taking the milk in, summer and winter, hail, rain or shine. But there was a lot of activity at the station as well.

Guy Brown remembers that the whey was used by local children as a substitute for the sweets which had to be purchased.

Guy Brown

We used to go and get dried whey as children. When you couldn't get sweets you got a bag of dried whey, there were rollers to dry it. And we got a bag of dried whey, it was quite nice if it was warm but probably very indigestible but you've got to take what you can get, you got it for nothing, you took your bag out and they gave you a handful of it and you chewed it for the rest of the night.

The crops, largely for the purpose of feeding the animals, were grown as part of a farming process which was still truly open to the risk and vagaries of the seasons. Tom McCreath describes a process of sowing and harvest which was an interplay of skill, luck and judgement which took place in the absence of technological insurance against risk, and whose more patient space and time were liberated by that absence. Judging the moment for the sowing and the harvest, awaiting the process of drying, protecting against winter rains, were all carried out against a horizon of the seasons, the opposition of the weather, the speed of the horse and the hard luck of breakdowns of fragile machinery. The time of storage and preservation would depend on the skill of the stack builder and thatcher and the circulation of the mills.

Tom describes the precision of measurement which worked according to the pace of a sower sowing broadcast and the skill and weather-eye of the harvesters.

Tom McCreath

And for sowing, was, do you remember anyone doing that broadcast or was there actually a seed machine?

We had a seed drill but it was quite interesting that there was a very wet spring and our neighbour, well everybody was behind because they couldn't get their drills onto the land so our neighbour decided, it being wartime and a big acreage that he and the foreman would sow by hand on top of the ploughing and the second man came behind with horse and harrow and it was all very well organised, the bags of seed were taken out and were placed at so many yards which meant that the kidney-shaped bag that held the seed for hand sowing was just about out when they reached the next bag and a woman was there with a bucket to fill it and all well organised. And he, at the end of a week, was all sown up whereas those with the drills hadn't started. But mostly sown by drills drawn by horse and at the grass seed, of course, with a grass seed barrow.

The biggest breakthrough in farm machinery, I think, was the self-tying binder. It was perfected in the 1890s, I think, or thereabout, and the one we had at the beginning of the War was 40 years old and made in Castle Douglas. But they were splendid machines, pulled by three horses, which had to be changed at lunchtime because they were so tired and another three put in for the afternoon. And also the reapers we had for cutting the hay, pulled by two horses, but they didn't need to be changed, they were important, carts of course, good carts, some made locally.

The binders must have been fairly complex pieces of machinery; I know John McNeillie's books talk about a lot going wrong or there being a panic if something went wrong with these things.

Well, yes indeed, and some of the blacksmiths were better than others. Tommy Woods, in Sorbie, got a name for being an expert in binders including the knotters, because the knotters could give trouble if they were, something was out of line, yes.

And what about the stack, after the bunches are on the ground, then somebody has to follow and stack?

We followed by hand stooking and you usually worked in pairs and took two rows each which you drew to the centre and made stooks, particularly of oats, six in a stook, which would sit there for at least a fortnight to dry out and be ready for stacking and after that period you waited for a good day, hopefully with a good drying wind and then you would tumble these stooks onto the ground to let the wind blow into the butt that had been resting on the ground and from there they were forked into carts and taken to the stackyard. Now, in the stackyard, mostly in this area, they were round stacks built on a foundation of rough stone that had been put in place and it was a skilled operation but we found on our farm we didn't seem to have chaps that could build a stack to run the water. Now, the secret of running the water was to keep the centre of the stack a shade higher than the outside particularly in the heading of it. And I went to a neighbour's farm to get instruction on this and came back and showed the men the way to do it, building stacks myself, and from then on we didn't have stacks that had grain ruined by drawing water. And what hasn't been said is that built into a stack and going through a winter with the wind and one thing and another, it's marvellous how the grain dried out. It had to be pretty dry to go into them but that said thereafter it got very much drier during the winter.

And about how many stacks would you have in your stackyard?

Oh, lose count, we had – particularly during the wartime – we had two or three stackyards because the grain acreage was just simply doubled. Counting the stacks in the stackyard, goodness me, some would be built big double stacks, they were called 'soo stacks', sow stacks if you like, and just to get it out of the way and thrash it early before it drew too much water. Oh, I'll have to dream about counting (laughter) I'm talking about, could have been 50 round stacks.

You wouldn't thrash them all at once or would you?

Oh, no, not at all because the cows liked fresh straw and you would thrash a bit, sell some grain and fill up the straw shed with straw and when the cows had eaten that then you would get the mill in again but I know one farm, it was a Ramsay farm, where they, during the week, they thrashed for a couple of hours every morning and that gave the cows fresh straw and fresh grain.

So, you would simply re-hire the mill to come back?

Very easy with the co-operative in Whithorn and Wyllie's mill, yes, and it would quite often come in for a day's thrashing or two days' thrashing and then go and then if you were left with a lot at the end, then you could have

OUTSIDE: THE FARMS

28. Stevensons at Broom Park.

a week of thrashing, that was a bit of a nightmare, because everybody got dirty and crusty and you name it (laughter).
And what happened to the grain once it had been thrashed?
A lot of it went to the barn where there was a bruiser which rolled it for cattle feeding. Any surplus would be sold, probably to the millers in Garlieston and sometimes they would sell it on or use it in their animal feeds.

One of the most important days in the calendar was the mill-day, when the mobile thrashing mill visited the farm, when the stacks were fed to the mill – technology which required a temporary increase of labour on the most sociable day of the year.

Prior to the advent of the steam mill, farms might mill their own corn, as at Blairbuy, or make use of the town mills, of which Bysbie and Port William mills were in use within living memory. Wind and water powered these: Jock McMaster describes the water-powered mill on his farm and Jack Niblock remembered the village mill at the Isle. Ultimately, tractor-driven mills were substituted for the steam mill, until milling in all its multiple forms was reduced by an economy of functions into the combine harvester.

Jock McMaster

Yea, we'd a thrashing mill in the barn. And Ah can remember it being used, it was water-driven, the loch supplied the water to the mill pond and there was a sluice in the mill pond that ye opened up, a big screw thing, this handle ye screwed and by the time ye got back tae the barn the water had got there with you and ye closed a flap and the water wheel started up and the barn machinery went from there. And then the mill was taken out in the late '50s and a corn crusher was installed, that's just to crush the grain to make it suitable for cattle feed and Ah used it often. Yes, it was water-powered, grand, very cheap way of– but the water wheel started to break up, it rusted and it was getting difficult to repair. There was a huge [unclear] bronze tooth mechanism right round the outside that drove the barn and it was starting to break up and it was very expensive to sort. So we took it out about 1960/61/62 and we put in a diesel engine instead, to drive the machinery, and funnily enough it was only eight horse power, the diesel engine which drove all that machinery, yet we thought this water wheel was enormous, it must have been hundreds of horsepower, but it wasn't, it probably was only seven or eight horse power. But very efficient.

So that was a piece of, what, Victorian engineering?

Aye, built by a firm from Cumnock, there's a plate on the wall down there to say that they'd put it in. But tremendous expensive system to put in, it must have cost a fortune.

The barn had to be built, because in the years gone by the steadings was away up the Fell [of Barhullion] road there before power was used, so they had to build brand new steadings and this barn was three storeys, because, naturally they used gravity, the sheaves went into the mill and the corn fell down onto the riddling mechanism, to clean it all and then it fell down again into wherever it was bagged to be taken away and the straw was, the straw came out one end into a shed where a, Ah can remember a woman with a fork spreading this straw round to make a– not a stack because it was inside four walls, she couldnae go wrong and it was all hard, hard work and dusty, very dusty, especially in a bad season, if the corn was damp when it was harvested it was mouldy and when they thrashed it the place was just full of white dust which must have been really bad for their lungs, aye. Because nobody wore a mask those days. If it was dusty Ah can remember the men tying their handkerchiefs roond their nose which would have very little effect, aye, and that was the threshing mill.

At the Isle of Whithorn, Bysbie Mill was still in use within living memory, Jack Niblock recalls.

Jack Niblock

I can remember it being worked and I can remember the wheel and, of course, I remember, I can remember the dam because it was a great day when I found that the handle to my grandmother's old mangle, with the wooden rollers on it. It fitted the sluice up at the dam (laughter). No, as kids, the old miller, Maxwell, [unclear] I think his nickname was– a crowd of kids, we used to get on to the big wheel and the weight of the children would turn it and of course that was turning all the machinery in the mill (laughs). And that was just to get chased by the miller. He had a big belt with all sorts of projections on it– he used to chase us, And the flats that are down in the harbour now, that used to be the main grain store. Now, I can remember there, grain being probably that depth in there, all over the floor and going in when they were turning it over. They had dogs in there catching the rats (laughs).

Jenny Jolly recalls a bruising mill in Whithorn.

Jenny Jolly

There was a mill at the fit of the toon there, but it didnae produce the same as the Isle and Port Yerrick but it did dae dressed corn and whatnot. Jist where the fire station is, it employed a man there all the time. And the corn was fetched in an it wis pit through this machine, an tied and whatnot. Ah hae mind o it for ma sister worked on it for a time ... Wyllie was a big man, he owned a lot. He owned a store in the Isle of Whithorn for the meal and he had one doon here in Whithorn, where the fire brigade is. Ye ken, it gave employment and he had a lot o lorries on the road tae ... Garlieston was the head bit though. He'd lorry drivers and folk working in them. He lived in that big hoose. And he owned it aw, Mrs Wyllie and she had maids.

At Port William, the mill is still prominent in the main Square, as Robin Kinnear recalls.

Robin Kinnear

Yes, yes. Mr Jardine was the miller and he was always white, he was always covered in dust. But I can remember it working and the actual water wheel working as well and they had a lade burn that came down to the water-wheel and it went under the square, round by the keep-left sign and ran into the harbour.

Oats, oats mainly, and a lot of the farmers would bring in their grain and it would be treated by the mill, bruised or made into a meal for feeding and most of the ... we called it, as young boys, corn, but it was actually oats, and very little barley or wheat that was grown then, much more barley now and of course it's a different type of straw and it's much, much better than the corn. Whereas the old oat straw was very good, still quite a good feeding, but it was used for, mainly for bedding. But the mill worked on for quite some time, it was Wyllie's and then Dalgety and then Monreith Estate, Dourie Farming Company bought it and they were storing their grain in it instead of in silos. They used to come and tip it in there.

The excitement and sheer noise and even the danger of the mill days were recalled by Tom McCreath, Cathy Miller, Jenny Jolly and Betty Stuart.

Tom McCreath

> They were extremely busy days and dirty days because of the dust. I found it, I was given a pretty mundane job as a teenager and for the first day I was fine and I could manage the second day, just, but at the end of that it was as if I had the flu. Because we had no masks, it wasn't thought to be important, and it did tell on the health, particularly of the mill men. I once asked the foreman on our farm, 'I don't remember many of these mill men retired in the village' 'Oh,' he said, 'they didn't retire, they just deid' (laughter). Says it all.
>
> *And the mill, obviously ... circulated different farms?*
>
> Yes. In the Whithorn area there was a farmers' co-operative mill, a steam pulled, steam engine pulled, travelling mill under the command of Hugh Smith who was a perfect gentleman, lovely man, and it travelled round the farms in this co-operative. The ... Sorbie and Garlieston areas were usually serviced by the mills, two or three units, that James Wyllie and Sons had at their feeding stuff business, feedings and fertiliser, and travelling mills and as a small boy, of course, you would hear the sound of this great steam tractor approaching and you would get behind the curtains to look out and see it come up the hill with sparks flying out of the funnel, very exciting. And I can remember a very big snow storm in 1936 and the mill was set in place at the dairy and – for thrashing – the grain being carted to it there but this snow storm came from the apex of the roof of a building and completely buried the mill. We had a fortnight's holiday from school, so that was fine, because all the roads were blocked level.

Cathy Miller

> Ah can go as far back as Ah can remember, when the steam engine come down to the farm. I would be about eight or nine, it was Bob McClymont and Bob from the Top of the Town. May Smith, Bob Smith, they had this and there was the brass on the front of her and they used to stand with a great big cloth, one at one side, one at the other and they polished her up

and down and up and down. And they filled it from the burn to be full of water so as start the next morning.

Jenny Jolly speaks about the sociability of the mill days.

Jenny Jolly

So tell me about the mill days.
Oh but they could be sair days, an if it was a windy day, if it was awfy windy, yer eyes would be gey sore I can tell ye. … Especially the bunches, ye were runnin aw day when ye yist tae be a bunch run then before they got the wee pick-up baler an ye were runnin wi these an they had tae be built up inside tae. Ye were runnin wi them, two at a time. An then ye had tae sweep up a the shaws intae a tattie basket, and put intae the baler, cause there's a lot o shaws, as they ca'd it, waste. And then they started wi the pick-up baler, Ah used tae dae the bales but they were the wee bales, they're no like what ye see in the fields or ocht nooadays; they used tae be big bales but they got the pick-up baler. But there was cheerie days tae, though, but they had some days they fought aw day, argued aw day and then laughed aw day, some days – it was funny.

The exposure of people to dust and moving parts before the increasing safety precautions and internalisation of the process betrays both the necessity for skilled hands and their easy replaceability.

Betty Stuart

Ah had a brother died when he was six. They were playing in the street and the steam mill went past and he jumped on some bar that knocked him, clean.
Molly: Killed him.
Killed him. Of course Ah wisnae born then, but he was killed, jumped – Ah think they were playin at – whatever they were playin at, jumpin on tae the mill, some bar, cross bar or something.
Molly: And it would throw him aff probably.

Greta Hawthorn

… when the mills came in, you see the mills were in nearly once a month, May Smith's father was the mill man, he had an engine that worked wi coal and then he had the thrashing mill and then he had the wee carriage at the end of it which was, they could stay overnight in it and it'd two bunks in it and they used to be lots o people that came extra to get the mill because there had to be two women up on the top o the mill cutting the bunches and givin them tae a man that put them in the thrasher and then when it came oot there was caff, well they had tae be put in bags and took away and then the corn had tae be put in bags and took away and then ye had tae get the straw, an it wis put in different places, jist for bedding doon for the beasts.

Jock McMaster speaks about the transition to the tractor-driven mill which replaced the farm's water-powered mill; though the new process still brought overnight visitors to the farm, the progression was gradually one of taking away the necessity for people within the process.

Jock McMaster

So, that's [the mill on the farm is] quite unusual because usually people got the mobile threshing mill?
Well, funnily enough that's the next step, once this barn mill, it was very slow in quantity so the next thing was the threshing mill, aye, Wyllie's at Garlieston provided a threshing mill and two guys came with it. A mill and a baler behind to bale the straw and they also towed a caravan behind that, they stayed on the farm till the thrashing was finished. They probably came for four or five days at a time, maybe even, aye probably the whole week. And the men ate their meals in the farmhouse but they slept in their caravan at night.

And so what sort of date was that, when Wyllie's?
That's '50s, that's '50s, yea, to my memory and way before as well, steam engines originally, I don't remember them. The one I do remember was a tractor called a Field Marshal and it was a single-cylinder tractor with a huge exhaust pipe, Ah can remember it comin in and it made a very distinctive beat – like a railway engine, a sort of 'chuff, chuff, chuff' as it pulled in this thing and it drove the mill with a belt– A big long end this belt drove the mill. And of course there was no Health and Safety in those days, there was no guards in this thing, people did actually fall into them occasionally or get their hands caught in them and all sorts. Oh, Ah remember the mill because Ah remember working at it. Ma dad actually bought one which we used for about ten or 15 years and it was my job to feed this thing. Ye stood up in a little box with a knife and two of you cut the sheaves and poured them in and aye, it was dusty. Ah can remember going to the cinema in Newton Stewart one night after thrashing and Ah couldnae open ma eyes to watch the film because they were so burning with dust (laughs). Thankfully those days are over.

But was it a sort of social day when the mill came, people have mentioned–?
> Well, we got guys fae Whithorn tae come and help if there was a big lot of thrashing to be done but normally we just did it ourselves. Because there was a pick-up baler behind the mill which took away the need for a man there, two of us on top and one body forking and instead of the corn coming off in bags, ma dad made a box with an auger in it that put it into a trailer, loose, so there was nobody needed at that end either so five of us could actually do the thrashing.

Kennedy Donnan and his brother were the owners of a contracting business, circulating round the farms with their mills.

Kennedy Donnan

> And after that Ah got a job at West Freugh for aboot two year and then when Ah finished there Ah got a job at Slaehabbert at Whauphill, Ah was there for four year. Ma brother and me started contracting after that. We had two mills, then we got a baler, stationary baler and then we had a small baler, then a combine and Ah had ma name in for a holding, Ah got the offer of a holding at Kilfillan but ah'd had tae hae contracted tae make a living so Ah turned it down. About a year later Ah got 3 High Boreland and one of the conditions was that Ah didn't contract.

Cathy Miller, Kennedy's niece, recalls how the mills were booked.

Cathy Miller

> Well, I would be about eleven year old, wouldn't ah? Because Ah was milking the cows. Ah was eleven year old because ma grandmother had a phone but it was a shared phone and with them being in business and people wantin tae get through, invariably when she went to the phone she couldn't, cause the other person was on the phone and they used to like a 'crack' as she talked about (laughter) so she used tae, until they got their own line.

So farms would call in and say that they were needed?
> Yes, yes. They mostly left the messages with ma mum, Mum had a book at the side of the telephone because there was that many came in in a day that she couldn't remember them all.

Kennedy Donnan

> Ah think it was maybe £1 an hour. It could hae been a little more, I'm not just sure.

And was it considered a good living or was it just a kind of bare living?
   No, a reasonable living, a reasonable living.
And can you describe ... how the mill worked?
   Well, ye had tae open it up, take the sheet off, open it up, get it ready for thrashing, two ladies come up, what ye called 'the lowsers', they cut the strings on the sheafs and handed then tae whoever was in the, was feedin the drum, and that was more or less what ... some o them liked it bunched and others liked it baled. Yes, Ah got the point of that finger stuck in the stationary baler (laughs).
   ...
   Latterly ye had tae take a net wi ye, an run it out round where ye were workin for the sake o keepin rats in, so as they couldnae get away. And there was quite a few rats about then. When Ah was standin feedin the mill ah've felt mice gaun up roon ma waist here. Ah had a belt on, Ah just gein them a squeeze (laughter).

With all the complex moving parts, breakdown was always on the horizon, entailing work and requiring readiness from agricultural joiners and blacksmiths.

Cathy Miller and John Wilson

   CM: Well, it was done about every third or fourth farm, ye just had tae do it in between your farms, cause they didn't give ye much time, if they wanted ye there you had to be there. And it also gave work to what they called the girls that went in. Were they stood, the man stood in like what it was a wee square with the sides up and the women cut the sheaves and handed them to him. And they just went with them mill, they had, Kennedy had certain ladies, Jim had certain ladies and it gave employment to them.
   JW: Ah think, although the mills were quite complicated, there was a lot of pieces on it, which if they broke were very easily repaired, there was a lot of wooden shakers, they had ash bars about, maybe about four foot long and like about three by half inch and they shook and these were the things really that tended to break, but they were very simple to be replaced. Because we always used to have a supply of them at the workshop.
   CM: There was only one thing that was nuisance and it happened over and over again was the belts. They were joined together with great big screws like that, about four of them and with usage and maybe three or four farms ye'd been to, they would snap so that held up a half-day and lost a half-day. Jim used tae get mad, couldn't understand how these belts kept– it was just the wear and tear.
      One [mill] was second-hand until they got on their feet and the second one, they thought with the amount of times the belt and that and

things were going wrong, they would buy a new one, so they bought the second one new, because they had enough work for the two.

JW: Yes, and then they were always painted up in the wintertime weren't they?

CM: Yes, they were all oiled down and covered up.

Were they always painted red?

CM: Mostly red or a sort of orangey-pinky–

JW: The combine harvesters killed these overnight, didn't they?

CM: Yes, yes, well, Jim and him went into the new combine harvester but the farmers decided that, 'Oh, we can do this' so a lot of them went into their own so that finished the whole thing.

So, about when did it finish?

CM: About 45 years ago, 40 years ago?

JW: Ah was going to say about 1965 roughly in aboot that time.

The 'squads', even by their name, signal the availability of people who came en masse; they would visit farms after a day's work elsewhere, to help with thinning, harvest or mill days.

Jock McMaster

But when Wyllie's mill came in, aye there was a couple of guys came from Whithorn to give us a hand. Before Ah was actually doing much work then, in ma kinna schooldays, Ah remember them comin in. But harvest time was more sociable when we cut corn with a binder. We used tae get squads out from Whithorn to help, five or six every day, and potato picking, turnip hoeing. Flannighan was the man from Whithorn and he supplied labour and they quite often came in a cattle float and Ah can remember them coming in the turnip field and the lorry, the back door coming down and jist a mass o humanity coming out and the girls and women all crawled up and down in the drills and they hoed the turnips by hand, just using their hands tae hold onto the small turnip and pulled the rest out, clean away the weeds, whereas the men, they used hoes, they stood behind and the gaffer, there was always a gaffer, he hoed as well but he used to help the slow people. He didn't actually take a drill of his own, he would help the slow ones and criticise and cajole them on to keep them moving. And aye, Ah think Ah can probably remember probably 40 or 50 people one, in it. They used to come in the evenings after work so they'd come here aboot back o six, this was in June it would be, aye, sort of mid, late June and work till half past nine. And they did their three hours and amazing how much work a number of people like that could do. A 20-acre field would be done in, quite happily, three evenings wi a squad like that.

29. Tattie howkers at Low Clone, Port William.

Jenny Jolly first joined the 'squads' as a worker, but then took over as the organiser of the Whithorn 'squad', for which she managed the weekly routine of payments and the reckoning up of credits and debits to each worker.

Jenny Jolly

Ye used tae scale dung, they used tae, tractors come through and they pit so mony heaps o dung alang that side and so mony alang this side and twa folk went tae scale it, you got it, ye met the body at this side in the middle wae it – through the middle – nasty, kinna heavy job but Ah didnae mind it and the harvest. I liked the harvest.

What about shawing turnips?

Oh, aye Ah liked the shawin, I didnae like the thinnin o them. Ma sister wis guid at thinnin turnips, she couldnae shaw wi her puir auld back. But Ah liked the shawin best. An at the mill tae Ah never wis much on the top o the mill lowsing, ye were standin all the time. I was either at the wee pick-up bales carryin them or something like that. Ye were used to gaun anywhere at the harvest. But yer body was fit for it, Julia, that's the hale story.

...

Well, it was efter Ah got married I went into the agriculture, an Ah just like it outside. There was a wee factory and aw. but it would have killed me, I was in for a short time, stuffing teddy bears, but ma chest an aw, jist gied it up but back to the usual. We were workin at the Wards tae though, we helped at, when Major Blakeman come and Mrs Blakeman, it was strawberries, we helped tae plant the strawberries and then we used to the picking o them and then ye had the weighin o them intae punnets and yin thing an another, cleaning and the raspberries, pulled raspberries tae.

So did you work in one of the squads first?

Yes, uh-huh, wi Hughie Smith an then he gave up.

And is that when you took over running the squads?

Aye Ah jist took ower. But then John Turner come an he took ower and I was quite happy, for ye never had a meenit's peace. Ah thocht, 'they can hunt you John' but oh, he widnae be bothered wi them though.

And how many people in a squad?

Oh, God, ye yist tae hae, when we wis at nights– folk that worked during the day, come oot at night tae work for the extra money and ah've seen us gaun, a guid squad, tae twa different places a night. Maybe aboot 40 or 60 or something like that.

So tell me about the work you used to do on the squads, what kind of work did you do?

Oh, the farmwork, aye, turnips, an shaw turnips and thrashing mills and whitewashed the steading. I liked the whitewashing though that was the inside and the outside.

How much did you earn a week if you were on a squad?
> Oh, different. Depends how mony days ye were oot an Ah got extra for, well Ah had tae get extra for the runnin a had tae dae. Ah mean, Ah neever had a meenit at hame for ye were runnin lookin for folk for this and folk for that and folk for the mills and ye were gettin money here and there. So I was quite … it was a big relief when Ah stopped it and John Turner took it ower.
>
> …
>
> Oh, it's a while. What was it to start wi? To start it was aboot ten shillings a day and then it went up and up tae aboot 18 shillings but then years efter Ah feenished a while it went right up. It went up, I think it'll be mair noo though but then it went up tae £8 a day, for farm or cas'l work. So I expect it'll be up since that. They had tae bring, they fetched oot these schedules, the wage schedules, and the wage board sent them in tae the farms for what they had tae pay. Oh, it'll be mair noo Ah would think, Julia, I don't know though. And the Kidsdale workers and the estate an aw they, they got, them that was employed, they got coals, benefit but it was kept oot their wage really. They got coal and they got tatties and milk but there was so much kept aff their wage for it. But they still, they were sure o that food.

There was nobody who was more skilled and got a bit more?
> Well, the younger yins, when ye were liftin tatties it was like two o the boys fae the school, two on one lift so it was a bit divided between the two.

Yes. And you had to keep all the money for them?
> It was a lot of money, there was a lot o tallying up, ye didnae get the money tae the weekend. Ah had tae start and get it earlier for they used tae no pay some o the farmers tae a Saturday and then you couldnae get your cheques cashed. So Ah got, Ah aye asked for them aye on a Friday tae get the money, get it sorted oot. And then Bill yist tae get in his fae his work, jist at his dinner, when the door got chapped. But hooever we managed.

And when did the squads die out, pretty much?
> Well, they started the combine. There's nae sheaves like ye see that auld wuman [in a picture] carrying. There were some big sheaves in thae days, fu o thistles. It wasn't very nice. There's no so much work noo for there's nae mills noo either.

Migrant Irish squads would come, symbol of the summer season, for the harvesting of the early potatoes, grown round the coast, and then move on to Ayrshire and into Angus. Judy Brown's father was the pioneer of the potato business, which employed not only the local squads but the Irish squads, who, according to Jenny Jolly, lived still more economically, in the most minimal of shelters, and worked still faster than the local squads.

Jenny Jolly

Oh, there's, there's early and late tatties. It was aye the beg–, when the early tatties starts, the same as when yer Drummore tatties comes in, but then they stopped growin them here. See, Christie didnae have them [the Irish], he got the locals, aw gathered up, a lot of folk for him. And he got aw the folk fae Port William, he gied aw the locals work, tae, rather than get the squads, the other squads in. And I seen big lorries comin in fae Glasgow for the market and Ah seen 60 ton gaun away in the morning. They had tae go every day, fresh, ye see. … Oh aye there was an awfy tatties, and first the tatties that come tae Whithorn, they never bothered hoo mony tatties they folk took, they took bags an aw, greed, ye ken. But he never stopped them. Ah, but when they went tae Kidsdale tae lift tatties they got a very little, they werenae gaun tae gie them onything but they got a very small dinner, what they called it, 'a small dinner'. They wisnae as saft as–

So where did the Irish come in, which farms did they got to?

Oh, up at the Morrach, cause I mind I was whitewashing at the Morrach for them comin for where they were sleepin, livin, cookin and ootside and inside. And, it was the Morrach but there was somewhere else tae, there's two or three farms they come tae.

So they grew potatoes for human consumption? It wasn't just animals?

No, what happened for the animals at Monreith, if the tatties was aw lifted an away tae get selt, ye gaithered the ground an then ye got a wee job sorting the seeds size and the wee yins for pigs, cause there's a piggery at the Dourie onyway. So they were aw made use o. Ye got paid by the job though, for gaitherin the grund, so much a bag. In thae days there was Irish tattie howkers come for the early potato liftin, for so mony weeks and they stayed in outhouses, no barns, but outhouses, on the Morrach at Willie Broon's and them. Tae start wi they hadnae a great bit at all, away back before Ah started, like, but there was a priest come roond tae see what way they were treated and he kicked up Dublin and they had tae have a decent place for them tae sleep in and beds, something comfortable tae lie on and they had tae have a place tae cook. So they put in one of thae big set pots and there was a lassie stood at it, a wuman, cooked tatties for them at dinner time and they aw bought their ain wee tins o meat or what have ye. It was a rough life. But they worked, oh God, but ye couldnae hae lifted tattie wi them, never seen them, they jist, oot at yin hand intae the other, ye never it, they were that quick. They were speedy right enough, they're trained tae it Ah think. But we were workin wi them but nocht tae dae wi it, ye ken, different foremen. Their foreman, they say he robbed them tae, worked them like hell, instead o, he didnae pay them right either. I mind o one o the women asking me yin day what our pay was and she was quite, and she said aboot the big difference. You see some o thae foremen was dirty.

Greta Hawthorn

And there were potato diggers came and– they came from Ireland and they stayed in which we called the bothies but they were just shed places but they were always cleaned out before they came. And they had [turnip?] boxes and they turned them different ways so that it made them into beds or wee drawers and they filled their sacks with straw or the chaff that came from when the mill was there, it was always saved for them. And they had the big range, there was always a cook there, and they used to put the turnips into the horse trough that had been cleaned out and they just swilled them round with a stick to get the skins off them because they were always just newly dug and we used to gaun and help them, making jellies and putting names on them. They always left a note of what they wanted for their dinner at night.

...

But they'd always plenty potatoes because they'd potato workers came over from Ireland, as I say, from June until August and they just did all the digging and Mr [Forry?] was their manager that came over from Ireland with them and there used to be a couple stayed in The Grapes, from Fife, that ordered where the potatoes were to go to and the lorries went in and they made staging with sleepers in those days so that they could just reverse the lorry on and wheel them on tae the lorry, the bags of potatoes, new potatoes.

Judy Brown's father was the pioneer of the potato trade and provided accommodation for the Irish squads on their farm near the Isle of Whithorn.

Judy Brown

Oh, yes. We had both beef and sheep and arable because there was 640 acres, approximately, and 300 was arable and the rest for rough, or grazing. So we had that, then just after the War we started the dairy and in 1947 the dairyman and his wife were milking 63 cows, night and morning, and looking after all the young stock for a wage of £7 a week (laughs) plus they got free milk and free coal and that sort of thing, but £7 a week that was a big– and my father started growing early potatoes in 1938 and he was first into the Glasgow market with them, then.

And so was he unusual in growing potatoes round here?
> Yes, he was the first one in this area, they were all grown up Girvan shore then before that and we were the first down here and Claymoddie and Kidsdale grew them too … (laughs) they were planted by women. They took the horse and machine along to make the drills and then the women carried a box between them and they did two drills, one each, as they went along planting and when they were ready we got a potato squad over from Ireland with all his workers and they dug them and lifted them.

So were the women who planted, were they local?
> Largely Isle of Whithorn but other people who worked on the farms, lived on the farms. Because there were ten men on Cutreoch and the Morrach at that time because it was horses and tractors had not long started and it was much more manual labour than it is now, so you had all the families and the kids would come out as well.

Yes. Now, I've heard about 'the tattie holidays' is that for lifting?
> Yes, that's for lifting the late potatoes in October.

How did your father have the idea of getting Irish squads in?
> I suppose it would be his potato merchant in Glasgow that would recommend, there were certain squads that came over to certain farms every year and once we had them it was the same ones that came every year, to us, and then they moved onto wherever was next.

And were the Irish people just quicker at it or were they cheaper or–?
> No, I don't think there was anything like that but they were Catholics and they were controlled by, 'You will be at Chapel on a Sunday morning' and 'you will be …' so I suppose they were more regimented. And they slept on potato boxes with straw on top, for the duration, and they lived on potatoes.

It seems quite a monotonous diet, did they have it for all three meals of the day?
> I think so, I think so. Never seemed to see them at– they were never off the place except to go to Chapel on a Sunday.

So they'd go into Whithorn, presumably?
> …
> My father got a tractor and a trailer and took [them], got one of the men to drive it in, so they had no excuse (laughs).

So, once they'd got the potatoes up what happened then?
> Well, they bagged them and they were stacked outside the field, on the roadside, and then the potato merchant sent his lorry down to get whatever and from the next place, whatever amount they wanted that day, because he sold them daily at the price they were that day so you wanted to always get the best price and, of course, first in the market got the best price. So, the earlier in the season that you could grow them, the better.

Although much of the Machars economy centred on dairying, there were still farms which had large flocks of sheep, enough to require a full-time shepherd, as at Blairbuy; whereas on the eastern coasts, Cruggleton was part of an estate engaging in a truly international beef trade.

Robin Kinnear speaks about the occupational costume of the shepherd.

Robin Kinnear

> Well, there were, in the early twentieth century, late nineteenth century, there were a lot of shoemakers and boot makers, some of them repairers who would actually make 'kip' boots, the big curly toed boots but the main place for them was in Maybole, they manufactured boots and we usually got them from there, originally, but then you had shoe firms which came round from England selling them.
>
> *Now, you called them 'kip' boots?*
>
> Kip boots, yes, they were a herd's boot, they were a sort of one piece upper, they didn't have a toecap and they had a definite set on the sole, a curvature on the bottom of the sole, heavily tacketed with heel shods and toe shods, and you tended to roll along the grass in them when you were walking, going out, especially ... well I know a lot of herds wore them, shepherds, but a lot of farm workers wore that type of boot as well because they were completely waterproof. That would be before the Wellington boot would come out so would keep their feet dry and warm.

Jock McMaster's farm employed a full-time shepherd. The shearing was done by the farmworkers, some as efficient as machines, but now imported shearers can shear hundreds in a day.

Jock McMaster

> And that was his sole job, just looking after the sheep, morning and– he walked roond the stock every morning, he'd be finished aboot ten o'clock and he would go back round again in the afternoon, or the evening. And at lambing time he was just there all the time.
>
> ...
>
> Oh, yes, aye, jist as soon as we were old enough we rolled up the fleeces and packed them intae the big bags. In those days ye hung the bag up on ropes from the rafters and ye put in half a dozen fleeces and then you were chucked in as well because this bag was probably eight feet high, seven feet high? And the guys handed ye fleeces in and ye tramped them intae the corners. And we had a competition, as we got older we had a competition

every year to see who could pack the heaviest one. And Ah remember the wool then went to Kirkcowan to a chap called Milroy at Kirkcowan and he sent a note back saying he couldn't get the wool out because it was so tightly packed so in future we weren't tae pack them so hard (laughter).

…

Ah remember ma dad saying that at one time, Ah think before the War, when they took the wool up – they took it there, delivered it to them, and were paid for it, obviously, but they always got some cloth as discount, it was cloth given to them that you could use for a jacket or trousers, whatever. And it must just have been a sort of custom of the miller, gien ye some cloth, in lieu of cash, I suppose. William Milroy, Ah can remember wool bags with his name stamped on them, they were stencilled on the wool bags. But yea, we sheared sheep from about 14 years, I suppose we'd be 14, 15 year old, with hand shears, just the hand clippers. By the time Ah finished using the hand shears, electric shears were common and we jist used a contractor for that. But it was a very sociable thing, we only clipped 40 or 50 every day, among three or four of us, because we dosed the lambs, cleaned their tails and sheared that group o sheep and then the next day we did another lot and so on and so on until it was done. Now the guys come in and can do 400 or 500 in a day, 250 each, just the way it's done. The way it has changed.

30. Hand shearing sheep, Glasserton, 1934.

And, did you use the shearing stool?
> Well, we didn't but was one shepherd that we had, he and his brothers came and did the clippin then and they used the stool, yea. And one o the brothers in particular was ambidextrous, he could shear with both hands and he never had tae turn his sheep, the sheep sat on the stool and he clipped the one side wi his right hand and the other side with his left hand. It was beautiful to watch, he was just, he was just like a machine, himself, aye. And that was on a stool, it was a narrow seat at one end for the man to sit on and a sort of broader shape for the ewe to lie on and of course it's easy on the back, you didn't have to bend over because you, your work was just at your level.

Beef farming on the eastern coast of the Machars was on a large scale, and opened up a horizon far beyond the Newton Stewart cattle market: there was international trade on farms owned by A. B. Marshall, with trips by train to shows and export to faraway Iowa and the Argentine, where Cruggleton stock must have founded the significant cattle trade there. A regime of care and feeding, often better than the farmhands' own and sufficiently tempting to lure them to try the bulls' morning porridge, resulted in world-class stock.

Cathy Doughty tells of her family's involvement with the Shorthorns.

Cathy Doughty

> I was born in Cruggleton, in 1924, and we moved to the Cults in May, 28th of May, term-time. I was 28 year there. In Whithorn, in Cults. And my eldest brother worked a lot wi the Shorthorns, he left the school when he was young, cause, well, probably we needit the money, I don't know. But he got off, Marshall got him off to work at that time wi Pat MacDonal, come over Ireland, and my mother fed him and everything and he stayed in the farmhouse on his own. And they worked wi these bulls. And these Shorthorns, they had boxes their own, each one had their own box, they suckled the cows when they were younger, and then they were fed the cows' milk, they only kept a cow for farm workers, they got a whatever milk they were to get every day. And these bulls were fed on the best, they were going to the shows, they were fed on eggs, and malt, they got everything they wanted. They were taken out for exercise every day, three men took two bulls each and they walked them out every day, brought them back, put them in. A lot o them went to the Argentine, they went there. And that's aboot it really, the— I'll tell ye something, the bulls were better done to them than working folk!

Robert Galashan, whose father and uncle were experts brought in from the north east of Scotland, describes the special diet developed for the bulls.

Robert Galashan

And the feeding stuff, they couldna feed cattle the way they fed them in these days. Do ye want to know the sort o recipes?
Oh yes!
There used to be, the train would have brought in a big full carriage of late maize, bran, cotton cake, it was like a big slab, linseed cake, they grew their own barley and oats, and the first thing in the morning that was done was to put the boiler on. They never fed dry barley to the bulls. It was always cooked. It was like porridge, when you went past you could hae ate it, the smell o it was lovely! And that was the first job in the morning, getting this boiler going. And they had a – do ye know what a cooler is? Well, we call them killers, but the right name's a cooler, it's like a big trough shaped like that, two wheels, two handles. And the food that was made up for the bulls, it was like a sandwich, they put late maize, bran, maybe some oats, cotton cake, linseed cake, and then tae top it all, to finish up, they went to the boiler and got a big pail o this cooked barley, and spread it across the top, boiling hot. And then put jute bags over it to let it steam. And when they went tae feed it, they mixed it wi a shovel, and it was all in layers, like a sandwich, and they mixed it all up. And ye went round the bulls wi a basket, and ye gave them allocation into the trough. And then ye come round behind that, they bought 40-gallon barrels o malt, and they got a big dollop o malt on the top o the mixture, the mash, and boy, they enjoyed that. And more than the bulls enjoyed it, we used to get it roond wir fingers! But it wid be too costly now, people couldnae afford tae feed them the way they did in these days.

Aye, and the bulls, they were always exercised. They were taken maybe couple o mile doon the road on halters, to keep their feet right, but they also had what they called stocks, and Mr Marshall used to do this himself, they would put a bull into this stocks, and he couldnae move, there wis a clamp went roond their neck, and their legs, you could lift their foot and put it ontae a bit like that. And he used tae use a wood chisel, just what a joiner would have, and a mallet, and he would pare their feet, cut the hoofs doon to they were level. Sometimes he had them bleeding. But he aye said they walked better after that. It used tae get them tae walk properly. And they were shampooed and groomed, and all their coat and that brushed, and, oh, they were well looked after. They would be taken to shows and things like that. And when the buyers came there were always a big day before that to get them all intae order and looking their best.

Cathy Doughty

> He had five farms. He had Cruggleton, he'd Palmallet and Crugglelton, Brownhill, the Cults, and Bridgebank in Stranraer.

And did you ever see him?

> Oh, aye, twice a week. First of all it was his father, he was Matthew, and then the other one was Bertie took it, Bertie. … I remember a Lord Lovat coming and there used to be people aboot Castle Douglas, I cannae remember their name just now, they used to come, they knew when Mr Marshall was coming and they came and met him, and he showed them round. They'd, us kids could open up the bull boxes and went to where the bulls were, they never bothered us. But see the cows, aye, ye'd to watch them, they would go for ye.

And did the bulls get sold and go on the trains?

> They went … I don't know how they got, but they went on the trains to the shows, they had tae, they got a carriage, a special carriage tae go to the shows. And 'Paymaster' was a great, it was a great bull. It would be the bull of all bulls, I think, Shorthorns. And there was one called 'Silver Wedding', it was white. I don't know why it got Silver Wedding, but Silver Wedding, it won prizes. But the men, my brother and some o the other ones, had to go to York or wherever the show was, go on the trains wi the bulls and look after them for a week, the shows on. They met King George VI and his wife. And she spoke to them all, my brother had a wee bit o a stammer, and she said tae him, when she went up tae speak tae him, 'Just take your time, because ye just speak like the king. So just take it easy and it'll come out easier'. And then they went to the next boy and asked it to him and he's, well, very ill to hold and work with, but he says, 'They're nae bother at aa', he says, tae her. And she says, 'Oh, the Scots, how I love the Scots', she says, 'I do wish more people would speak it to me!' So they were very nice. They'd to take them round the ring, and different ones, he met the, well, the one who abdicated, he met him at the shows. Met a few o the royalty there, to see the bulls, and spoke to them. They were very nice.

Inside-Outside: Farmhouses

The farmhouse, like the townhouse, was welcoming to surplus people, outside the family unit – boys who stayed in the bothy, hired men, as well as those who lived in, like maids and housekeepers – whose many hands were needed, in the absence of extensive domestic technology.

Tom McCreath

And did you provide a lunch in the farm kitchen or did they go back their own cottages?

They went back to their own cottages, but very often there were extra people that were fed in the farmhouse, particularly on a mill day, there could be two mill men or three sometimes if they'd a baler in and the extra hands all had to have a big lunch and then, come wartime, land girls. I don't think the prisoners of war had a midday meal, they brought it with them, I think. And then we had the medical students to help with the harvest in wartime. Farmhouse organisation had to be good to cope and Mother's mother, my grandmother, couldn't cope so she was brought back from school to run the household, which made her, in her day quite formidable, although very nice, I've got to say.

It has an implication for how much women had to do in the household and of course not having all the aids that we have now, it must have been pretty hard work in the farm kitchen as well?

Oh very much, yes, but of course there was help in most of the farm-houses. We had two maids before the War broke out and they were kept very busy and a lot of their parents looked at it as an opportunity for their girls to get a training in cooking and baking and other things that stood them in good stead once they got married.

And of course everything would be made from scratch ... you'd be making scones or pancakes or something for every day, I suppose?

Absolutely, and you always made sure at the beginning of winter that there was a full sack of oatmeal and a full sack of flour in the meal ark and of course the gardens had to be good and produce all sorts of potatoes and veggies.

Jock McMaster

Did she [Jock's mother] have to cook a lunch for people coming in from the fields or–?

No, there was teas taken out, mostly, there wasnae sae much eatin in. The mill men were the only folk Ah remember actually eating in but at harvest time there was always tea and sandwiches taken out in the afternoon, especially if it was a good day and you were gonna work on till maybe eight at night, so she would make tea and, a harvest tea and take it out to the field. But of course in those days we had a three-course lunch and a high tea as well. We seemed to eat all day, although we never had breakfast, Dad and I just had a cup o tea and a bit o toast but we always had either a two- or three-course lunch and then we had a good big hearty tea as well. Of course ye were doing a lot more hard work – ye were physically liftin

31. Oat harvest tea at Torhousemuir, Wigtown, 1935.

things and Ah suppose yer appetite was better. But no, well Ah think they had pin money, was hens, she kept a few hens, and she made butter cause we had a couple o cows in the byre and she used tae make butter and Ah can remember her selling it, or selling butter to various folk, it would only be pennies, Ah suppose, but it would be a little extra. But Mum didn't help outside as such, a lot of farmers' wives do. She didn't do any outside, she did a lot of gardening and stuff and she jist done her housework. But a lot of farmers' wives actually physically work outside, especially dairy farmers, a lot of them do the dairy, or part of it.

The provision of a meal to the field workers was a favour, not always offered, which helped stretch the wages.

Betty Stuart

But it was different times and some o the farmers tae the aulder folk were nice and some o them werenae. I was saying to Elena, she was the sister of auld Mrs Kerr, and she took them all meals, and they had them fae they were say in a steading or in a shed. 'Come here a minute, Hetty' and there was a special dinner for ma mother. She got aw right in that.

Betty Stuart and Jenny Jolly reveal that leaving home for the life of a young live-in housemaid on a farm was traumatic. Employment of young girls, with accommodation, food and training provided on the premises, was an important relief to the family expenses back home. Jenny Jolly was a live-in maid at Catyans.

Jenny Jolly

And that was what? General housework?

General housework in the house, uh-huh. Oh, she'd yon wee 'piggy', ken the auld fashioned water bottles? Thae yins an there was aye a big yin put in every– aboot tea time in Mr, the auld man's bed, tae, the bed, tae heat it up. And God, yin night Ah had it up and she was oot feedin her hens when she heerd the explosion. Did Ah no drop it! Oh, the mess, got it aw dried, cleaned up an aw, but it was the bang, it was like a bomb going off. She come tearin in tae the hoose, because she heerd the bang outside, tae see what happened. 'I'll take it out of your pay', she says, but never did. Miss Laurie was awfy guid tae me compared tae some maids got. Maids in thae days didnae get weel treated, ye know?

…

But I was to stay in, they had a wee bedroom for me, but I was aye spoiled by ma– I was aye shoutin for ma mother and I stayed a night and that was it so I said I'd just walk if it was a'right I could walk across, so I did that, aw weathers. But they kept, the wee bedroom was kept for me, for ma– changing in the afternoon, after lunchtime for teatime, I was [unclear] ma comb an aw was there for ma hair. It was a nice hoose the Catyans hoose.

What time did you start work in the morning, then?

Oh, early, I was across early because ye had the fireplace to do in the dining room and light the fire and the dining room tae dae oot and then set the breakfast table for the auld man getting up, for he was a solicitor. He was in an office in George Street and he never went home at dinner time, he aye went into The Commercial pub at– where your hoose is. He aye went in there and had a whisky for his lunch and he had a crooked kinna stick he walked wi [unclear].

…

Catyans Hoose was a lovely hoose but there was a big kitchen and pantry, there was a big kitchen that ye ate in and aw that was square and big lovely stove in it wi the tiles, aw white tiles aw roond the side o it. Then there was the pantry, and these old crocks, [unclear] in there but [unclear] the old crocks and they had lids on them and the pantry sat on the flair because it was just a tiled floor. And she baked, every Thursday she did an big baking in the forenin and she aye made, always the same Ah can mind, she did a batch o rock buns and shortbread. That was for wur cup o tea ye see at night and she made tattie scones, meal scones and soda scones. And they scones kept fae this Thursday tae the next yin and they were still lovely. On no, it was a guid meat hoose. And then she got – it was a secret though – so I never said ocht aboot it, she got auld Kennedy man … was it Bob ye ca'd im? He was a butcher, onyway, he was trained a butcher and he was a butcher wi Owen's in Garlieston and she got him across the field but he had the things an aw hid doon his jacket and here he was jist oot for a walk wi his way o it and he killed a pig, ye see ye werenae allowed tae dae that [during the War].

...

Well, I just went to another hoose to work an Ah hated it, Ah didn't like it and they were very mean, ye were rationed, that's what ah'm saying tae ye. An she would come through in the morning, she took my jam, a pund o jam a month or something ye got, she took my jam for wee Lesley, her daughter's parritch to encourage her to eat. I mean she had her father's jam and her own jam but she aye come for mine. And see in the Catyans, Miss Laurie left ye the pots o stuff and ye helped yersel tae as much as ye wanted and us, maybe if I hadnae been spoiled that way. Onyway Mrs Jones, ye had tae go through to the– everything, all the food was took to the dining room table and ye had tae wait till she rung a bell fur ye to go tae get yer first coorse and then ye had tae wait again for your second and so on. You didnae help yourself. ... They wis mean in the old days. Some of them wis, onyway.

Betty Stuart

Mary left school at 14, on Friday, ma Ma had her waged in service on Monday morning. Mary got on well in her job and was very well-liked, she stayed in the job for years. Alas, I was different, I also left at 14 years old on a Friday and was waged on Monday. Ah went off on the Monday morning on a milk cairt, crying, Ah didnae want tae go but I had tae go but I hated it. One of the many, ma duties, the mistress told me, was to empty the master's po in the morning so I did not. On the third morning I got a right doing and was told to empty the po at once. I refused and told the mistress, 'The master's as like doing it as I was' as he'd be an old man and I was just 14. The result was I got sent home. Ma Ma immediately took me back and made me apologise but I carried on that much they were glad to get rid of me. I had a good few jobs after that, I worked in Miss Hannah's tearoom, I liked it very much, and Molly and Joanne were very good to me. It was very busy as the War was on, the soldiers and airmen came in at nights for their supper. The supper was bacon, sausage, tomatoes and egg and tattie scones, all for the sum of one and six, so you can imagine it was a very popular eating house.

And did you have to give some of your wages to your mother?

No. Some of them – you handed them over.

All of it?

Aye. My first wage was ten shillings, it was over at The Mains there.

Molly: Was that a month?

A week. And, Ah think it was ten shillings a week, aye, and Ah hated every minute o it. Ah was frightened and there was an auld man worked at it and he yaist tae frighten me– Ah wis only four– that's when Ah left school, that was ma first job, an Ah wis over there and a Tuesday night, I think it was a Tuesday night Ah was in ma bedroom and a wee rap come tae the door and it was ma Ma wi a comic for me an a sweetie, every Tuesday night (laughter) *The Film Fun.*

So that's what you got out of it?

That's what Ah got.

On a Tuesday, a sweetie and that, Ah didnae really like it, they were what de ye call it, Ah dunno if it was Plymouth Brethren, they was some kinna Brethren, anyway, an they had meetings an ye had tae gae intae, it was an awfu palaver. Aye, they were religious people.

So, you had to live in?

Yes, you lived in, there.

And so what were your duties?

Ye did the housework an that, Ah didnae have any washin to do. She had what she called a hall, well, I'm quite sure it was wee'er than this carpet and she, 'Before you go away the night, polish that hall'. Of course Ah never bothered, an that was me got intae bother the next time Ah went. 'Did ye polish the hall? Ye never did.' We didnae really get on an Ah didnae like gaun tae the meetins for Ah didnae understand them cause they werenae the same as us, ken what Ah mean? Ah had tae go to them but Ah didnae really understand them and they were away singing high, away. But Ah cried that much one night she said, 'Ah'll just tak ye hame wi me'. That was it. After that Cherry Valley, tae the Christies.

4

Work and Rest: The Timing of Pleasures

In the margins of the day and on the seventh day, there was just time to snatch rest and recreation, all the more anticipated because of the relentlessness of daily toil. Most, like the social gathering on the dyke at Glasserton village, or Sunday picnics at Monreith sands, or dances in the town, involved face-to-face congregations of people, rather than the enjoyment of private pleasures sourced from elsewhere. These occasions loomed large in anticipation and in memory, magnified by their sparseness and the rush to cross the countryside on foot or bike, and return in time for the milking next day.

Robert Galashan

> [Speaking of his uncle, stud groom at Cruggleton] Oh aye, aye. He wis a very quiet man. He'd be one o the strongest men in this area, if ye could have seen the things he could lift, it wis unbelievable. Very, very strong man, aye. But he wasnae one tae– never went tae a pub, he wasnae a drinker. And he used tae smoke a pipe. He had one fill o Three Nuns tobacca when he wis sitting reading the *Glasga Herald* at night. He never would refill it. One pipe o tobacca, and that was im relaxin after his day's work. He worked fae daylight tae dark, oh aye.

Cathy Miller

> Ma grandmother's one relaxation was, there was Beanie Anderson, the Miss Andersons, they used to come once a week and it was all the china and everything and the wee fancy doilies and when they had finished their tea, it was leaves in these days, they turned their cup upside down and ma grandmother went round them all tellin their tea leaves. … That was the highlight of the week.

John Wilson

Well yes, they come in there and they'd blether but in ma father's day Ah can remember ma father saying that the young men always used to meet at Glasserton, ma father was born at Glasserton, they used to meet and there would be, they would sit on the dyke at night, all the local boys would come in and they'd have a game of football or what and then they would have a blether on the dyke.

We used to go up to the Black Rocks at Monreith which was about three-quarters of a mile from where Ah was, where Ah lived, on a Sunday, and there used to be busloads of people came up from Whithorn up there and there'd be two ice-cream vans there and there would be 50, 60 people there. That was the main place at the weekends.

Betty Stuart

[Speaking of these Sunday School parties] Well, at the beginning there was some pony and traps but in my day it mostly was the bus, Caledonian. But ah've been in the pony thing. It must have been years and years ago but that's what we used to go in. Rows and rows o the pony and traps to the picnic.
Was that just once a year or several times?
No, it was once a year. And ye had a party once a year too.
...
Do you remember curling going on in the neighbourhood?
Yes, doon in the field on Nummerston Loch. ... Ah can remember that. Frances Wyllie used to go and some o these, aye that's right, Frances used tae go curling.
Because it must have been pretty cold to get the loch frozen.
Molly: *Frozen enough for curling anyway.*
That's right, aye. Aye, it was very popular with quite a lot of people, the loch then, they went curling and that and then when we went sliding on it.
That was not far from the town?
That's right, just down the field.

Betty recalls the anxiety about not having enough money to purchase a new dress for the ball, finale for the dancing class.

Ah wis intae the dancing class, Mrs Mulhench's, an we really hadnae much money. An they were aw talkin aboot their, what they were putting on tae the ball, the last, the night o the– an Ah said tae ma mother, Ah says, 'They're aw putting on new frocks'. She says, 'They'll just hae to put them on' and Ah was worried aboot that and then this day Ah come in fae the school, Ah can remember it, an ma, the bedroom door was open, which was unusual, it was aye shut, an a went in an there, lyin on the paper, was this blue silky dress wi wee kinna diamonds wi wee flooers on them and Ah stood an Ah would greet likely and that and she had went intae a club just tae get that, Mrs Murray's club, tae get me that frock to be like the rest and Ah had socks and Ah even had pumps. But a got the pumps fae Mrs Costley, Billy Costley was ma partner, and she had an extra pair o pumps and she gaed me the pumps tae be like the rest, at the ball.

So where was the dancing class?

In the town hall, Mrs Mulhench had it, it was in town hall and the ball was in the hall.

Molly: Did ye pay for that?

Aye, ye paid sixpence. Ah hadnae that much money an ma sixpence was left oot and a certain person came into the hoose, he was leevin just roond the corner and stole ma sixpence. Ah never forgot it. Aye that's right, but Ah was the only one, ma sister never was at the dancing class but Ah was at it, Mrs Mulhench's and, as I say, Billy Costley, was ma partner, and he was aye runnin away ower tae his mother that he didnae want tae dance (laughter). But Ah can see that dress, it was a kinna– it wouldnae be silk, but it would be like silky stuff, she got it oot o Mrs Murray's club, and a wee pattern up here. And there was the Little White Ribboners [the junior section of the World Women's Christian Temperance Union] an that, cawd it the Little White Ribboners, ye were very young when ye went tae it, it was in the, up in the Belmont, where ye went to it, the Little White Ribboners. It was just like a Sunday School.

And what about youth organisations like the Boys' Brigade and the Girl Guides?

Well, the Boys' Brigade come on later than that. For Robert was in them. And the Girl Guides, well I was in the Girl Guides and Ah was in the Brownies, Ah was in the Girl Guides. Then Ah was in something else further up tae the Guides, Ah cannae remember what they cawd them.

So, would most children join something like that?

Yes. Ah think ye were more or less told ye were going. But Ah liked it, Ah liked the Girl Guides. We'd wur uniforms an that, and the hat, mine's was put intae a polythene bag, Ah can remember, to keep the stoor aff it (laughter).

In general, unnecessary display was frowned upon: community disapproval thwarted Jenny Jolly, when she attempted to buy make-up from the chemist, Mr Hannah, in Whithorn.

Jenny Jolly

Ah mind when we were young Ah seen folk wi nail varnish on and Ah went in, wanted nail varnish, 'What are ye wantin nail varnish for?' Ah says, 'Ma nails', 'You're no getting it' he says, 'don't need them, no startin that carry on, don't need it'. The next thing I went for wis rouge and a didnae need it, really, for I'd aye red cheeks, Ah didnae get it either (laughter). Nae nonsense wi him. Ah liked him though. He used tae dae nice pictures aw roon aboot and o Whithorn.

The basket tea, held at remote halls and schools throughout the Machars, was eagerly anticipated and attended on foot and by bicycle.

Cathy Miller

No, my first dance was at Ravenstone School. The harvest moon, Ah was 15 and ma mum and dad took me ... and it was what ye call a basket tea, took a basket of food with ye and asked someone to join ye that didn't have– passed it round. That was in the September, the October, November and Ah couldn't wait until January still they started again and they went from January, February, March.

And was that quite common to have dances in the country?
That's where they were held, yes, and Glasserton School and The Isle hall, Whauphill hall, Port William, Highland music, just. Well, quite a lot of them played live on the accordion and the fiddle. There was two or three bands in these days, well-known. And mostly in schools as well, out in the country because it was the only bit that they had.

Robert Galashan recalls the dance band at Whithorn and how Saturday dances punctuated the week, a day of release from the routine of the week.

Robert Galashan

But he wis a big man, the butcher's Douglas, and he used to have a band here, it wis Douglas, there wis James Kerr, there wis Anton Griffin, and who else? Aa the kind o auld worthies, fiddles, and banjos, and Whithorn had its band! A dance band.
...
I remember the first night I come in here, it was a Saturday night, and they were running the football buses tae Glasgow on a Saturday, to the Rangers–Celtic. Well we went to wir bed that night and the row got up! And shouting and swearing and kicking at doors, they were up on the top

o people's cars. So Ben went oot and chased some o them up the street, he wis on the pavement wi the car, he wis gonnae run them doon! [Byron's?] father went oot wi a golf club, he was gonnae kill someone! And I says tae Molly, well, if this is town living, we'll no be long here! I says, a month on that'll dae us til we get another house in the country. But we've been here 37 year. Oh, that wis— after The Grapes closed, and things like that, everything kind o. The town's a different place now fae what it used to be.

Well, it certainly has a lot less employment in it.

Oh aye. See when the soldiers were here and that. Oh, it was wild. Fighting and, oh, gee! Do you know, I have stood in a queue up almost at the post office tae get into the picture hoose? Aye.

Aye. The soldiers, the big convoys used to come by, they were going to Kidsdale and Burrowhead. And oh, maybe aboot 40 lorries wid go through the toon. Soldiers and that. Then they come in on a Saturday night. Oh.

Was it a flash point wi the local boys?

Oh aye. Aye. And then there was Poles come in on the scene, and Italians, Italian prisoners, there was wars in Wigtown and that wi them. But I never got much involved in onything like that, I kept mysel clear o that. But oh, aye, been in that dance hall doon there and one half o it there wis women fightin and the other half wis men! Oh, what a place! Night at the dancing, Kirkinner, and I don't know if you knew, what was his name, Willie, oh, I forgot his name, he was an affa man tae fight. And then a fight broke oot and one thing and another and he got up onto the stage, he got a hold o the piana, flung it off the stage onto the floor, there was bits lying everywhere! Oh, there wis some wild folk aboot at one time. The women were as bad tae. Fighting at the drop o a flag.

John Wilson

So that was aboot the only social thing or gaun intae the pubs. But when we came here first they had this three-mile limit that ye couldnae get a drink on a Sunday unless you were a bona fide traveller so ye had to travel three miles. So people from Whithorn would walk down to The Isle or get down tae Isle of Whithorn tae get a drink because it was just outside three miles. That is the way it was.

The place which the public house held in community life is now almost forgotten, with Whithorn's Brunswick, Star, Calcutta, Temperance and Commercial, as well as others which dotted the town, mostly closed and the Saturday rituals changed for good. While the rule was generally observed that women were discouraged from drinking in public houses, they nonetheless seemed to dominate the publican's trade and control the potential for disorder through a strict allowance of time for drinking. The lack of oversight by external agencies and the proliferation of inns, formed largely out of front rooms in the townhouses, was compensated by this sense of responsibility on the part of the landladies.

Jessie McLean

>Yes, there was The Kelvingrove pub and The Calcutta, it wisnae cawd The Calcutta, it was jist cawd Torrance Hoose.
>
>*Torrances, yes. But you would never be in it, would you?*
>
>Naw, never was in it.
>
>*Did you see people drinking a lot?*
>
>Aye, the farmers on a Saturday night and the farmers aw came intae thae twa pubs at the Top of the Toon. Oh, Ah never mind o bother [unclear] a policeman or ocht.

Betty Stuart

>*And who owned the pubs at the time?*
>
>It was Mrs Flannighan had the first one and Miss Torrance the next one. They were there for years and years.
>
>*It always seems to have been women in Whithorn who owned the pubs?*
>
>Aye, it was. Well Mrs Flannighan's eldest son helped her too. He helped in the pub too and Miss Torrance, there was two ladies, Maddie and Margaret Torrance, they were in the [unclear] pub. They were very popular but straight at nine o'clock everybody was put out, definitely nine o'clock.
>
>*Nine o'clock, even on a Saturday?*
>
>Even on a Saturday, nine o'clock and Sunday it wisnae open.
>
>*And they perhaps didn't tolerate much drunkenness either?*
>
>No. There'd be the odd one– kinna over their stick an that but there was no kina, no fightin or that, no, there wasnae. But it was very popular the pub.

Jenny Jolly

>Miss Torrances was at the top o the toon. They were twa sisters, the Miss Torrance.
>
>*Was that The Calcutta?*
>
>Uh-huh. And they used to get me on ma [unclear] at the turnip shawing to bring them a turnip and when ye went in there was nae bar in it in their day there was jist barrels o beer wi a tap on them, that they got the beer straight fae the barrel, big wooden barrel things. They didn't like women in the pub drinking, actually you would have got one but you didn't get drunk on it, they didn't want women drinking. And every, Monday

especially, they were oot wi big buckets o water and the brushes and runnin aboot the door, roond aboot, they wanted ... everything was thoroughly washed and then the pavement got washed and then, after they did that, there was mair water to come for the– the brush shafts had tae get all washed, dried off and left up tae dry tae. They were very precise. They were more strictly in thae days. But still, not Miss Torrances', but still they could be kept in after closing time. Hamish McLachlan was in The Grapes Hotel and it never was closed.

Betty Murray

And the house at The Pend was a public house. That was Kate McQueen, and I remember that. I remember Kate McQueen's pub, because I was wheeling a friend who was much younger in a pram – because we loved to wheel prams – and I used to stand at the butcher shop and let go! And then I used to run and catch it at The Pend, and it went over. The old lawyer came out of Kate McQueen's, and gave me a dressing down! (laughs)

There was a strict timetable of pleasures, largely dictated by the arrival and departure of the 'picture bus', which picked up customers in remote villages. As a result, Saturday night was one of the busiest for shopkeepers. In earlier times, anticipation would build over longer periods, awaiting the arrival of a travelling show which was put on in a tent. The popularity of the cinema signalled the ending of live entertainment provided locally, but the weekly event was still a shared experience.

Robin Kinnear

When I was in the shop, on a Saturday we went home for our evening meal at five o'clock and came back to the shop at six o'clock, and Robert McNally he went off for his tea at four o'clock and came back at five o'clock, and the girls, they just finished at six and then we had all the picture buses coming. You had a bus coming in from Elrig, which it didn't come down till seven o'clock, and then there was Crawford's bus would come from the Whauphill area into Port William and they would all come into the shop and buy things and do a lot of their grocery from the Dewar's, these shops were all open until seven-thirty at night and the last bus was in from Elrig at half past seven, there was one at seven and it went on to the pictures in Whithorn. And then there was another bus went to the pictures in Wigtown and then the big bus went to Newton Stewart for the pictures there so there were picture shows in the Kingsway cinema, the Wigtown cinema, Whithorn cinema and then we had a travelling cinema that came round the halls during the week from Byron Chamberlain's father, he had the– was it– his was the Kingsway, can't remember the one of, the Rex, I think it was in Wigtown, 'the bug hut' they called it (laughter). But Saturday was a very busy night.

Greta Hawthorn describes the evolution of travelling shows from outdoors to indoors, when the King's Road Cinema became established.

Greta Hawthorn

Oh, yes, ninepence and one and three and two and six. That was when you were sitting up in the balcony but we were never in the balcony, we were in the ninepennies (laughter). And there used tae be a tent down at Ketburn where the first bungalow is and that was the cinema at one time. It belonged to show people and they used to show films in it and some of the wee-er yins used to wait till it got started and then they went underneath tae get in for nothing (laughter). They still did it in those days.

And the shows used to come in and the circus used to come in to the field where the police houses are and there's a wee show boy, Paris something, that's buried up in the graveyard and it was jist a wee cairn o stones, he was only six months old. And there was just a wee cairn o stones and Miss Hughes and I used to go through, that's where I got all my information, was fae Miss Hughes, she wis great, Miss Hughes, she yist tae come in maybe aboot seven o'clock in the morning and if there was a royal wedding or anything to do wi royalty she was in to see the television then and she went away when they went away on their honeymoon. She showed me that wee grave where this wee person was buried and there were shows in at, they were up nearer John's end in The Park then in these days and they come into The Grapes and they'd had a whole load o mackerel, somebody had gave to them and they didnae know what to do wi them. And when I was working in The Grapes then and I says, 'I'll clean the mackerel for ye' and I took it away intae the kitchen and brought it back and I says to them, he says, 'How much are ye wantin for that' and I says, 'I don't want anything' I says 'I want ye tae find out' and I took him up the graveyard the next day to show him this and they put up a wee headstone for the wee yin. So I planted lilies at one time and they're nice and they're getting more and more and more every time. So when they were 80 I put on a nice wee spray of flowers.

John Wilson

Yea, yea. We used to come in, when Ah lived at Monreith, we used to come in here every Saturday night to the pictures, there was a cinema here, and we would come in. There used to be a bus run from Port William to Whithorn, it was a 29-seater, and there'd be normally maybe aboot 40 on it (laughs). In fact sometimes we were comin up past the police station and we had to sort of crouch down so that the policeman wouldnae see that this bus was overloaded because it was– there was aboot four in every seat and people standin down the aisle (laughs). But that– and then of course television come in and that just killed that. So as television started the trade just disappeared. And then you see, of course, that had a big impact on the chip shop, for example, because the chip shop was always open to late, late on, until after the last film show, every night, there was films on every night.

Jenny Jolly worked evenings at the picture house.

Jenny Jolly

Oh, jist wis young when Ah started in it. Tae start wi Ah just halved the tickets, Ah was working though, I was working in the forestry at the time and jist halved the tickets … . That was before Ah was in the pay box, when I was halving them and here Mr Henry fae … that owned the picture hoose in Whithorn and Wigtown, and he also showed them at the Burrowhead camp and at Kidsdale camp tae. Marjory Wilmot was the manageress, she was running the picture hooses, ye ken. She was in the top pay box and Ah was halving tickets at the bottom yin.

It was sixpence and then it went up in price at the bottom yins, the middle row seats, wis one and ninepence, and then the top yins was two and threepence. Ah had tae get a pen and paper because o folk come in and buyin maybe four or five tickets tae make sure Ah got it right. And then he selt aw up, Mr Henry, and Ah think he jist kept the Wigtown yin for a certain time but it closed through time and there was a group in Whithorn, there was Mr Costley the grocer, Jimmy Denton who had the baker's and was there a Little or something in it? Took ower the picture hoose. And then Ah used tae gaun in tae Mrs Wallace at the close hoose, auld woman, and her sister Mrs Smith, lived doon the high street a wee bit and she come and they played cairds and they fought and argued the bit oot, argued the bit oot, and Ah wis sitting there listening tae it aw. Fought the bit oot. Ye see when they come tae the picture hoose, God help onybody that sat in their seat, they had the very back of the cheap seats, but the furthest back row o the seats, next tae the one and ninepenny seats, ye ken. And God help onybody for they had tae move, they were shiftit (laughs).

WORK AND REST: THE TIMING OF PLEASURES

Jock McMaster describes how, at the very start of electrification and of the arrival of television, entertainment had not been wholly appropriated to a private space.

Jock McMaster

> But what Ah do remember is, when we got television, in the early '50s, talking about going out, and there was boxing on, my dad used to have them in to watch the boxing. And the three old guys up there and the one from Stellock and his wife all got all dressed up to come down and watch the telly and Ah can see him yet, this fellow, he had a collar and tie on and a great flowery tie outside his jumper, he had a jumper on but he'd this tie on the outside and they were all shining like shillings. So they obviously thought this was a special occasion and that's early '50s. And they would come in and, aye it would be early '50s, '55/56 and they would come in and ma mum would make a cup o tea and a sandwich or something, they had a great– they seemed to enjoy that. But gettin all dressed up for it, nowadays you'd just go jist wi yer shirt and a pair o jeans on but it's jist the way they were.
>
> Oh it [television] was a novelty, total, aye, total. Cause they'd no electricity in their houses ye see, they used to get an accumulator thing charged up in the garage in Port William sort of, it was a sort of glass battery with a handle on it, and that powered their radio. That's really all they had was their radio set and this thing, the wee knobs, Ah can remember them, they screwed the wires on and the radio cackled up and that was their that would be their only in-house entertainment. And Willie, up there, had a gramophone, Ah remember a huge thing with a great big trumpet on it that he wound up and played old scratchy music records on.

Both normal rules and also prevailing hostilities were suspended during the calendar events of Halloween and Hogmanay, when a little surplus time was allowed and modest generosities between neighbours and from farmer to worker were exchanged, as a mark of the exception to the routine.

Betty Stuart

> The best place to go for wur Halloween, when we were at school, wis was Wards. ... Wallaces were there then. They were great folk. ... Aye, it was a big event, we went oot, everybody went oot for it and some of the– like Annie Jolly, do you remember Annie Jolly? Norah Kane, they dressed up tae, and they were in their 30s, maybe, or something, 20s or 30s. And we went oot on Halloween tae. It used tae be a great bit Halloween. Ye went out for it, ye ken. An ye had tae say a magic word before ye got anything.

And what about Christmas, how has that changed?
> Oh, it's changed a lot. Gosh, Ah mean, Ah cannae remember but Ah never got anything like– we got sweeties, a box, Ah don't know where they got them, wi animals, chocolate animals, Ah can mind o getting that and ye put yer stockin, ye got stuff in yer stocking, that was it, nae toys or– we widnae hae the money, but still ye believed in it …. Oh, there was nae Christmas trees in my day.

Molly: Did ye get a Christmas pairty fae the burgh or was there–? No?
> The Sunday School, doon King's Road, doon at, aye, doon King's Road, Belmont Hall.

Now, was New Year bigger than Christmas?
> Yes. Hogmanay was really wild, you would say, everybody, an ye even went oot beggin for yer Hogmanay, same as Halloween, ye went roond the doors asked, 'Could you please [gie me ma] Hogmanay?' Aye, it was big, they made a lot o Hogmanay and ye yist tae have yer food aboot midnicht often and aw they kinna things.

So, houses would be open for visits?
> Aw the shops an the pubs.

Molly: What kinna Christmas dinner did yis get?
> Oh, well, it would be a hen, because they'd get it at the farm (laughter). We always got, the family always gave ye a hen. Aye, it was always a hen. And nae Christmas pudding or onything. It would be maybe, rice pudding or something. Aye, it would be jelly, we got a lot o jelly, aye. But it was a hen at Christmas, because the farmers gave ye that, a hen home wi ye.

Somebody told me about– on Hogmanay there would be some sort of a parade with–
> That's right, fancy dress parade. Every Hogmanay night there was, a big parade. And big Pat Flannighan an aw them dressed up as a wuman an that, wi a wee skirt on and that. It was really very good, the Hogmanay parade.

So where did that start from?
> It would start fae the top o the toon richt doon tae the bottom, tae the station, Ah think, very near tae the station, anyway. … I think there was an organisation started [the parade] but Ah don't know what it would be. … Aye, they had torches, Ah mind, they would make them themselves likely, they'd torches an that. … And then at midnight come, everybody was oot, chappin hands wi their neighbours. No like, no jist noo and again, they were aw oot, doors opened at midnight and ye went tae next door this side, next door that and across the street and–

And was there food and drink?
> There was food and drink, uh-huh. Ginger wine. And black bun. Aye, there was definitely that and everybody was friendly, ken what Ah mean, for the meenit onyway, before the pubs maybe come oot. Aye, it was cheery.

5

Up and Down: Wealth and Poverty

Whithorn's social life was inextricably bound up with the existence of Glasserton Estate, just on its outskirts. The influence of the estate owners reinforced by many generations of heredity, was acknowledged, in a society where time counted, more than money, and there was always the reward of employment on the Laird's property or within the 'Big House', which had its own stratified society within. The multiplication of staff within the economy of the landed estate was aimed at creating a surplus of time and leisure for the owners.

As the son of the local minister at Glasserton, John Scoular saw both the high and the low of the social spectrum.

John Scoular

> My earliest memories of the '30s, when the area was recovering from the effects of the First World War and was a very depressed area, it was just starting to revive a bit in agricultural terms, one of the best things that happened was the Milk Marketing Board, when the farming community began to see the benefits of a monthly pay cheque, but it was still a very, very backward, rural area. When I think of some of the places I visited in the parish with my father, the conditions were really abysmal, earth floors, outside toilets, no running water, the rural community was really a very deprived place and not so far removed from that depicted in the *Wigtownshire Ploughman*. People didn't move about much, this is the big change over the years, mobility … . In those days the majority of people lived on the land and transport was negligible, really we're talking about the end of the horse drawn era but in this part of the world, in the rural parishes, people just didn't move about.
>
> This part of the world wasn't, hadn't much in the way of big estates, Glasserton would be– was in its twilight era, even then, the Admiral lived at Glasserton House, and lived in some style but even then decay was setting in among that kind of influence in the community, Glasserton village

still, in the late '30s was mainly staffed by people who worked at the big house or on the estate.

...

It was an estate church, even then the Admiral and his family had no influence on who was chosen. There was no influence in that sense but obviously as one of the richest people in the area, he had a strong influence and he and his wife, my father got on very well. ... even then he had a chauffeur, he had gamekeepers, it was the last of the old era. This was Stewart territory, you see, long before Garlieston, they go back to the 1600s. At Glasserton church, the oldest thing is a panel on the wall of a ruined building at the end which goes right back to when the Stewarts, or branches of the Stewarts, were down here long before the House of Garlieston or Galloway Estate. They were in this part of the world for a long time, both Glasserton House, Physgill and Tonderghie were all Stewart Houses going back to the 1600s.

I can remember the old Admiral, he was a wonderful old character, he made sure that every– he and his housekeeper, Miss Robb, went on a shopping spree before Christmas every year and every child in the parish got a present. I've still got books inscribed from the Admiral to myself and my sister. They were the best kind of feature of that kind of landed estate, they did look after their people.

Upstairs-Downstairs

Elsie McShane's father was eventually head gardener at Glasserton and grew up on the estate. Just as on the land, the big houses required large numbers of people to run them and the grounds.

Elsie McShane

So how many people do you think were running [it] in terms of staff, how many people do you think were running Glasserton?
   On the estate? Well, I've told you, five, six, were in the gardens. There was woodcutters, you know. You're talking maybe 40, easily.
And would some of the maids live in?
   Yes, yes. All of them, I expect.

Robin Kinnear remembers the effect of full employment at the big house (Monreith House, in particular) on sales in his family drapery shop.

UP AND DOWN: WEALTH AND POVERTY

Robin Kinnear

To a certain extent, yes, because you had a lot of people employed in the house, in domestic service, and they would come and spend their money in the shop and of course they had to get their uniform, they had a uniform, and the proper pinafore, lace-edged pinafores and things and then there were so many that was the sort of upstairs or the downstairs: there were a lot of dishwashers, people preparing vegetables, out digging vegetables, the sort of lower strata of the staff but they were all in full employment and they were making money and they didn't have a house to have to spend money on, they were provided with a house, albeit not very good conditions. They would have a well or there would be water near at hand but they would have to cart it, there would be no running well and conditions were difficult, very difficult.

The indoor staff were ranked in a complex hierarchy, echoing the social pyramid in which their masters were at the apex.

Jenny Jolly

But they had a kitchen maid that did the fireplaces in the morning early. That was for the auld, as you say, the auld man. They were up early, early, aboot five o'clock for they'd all the fireplaces tae clean and they were properly cleaned and the fire burning an the dining room all oot an the breakfast set for them comin doon the stair. Kitchen maid had it kinna hard.

Elsie McShane

Yes, I remember two cooks; Mrs Forbes, was one. I don't know if they were Mrs, they tended to take the title Mistress. You know, if they weren't married, that's the way they were referred to. But there was Mrs Forbes, and then there was Miss Robb, and she retired to the Isle of course. I remember these two. There was some nice maids, some young girls. There was two in particular came; they were Mrs Forbes' nieces, and they came from the Outer Hebrides. She brought them down to work in the mansion house. I remember one was called Joanne– Forlow, was their name, but they were no connected to local family.

Elsie McShane recalls the operation of the outdoor staff. She began life at Sawmill Cottages, Glasserton.

Elsie McShane

That's where I started off. Then [when] I was about six years old, my father was the head gardener on Glasserton estate. He was the head gardener for the mansion house, which was in operation then. We moved from Sawmill Cottages to the garden house itself. Then the previous head gardener moved, down to Carlisle direction, and my father was promoted to head gardener; he had five other gardeners under him. Now they call it Woodfall, of course, but in these days, it was just Glasserton Gardens. So, the mansion house of course was in operation then, it was Robin's grandfather, [he] was there: he was Admiral Robert Johnston Stewart.

So, did he [your father] live in when he was an apprentice, or did he go from the town?
Well he would come from the town, but next to the gardener's house, where we lived, was what was called the bothy, and some of the younger ones slept in the bothy.

All his training was given to him by a senior gardener, was it?
Oh yes, uh-huh.

Do you remember any of the names of the senior gardeners?
Mr Hamilton, I remember him. He went to, Lonsdale, in Carlisle. He went to this place, he left Glasserton and went there. Because the writing was on the wall by then, we knew that the mansion house wasn't going to go on. So that's where he went, that was in the later stages of the War .... And that's when we moved over to Glasserton, to the gardener's .... Yes, I can tell you what my father's wages were. I've heard him saying this. Thirty five shillings a week, when we were living in where I was born, in the cottages, and they went up to two pounds, when we moved to Glasserton Gardens.

Oh it's all walled garden. Because there was peaches, and plums and figs, grew a lot in the walls. Actually, part of the inside walls were hearted: there was two stoke walls, we called them, because we got the lovely job on a Sunday afternoon of stoking them up. Yes, there was two– three– greenhouses at the top garden, and another vinery down where the third garden, where the bottom garden is. There was fireplaces to heat the wa'. A lot of work–

... Were those fruits to supply the main house?
Yes, aye, they were. Beautiful grapes. The green ones and the black ones .... And Glasserton tomatoes were famous.

And did your father take his orders from the house?
Oh yes – the order probably came down the day before they wanted it. And we had, my brother and I, we took them, the baskets up– and we delivered them to, I'd say the back door, but that's not what they called it, the hall door. We were invited into the kitchen until we unloaded the

baskets and all the rest of it. An' we always got something, maybe a rock bun – it wasn't very much – but we always got a wee treat. You know, from either Mrs Forbes or Miss Robb.

So what do you remember about the kitchen?

Oh, well, just yer big kitchen; everything was big, you know. Everything's big when you're young and small. I've told Robin about this often– we went to the hall door, and somebody rang the bell, and somebody came; and of course we were taken through to the kitchen. But along this long corridor were glass cases, I've told Robin about them. They were full of china and glass, and everything glistened, you know. It was absolutely gorgeous.

Greta Hawthorn, also born on the estate, describes how spaces were clearly differentiated, and access permitted and denied, according to position, even within the church.

Greta Hawthorn

And the Admiral stayed in the big house at Glasserton and that was Mr Johnston Stewart's now, his grandfather, and it was a beautiful big house, it had terraces into the gardens and we used to have wur Sunday School picnics there. But when we came up from Claymoddie it was an old road and ye had to go round by the laundry but on a Sunday we were allowed to pass the big house and he used to be standing at the front door saying, 'Girls, you come this way for to go to the Sunday School, you don't go round by the laundry, ye'll get your feet dirty', and this. … Yes, he was a very nice gentleman and the lords and ladies went to the church at Glasserton and they had their own special seats, they go up the outside and the Johnston Stewarts were at one side and the maids were at the other side, that went up the outside steps. And nearly all the people that were in the houses were at the church, there was a big congregation, it was Mr John Scoular's father was there and he was gassed during the First World War and he had his throat, but ye could still make him out and he was really an excellent minister. He was the minister that christened us and he came to the house to do that if you wanted.

Yes, we were allowed in when we got wur picnic and we had, if it was not a very nice day we had wur tea in there but they were always very nice to us. I was really sorry when they pulled down Glasserton big house. Glasserton big house was– the sale of the furniture and everything that was in it was the day that Lorna Hall was born, Mrs Hall's daughter was born that day, and there was lots of people there buying it. They had baths which looked like chairs, that was the baths that they had and the lawns were beautiful kept, they had gardeners there was well, and there used to

32. Fox hunter with hounds, Whithorn, 1902.

be a horse out at the side of the house and it kept going round and round and round and that was it pumping the water. That was the way that the water was pumped, with this horse, a big Clydesdale horse. And in the wood there was the cold place where the ... when they were out shooting they had the pheasants and rabbits and whatever they got, and they were kept in there outside. ... they did fox hunting after the pheasant shooting was finished but they had always pheasant shootings there.

...

And the ladies visit to go to St Ninian's– near enough St Ninian's Cave but they went down by the Glasserton Hill, which ye went through the woods and come to Glasserton Hill and then along one of the fields, down the road, or sometimes they went along the cliffs and they come down the Ladies' Steps, they were called the Ladies' Steps, and the ladies always went down there to do their swimming. And there's two wrecks o boats there, I don't know what they're like now for I havenae been down that way for a long, long time, maybe the sand has buried them but ye can still see the big hold and everything, there were two boats sunk over there. And the ladies used to come into the town on their horses and there's a double fence just past Cathy Christie's, on that side of the road going out, and it was my mother's uncle that used to cut that for the ladies and that was the way that the horses came to keep them off the main road till they come nearly to Longhill and then they had to have a wee detour and then it went on nearly down to New England.

Elsie McShane

> Did you see the little place that's walled off in the front garden, in the first garden, when you come to it? There's a fireplace there. Well, the ladies that were staying at the big house, they used to come down there— I think they were the Admiral's sisters. Well, anyway, they used to come down there, and the fire was put on for them, and they sat there in the summer. Big hats and parasols.

The War marked a watershed in the existence of many of the Machars estates and the little round of estate generosities ceased.

Elsie McShane

> My sister and I, I remember that quite clearly, we got boxes of hankies with little– remember them?– you used to get them with flowers on the corners. Yes, we each got one of these, and we had piles of them! (laughs) Maybe I've got some yet. And the boys used to get gloves, and that all stopped.
>
> Yes, well, that's where [at the House] we had our Sunday school picnic; we were taken up to the big house and allowed to run riot! (laughs) Roll down the terraces. Yes, it was good, it was a nice little life. But as I say, the War changed everything…

John Wilson's family were the estate carpenters on the Glasserton Estate, with almost as long a pedigree as the estate owners themselves.

John Wilson

> So, they came from Glenvernoch down here and my grandfather was– came down as joiner, at Glasserton, and he continued to be a joiner there until his death. At the time of his death my father and my uncle continued the business. That continued until ma father saw that there wasn't a living in it for the two of them and he went away to America. He came back to see his father, who was dying at the time, and this was at the time of the Depression and when he came back he had other, he had two other brothers in New York, and they kept writing back to him to say, 'Don't come back' or 'Don't come back, there's no work'. And eventually he met ma mother and the week that his work permit expired he got a letter to say that work was pickin up and he could go back but ma mother didn't want to go to America and that's how we stayed here. Ah was born in Monreith, in 1938. It's a good job Ah was born here because Ah would have finished up in Vietnam!
>
> …

The business had been going for about 120 years at that time. So, it was just a continuation. At that time the workshop was at Glasserton and there was no electricity or anything like that at all so it was, and it was mainly agricultural work we did. Mainly we were mainly on farms and we'd repair bits and bobs about the farms and repair carts, things like that. Ah made, well, Ah helped ma father make a pair of wheels one time, the only time Ah ever did that. But we made, we made a cart one time when Ah was– this was at the very early days or the very last o the horses and carts basically, early– this was 1954, as Ah said. So it was a time of great change in agriculture. But we repaired horse troughs, there was always fork shafts, aw this sort of stuff to do so it was basically agricultural work we did but there was a lot of cottages being renovated at that time as well so we did that sort of work as well. And of course there wasn't very many different tradesmen around at that time, ye adapted, an ye could, although Ah was trained as a joiner you could lay bricks and do things, bits and pieces like that, simply because these other people weren't there so ye got a sort of general all-round trade. … We did a lot of work for Glasserton Estate but at that time the farms were all tenanted so we did a lot of work for the tenants but yes, Ah think from memory, the estate had to do the repairs to the farms and we did a lot of work on the estate, yes. But the workshop at Glasserton, it was just, it was just a basic, just a basic house. It had earth floors on it, it had an earth floor in it and we had no electricity so everything was done by hand so I suppose ye could say we were trained the hard way, or I was trained the hard way, that everything had to be done by hand. … One of the memories, as well, was there was a blacksmith had his forge across the road and he lived next to the workshop and he kept hens and the hens, we always knew what time it was if by chance we forgot to bring a watch or whatever, the hens knew the time because they always come into the workshop at ten o'clock when we were havin a cup of tea and twelve o'clock, they always come in, on the dot for the crusts. So we always knew when the hens arrived it was either teatime or lunchtime. And there used to be a red squirrel, there was trees roond aboot the workshop at that time and there used to be a squirrel used to come in to the workshop and run roond aboot the workshops so it was really agricultural ye know (laughs).

And I guess if your grandfather had already been in the business you would have inherited a lot of tools and techniques?

Yes. In fact, to this day, ah've got a mortise machine that was my grandfather's. It's just a hand operated mortise machine, but yea, all the tools were there until I retired. In fact, in ma workshop before– I've been retired now for eight years, the workshop's still there, and in the workshop there is a gig shaft sittin there, a broken one, which came from

UP AND DOWN: WEALTH AND POVERTY

Glasserton Estate and it was, Ah kept it because it was lancewood it was made of which is a very springy type of wood. So, aye, there's plenty stuff there, Ah still have a barrow that my uncle had made, we used to make barrows for the dairy farms, for the manure, and there's still a barrow there which now must be 80-year-old, that was made and we always had a barrow sittin there for the farmers to get but again that was a time of change, suddenly they discovered that they could buy steel barrows cheaper and this barrow was left and to this day it still sits in the workshop (laughter). We yaised it for takin oot the shavins oot the workshop. This was one o the funny things as well, ma father always said to me, 'If anybody comes into the workshop and there's no much to do' he says, 'never stand about, always be busy and if nothing else clean up the floor'. But he always, he was quite funny actually, he always said, 'Never clean it out completely, make it look as if there's work going on' (laughter). But this was one o the funny things as well, ma father, in the wintertime, because the workshop was surrounded wi trees it was always quite dark in it and come about three o'clock in the afternoon when it was quite dark he would say, 'It's no worth lightin, putting a lamp on' and he would work at the bench with a candle on the end o the bench. I managed to get him to get some Tilley lamps, at least we could get a wee bitty more light but it was terrible, it really was, it was hard. So this is why I have to wear glasses now (laughs). But that was the way it was, we used to get glass sent down from Glasgow, we used to get a crate of glass at a time and it would come down on the train into Whithorn and then the local haulier would bring it oot tae Glasserton. But we used to get timber down, there used to be a delivery once a fortnight from Ayr and any other times we used to nip down to Garlieston to get local, if we needed something in a hurry. So that's the way, that was the way it was at that time.

We used to sharpen the tools, ma father had a labourer who worked for him and every Saturday morning we sharpened the tools and my job was tae crank the big, we had a grindstone which was about two foot six in diameter and my job was to crank the handle of this grind stone and get the tools all sharpened up. That was normally on a Saturday morning we did that.

So it was what, a six day week or a five and a half?

A five and a half-day week.

Betty Stuart describes how the existence of the Estate affected the town.

Betty Stuart

An him an his men an the horses an we were told that they were comin so

the weans, the young ones, were aw oot on the– and when they come ye had tae bow. And the men took off their caps. Ah remember that.
Would that have been the old Admiral?
Yes, the men sat wi him and the females bowed and the men stood. ... But oh, when the Admiral and them come, there was a line and ye were told to bow and that. ... The men saluted them and had their caps off. And we bowed. Seein the horses comin in.

Cathy Miller, remembering Glasserton Estate, now lives in one of the lodge houses.

Cathy Miller

Ah do know that everybody on the estate, every house. The lady that was in this house, she opened that gate for the lady and for all the gentry that got up and down there but she had to have a white apron, a white hat, and she wasn't allowed to have washing on the line. And when the shooting was on, it was all done in here, they all came in here and she fed them and poured the wine, that was her chores. There was also 16 gardeners, they scythed the whole of the grounds.

33. The Meet, Craiglemine, 1902.

Clothing too reflected this hierarchy, both between estates and between occupations. The House of Elrig, where Gavin Maxwell's mother was closely related to the Percy family, ranked, in sartorial terms, more highly than Monreith House, home of the baronets of Monreith.

Robin Kinnear

> And you had to keep a register of all these people that you had and I still have these figures there. Pricing, I think, was really quite interesting, the difference between a gent's made to measure suit, 52 and sixpence, say £2.75, to a gent's livery suit which was £5.00, £5.50 for Monreith House, which had silver buttons, and a livery suit for Elrig House which was over £7.00 because they had gold buttons, so there was quite a big rise between the ordinary gentlemen's suit – that would be a business man's suit which would be about 50 shillings, there's an enormous rise to clothing for the employees of the estate, they spent that amount on it.
>
> *So those would be household servants that would wear the livery, would they?*
>
> Yea, they were the coachmen that drove the coaches back and forward. And the pony and traps and gigs, they would always be in uniform and then the butler always had a uniform, he would have a livery as well.
>
> ...
>
> Yes, well, during my time, of course, a big lot of agricultural clothing was sold, bib and brace overalls, all the dairymen always got bib and brace overalls with very long legs and then cut the bottoms of the legs and made patches for the knees because when they were couping milk buckets, milk butts, they were always doing it with their [knees], that went into a cooler and ran down because we didn't have bulk tanks and things in those days. But we sold milking feckets which were striped tunic jacket but was known as a fecket and it was blue and white striped, the same stripe as a butcher's apron, and then they had, of course, bunnets and socks and all the other general wear that they would wear for milking and for ploughing and latterly, after the Second World War, there was a lot of army surplus which was distributed by a firm, Mallet Porter and Dowd, in London, and they would sell on these second hand uniforms which were ideal for tractor men and for ploughmen walking along because they had a big greatcoat or and they had some of the big parkas with the fur hoods and they had to have completely waterproof trousers because there was no cabs and things then on the carts or tractors, they needed to be very, very well clad so we did sell a big lot of that.
>
> Yes, yes, and you had a lot of lady agricultural workers so they bought bib and brace overalls but without a fly, so we had ladies' bib and brace overalls as well as– sometimes when some of the ladies came in, mind, you

never knew whether you should sell them ladies' or gent's, (laughter) they were pretty rough, tough characters. They could work every bit as well as the men could.

Yes, well I can remember, as a young boy, always putting in a hat, a ladies hat window, a millinery window, the week before Communion and most people would come in and see the hats but they wanted to come upstairs to see the hats that hadn't been shown in the window because they didn't want to go to church on Sunday and let the people see that they had bought their hat out of the front of the window in Kinnear's. So there was quite a lot of rivalry then but no one ever went to church without a hat and they nearly always wore a ladies' costume, very often with a fur, a separate fur clipped on, and they're very much in their Sunday best and they were very well turned out for that and we used to make ladies' costumes as well, we had again, a firm, when we discovered it was becoming so expensive to make suits in the premises, we could get them cheaper from Yorkshire so we got ladies' costumes made there as well but we still had our tailors to do the alterations. But that would all finish coming up to just after the, the First World War. But that would be when the actual manufacturing side would break down, we were much better buying the suits in or getting them made to measure actually, down south, just sending the measurements off, which was common trade then.

Yea, well, we had Dutch aprons which was just an apron from the waist down, then you had a pinafore which was round your neck and tied behind you and had a bib on it. Then there were Dutch overalls which were a pull-over, a complete overall, which came right down to your ankles, more or less, and had a tie and then there was a wrap-over, all cotton, all patterned cotton for ladies, and then you had proper pinarettes which were very fancy, afternoon tea ... things for serving. So we had a big selection of Dutch aprons, pinarettes, ordinary pinafores, and the overalls, Dutch overall and wrap-about overall.

...

... the grocers in the village all wore warehouse coats and they were all either white or a khaki coloured. ... The hairdressers always wore a grey warehouse coat or short jacket. The butchers, of course, they had their own sort of uniform as well. The fishmonger was, just again, a khaki warehouse coat. We sold warehouse coats and then of course all your mechanics and a lot of lorry, truck drivers wore boiler suits and the– I think, although I can't remember it myself, but all the carters and hiring coaches, horse, maybe four horse and a coach who were going a distance, they all had a sort of uniform. But then, of course, on Sunday everyone was dressed up to the nines in their best suit and similar attire when they went to funerals, everyone was very, very smart for funerals, always got the day off work to go attend the funerals.

Cathy Doughty describes her work as a 'between' maid at Physgill, working for Miss Hopkins, where her uniform changed according to the time of day. Wages were saved thanks to the board and lodging provided as part of the living-in job, and given back to the family on brief visits during days off.

Cathy Doughty

> She'd [Miss Hopkins] a lovely [garden], and it was just all white flowers, and she looked after them herself. In the morning she got up and she put on an old coat, tied it wi binder twine, an old bunnet on her head, crochet bunnet, and her wellingtons. And she went to work in the gardens, and potter about the gardens, and she brought her flowers in, and did her flowers, and passed the day like that. … They rented, well, I think they owned Physgill, though latterly they would sell, when they went to Connel during the war years. And they– it was just the two o them, and they were catered for. I was what they called the between maid, between the house maid and the table maid. The house maid in the morning, the table maid at one o' clock. And you wore a wrapper in the morning, in the afternoon you dressed for the dinner, lunch, to start wi, wi your collar and your cuffs and your wee aprons and that. Your white dress. You'd a black dress, you'd a wrapper in the morning, flat shoes, and then at lunchtime you had on a black dress, you had your wee thing roond your hair and your collars and your cuffs, waitit the tables, just for the two o them. Then ye had to learn. The first time she said to wait tae he says grace, so I was standing at table there, and there five places, a table over there and a table here, and I stood here, I'd to open the door to let them in from their sitting room, and they come into the dining room, opened this door, there was two doors, in between doors, you see, they come in, opened the door fae their sitting room, and I had tae have this dining room door open, and shut it when they went through, and they would take their place at the table, and he said grace. You'd tae attend to the, serve fae one side, lift tae the other side, just for brother and sister, this much carry on. And aa the table had to be laid wi, the spoons, she arranged, the things with, you'd to watch what. I had to watch what Nancy was doing, cause I had to cook when she was off, I had to do it, and I had to hae a different way fae her. And the housekeeper, they changed for dinner every night so he changed right out, vest, pants, everything, socks and things, and she did the same. I come down and I had to watch what evening dress she'd on that I didnae put on one that she'd on before, when the housekeeper was off, so ye had to take note on aa these kind o things. Ye'd to live and learn.

And how old were you then?

Oh, just young, about 14, 15, maybe. ... And I used to be kind o naughty, she'd a wee chest o drawers where the phone sat, and she'd wee ornaments, and I used to change these ornaments, ye see. And I'm saying to the housekeeper, 'Madam will be up this morning because I shiftit they vases'. And then she'd come up and she'd say, 'You must come down'. So she took me down into the front hall, ye see, where I'm supposed to be daein it, and she'd say, 'You must try and remember, child, to put these, that's where that sits, and that's where this sits'. So I would do it right for a wheen o weeks and then said to Nancy, 'She went back up the day because I shiftit they things for badness!' I says,' It gies her something to dae!' Nancy used tae say, 'Ye shouldnae dae that!' And I would say, 'That gies her something to dae' so sure enough, up she would come. And she says, 'Ye must try and remember, child!'

And did you live in at Physgill? Was it a bedroom on the top floor?

Yeah, the top floor. And then there was a big kitchen, and as far as I know that's away. But outside her kitchen window's a huge big kitchen, a scullery, it wis lovely. So that was it then. And they went away to Connel, and surely had a daily help there. That was after the war, everything changed.

So how long were you at Physgill?

Oh, maybe a year, couple o years or something.

And how big was the staff?

It was five. There was the cook, the scullery maid, the housekeeper, the table maid and I was whit they caaed the 'between maid', between the housekeeper and the table.

And did they keep strict discipline on you, the other house staff?

Oh aye, you had tae have everything, and whiles, she used to– I remember one night she rang the bell and I had to go all the way upstairs, you had two or three flights o stairs, away along a long corridor, through into a big hall, and ye went to the sitting room, opened the door, and she had tae tell you tae enter. And ye went in and I was, 'You rang, madam?' And she would say, 'Are all these doors shut?' And I would say, 'Yes, they're all shut'. 'Well, were they all shut when you come through, every one? Well, I can smell the cabbage boiling, I shouldn't smell the cabbage here'. And I went the kitchen, and said, 'See that auld woman! Hope some day she has tae cook the cabbage hersel!' Imagine making me go away up there just because she smells the cabbage! It's a great life. Funnily enough some o them went to visit her in Connel and she only had a daily help, so I wonder how she got on wi the cabbage!

And when you were at Physgill, what did they call you, the people of the house, did they call you by your first name, or–?

Wir first name, always just wir first name. So that was it, it was Dotty and

Nannie, and Mamie was the cook, and she came tae give her orders for the day to the cook, ye see, and she come down and knocked on the kitchen door to be admitted into the kitchen to give her orders for what she wanted for their lunch and what was for their dinner. And then she went back, but that was the only time she was in the kitchen. We'd wir own wee sitting room.

And what was the, was the cooking a range?

It was a big old-fashionet range. Cook would mainly do the cooking, all sorts of things she had.

Was it powered by coal?

It was coal. And he'd the stoves, and that, ye had tae fill they stoves wi, ken the anthracite, I think, was put into these big stoves, that's where they got heating. And then they'd their own burner for doing the, like, the lights, and it was gas mantles getting used, and ye had to watch ye didnae touch these when ye're putting them on, cause they fell tae bits if ye did, after ye lit them, ye see. Ye darnae touch them wi the match when ye were thingmying them, just sort of disintegrated. So ye had to watch putting these gas things on. They used tae break down and the garage used to come out to repair the engine.

Did you like your employers?

I did. Nice people, the Hopkinses were nice, they seemed really nice people.

And did you get a day off?

We'd an afternoon off, and every other Sunday off. But ye had to be in at a certain time at night, nine o'clock. Six o'clock on the Sunday.

And do you remember what you got paid for being there?

Seven and six, seven and six.

And what did you do with your pay?

Well, ye had to buy your own uniform, she didnae supply it. Ye had to buy your own wrappers and your own things. ... I got my Auntie Bessie's collars and cuffs and things. But other than that ye had tae buy your own frocks and things. Oh, she never supplied anything like that, she just sent your things tae laundries.

So where did you get your uniform?

Just Brown and Charters'.

In Whithorn? So they sold uniforms for maids?

They sold all these things.

But presumably you didn't pay for your board and lodging, was that free of charge?

That was free of charge, bought wir food, of course, and ye got your bed, and that sort o thing.

So did you have any money left over for yourself?

No a lot! Ye had to take so much home. Ye kept, when I startit work first I had five shillings a week and I bought a bicycle, saved £1.00 a week, [Anton Murchie?] in Newton Stewart, and the bicycle cost £5.00, and I

paid £1.00 out and I saved a shilling tae the £1.00, and then I paid it up a shilling a week, tae Anton Murchie, come every week and collectit money. Ye'd always tae be there wi your money to gie him his shilling. And then ye had tae buy whatever else ye needed wi the rest.
So did all of you give a bit of your wages to your mother?
Ye went home tae see your parents, give them what money ye could give them, or whatever, and then back to work.

When Cathy Doughty left Physgill, she went to the Monreith Estate, owned by the Maxwells, the family of Gavin Maxwell. The Maxwells were already by and large absent from the estate, and the dower house at Airlour rented out. A broader perspective, the reach of distant London, was opened up for the maids by the presence of the telephone, and the coming and going of wealthy and famous visitors.

Cathy Doughty

I startit work, I worked in The Airlour with a Mrs Philimore. I worked there for a while, she was very nice. She came from– she rented the place from Sir Aymer Maxwell. … He was away a lot, but when he was there he was round about the places. But usually Mr Christie did the, he wis the kind o manager then.
And did you ever see Gavin Maxwell?
Gavin, two or three times, I spoke tae Gavin, aye. Very nice. … He was up in years then, he went then when I was wi Mrs Philimore, and she didnae like Gavin, by the way, because he was an author and so was she, and they never got on very well. And she used tae say tae us, 'Sir Aymer's coming in today and Gavin's coming with him, but don't put the whisky on the thing today, just put sherry on it, Gavin doesn't like sherry!' We used tae get a whisky and put it in the hall table, and Gavin sat at the bit where he could look onto the hall, and we waved this whisky, he made an excuse and had his whisky, getting back in and she says, 'Wouldn't you think', she says, 'Gavin would go to the toilet before he came here!' We says, 'He's a weak bladder'. … he used to laugh, we used to laugh at it.
Did you ever see the otter?
Oh yes, we've seen his otter, in fact, Davie [Doughty], one of the times fed it wi herring but it wis fed, he says, it might not take anything because it's already been fed, he had him down at the loch one morning. It was quite nice; Gavin, he could speak tae anybody. So was Sir Aymer, we got on fine wi him when they came about and that, they were nice. I liked Sir Aymer. … he always came, he never went out, without coming to the kitchen to thank us for the meal.

So were you trained by the cook there, did she teach you how to cook? So how old were you when you started that work?

Oh, I'd be getting up in years. Well, I was 28 when I left the Cults, so it'd be then. Nearly 30 then.

And you had to live in at The Airlour?

I stayed in when the cook left, I had to stay in, stay wi the old lady, look efter her. Oh, she wasnae bother, apart fae her drinking. Pills, she'd pills scattered all over and I went tae Doctor Brown and it wis old Doctor Brown then, says tae him, 'I dinnae ken about the pills,' I says, 'that old wuman hid them aa scattered'. And he used to say, 'Oh, dinnae bother aboot them, they're just kid-on things', he says, 'just tae please her. She's no needing any pills!' But he used tae sort them out, when he came at night, and she used tae say tae me, 'Ye'll have to stay up to see Doctor Brown out', and whiles they had them for a meal, Doctor and Mrs Brown. But I never used to, when they went to bed, I used tae get Doctor Brown and say tae him, 'Snib the door afore ye go out and just pull it shut!' So when I met him, he always said, 'I won't forget to snib the door!'

…

And Attlee, she was very friendly wi Attlee. And she got us, Teen and I, one day, tae phone, we'd an affae job tae get through tae Attlee, ye've nae idea whit we had tae dae tae get through, ye went tae yin bit tae another bit and another bit and another bit … and then we got his secretary, eventually. And then when he came onto the phone, we never even got speaking tae him, because she was listening in on another phone, whenever he spoke, all we heard her saying was, 'Clem darling!' So we knew she was on the phone, so we pit it doon. She aye called him 'Clem darling'.

Did he ever come to stay?

No. Thingmy Russell used tae come, Bertie Russell.

Bertrand?

Bertrand Russell. Aye, and his son. Now, he wis the Marquis o Lorne or something, I think something like that, it's a name like that anyway, something of Lorne [more likely to have been John Conrad Russell, 4th Earl Russell].

So you knew a lot of important people!

That's right. A lot o rich folk. But I never bothered.

The fact that The Airlour was already rented out was a symptom of decline yet to come for the Monreith Estate. As the numbers of staff and hands disappeared, so did the possibility of maintaining a landed estate.

Jock McMaster

Ah know Sir Michael Maxwell who's the present laird. His uncle, Sir Aymer Maxwell, I didn't really know him, I knew him to see. In those days there was no connection, you paid your rent twice a year – and that was the job done. We dealt wi the factor, the factor was the man that was the go-between.

Yes, so you didn't really even see Sir Aymer?

No, but, funnily enough, going back to my great-grandfather's day, he and Sir Herbert Maxwell had a very, I wouldn't say a friendship, but they had a working relationship. Ma great-grandfather was an amateur photographer and he took a lot of photographs for Sir Herbert. Quite a few of which were used in some of Sir Herbert's books. And they had a very good– there's quite a few letters in the house back and forward from the two of them. ... Diverse things like being allowed to plant the same crop twice in succession in one field, or the fact there was no hot water at Dumfries Station for Granny McMaster's tea. That is just the sort of scale of jobs they got involved in.

And that was, presumably the lack of contact with Sir Aymer was simply the Maxwells kept themselves to themselves, they didn't–?

Well, the fact that Aymer was never here. They lived mostly in London and Ah think he had an island in Greece somewhere and he was just never here. And he was, after ... well, before the last War and also after the last War he was selling a farm every year or so from the estate to pay for his high lifestyle.

And do you ever remember seeing or hearing of Gavin Maxwell coming?

Yes, and I actually stroked the otter. There you are now. And in the book, in the book *Ring of Bright Water* he mentions the black cattle chasing the otter at the mill pond. I was there that day, it was our mill pond. So that's my claim to fame. Didn't know Gavin at all, just met him that day, spoke to him once when he– the premiere of, was it *Ring of Bright Water*? ... It was at Newton Stewart and he was there an spoke that night and ma dad and I spoke to him that night, Ah remember, aye. So that's our tentative connection with the Maxwells.

Guy Brown

Yes, my father was quite friendly with Sir Aymer, he tended Sir Herbert before he died. And Gavin appeared, generally looked in. One of my hairiest car rides was with Gavin – to Glasgow.

And he had just bought his long wheel-based Land Rover to go to North Africa for *Lords of the Atlas*, I think it was, and he offered to give me

UP AND DOWN: WEALTH AND POVERTY

a lift up. Well, I think the slowest we were was 70 miles an hour through Cairnryan and going across the Fenwick Moor from Kilmarnock to Glasgow, on one occasion we clipped the glass verge on the fourth – the other side of the fourth lane and I was really – he turned off to go to the Clyde Tunnel and up to … up north and dropped me and I really felt very happy rattling along in a tram to get back to university (laughs). Also, one of my friends was down, a classmate, and he was here with his otter, first one, and we had gone up to see it and not very happy with this thing running around our feet and it gave John a nip on the ankle.

… yea, Gavin was quite a character, without a doubt. And they had, there was a party at Monreith House, every Christmas, for the workers on the estate and Galloway House sent a darts team and Shennanton sent a darts team and one of the hotels catered for the meal, and had an entertainer. … That was always a big night for the estate.

So there were still quite a few people employed on it, were there?

No, numbers diminished, oh, six-fold I would say, five or six-fold. They used to, the estate and the Dourie used to employ about, I'm sure about 100 and probably about 20 now. It's gone right down, the numbers employed have gone right down.

Down and Out

At the other end of the spectrum, Tom McCreath describes the poverty on farms in the 1930s, the era of *Wigtown Ploughman*, and a slow change due to intervention from regulated markets and remote payments.

Tom McCreath

And agriculture in– had gone through a very serious depression, it was bad enough in 1895 when Grandfather came to the farm but it was worse in the 1930s and a lot of farmers went bankrupt and had to give up and Father just struggled to keep going so that by the time war broke out a lot of the buildings were in total disrepair but he was still there. And during wartime, with controlled prices, there was a slow improvement, as there had been also when the Milk Marketing Board was formed, in was it '34 or '35? A slow, well, a monthly milk check and a slow improvement. But it took a long time and often the debts weren't paid off until the '50s, post-war.

John Scoular

Quite a big, big countryside population in cottages then, an area which was poverty stricken in the extreme. As I say, I remember going with him to some of the big cottages in the backward farms, visiting the sick and whatnot and really, Julia, it was frightening, to even a wee boy, you just thought, 'How can people live like this?' Now that cottage, what we call 'The Halfway House', do you know where I'm talking about? It was a chap McShane who lived there for many years and I remember him telling me about the rats running over the beds. And that was by no means exceptional, you forget how much poverty there was in this area, right up to the War and during the War things were tight and then after the War there was a kind of stultifying period when nothing very much happened, really. There was social progress in the fact that council housing was built and what have you but there wasn't a lot happening. You had this tremendous effect of the incoming people over the war years, foreign faces, fresh faces and then it all came to an end and it was a very– I would say that from the end of the War into the 50s it was a very bleak period in Whithorn. …You look around at the pictures that were taken then and think, 'These people weren't well off'.

In Whithorn itself, before the Second World War and before the advent of payment systems which confirmed the reach of the State, the poor relied upon a patchwork of aid, partly supplied by the Burgh Council and churches, and in part due to the generosity of neighbours and family members.

Betty Stuart

Ah don't know but poorer people, ye went tae the council an ye got a chitty, a 'line', for £1.00 maybe, maybe it was more than £1.00, and ye took that up to the manse an ye got things for it. Clothes, clothing. Now you could maybe get, maybe, stockings, sandals, sometimes Ah think it was a bigger line, maybe, for a dress, but ye got lines. Cause ah've had– Ah have had– ma mother got a line, Ah can remember once going and getting.

This was the manse up Bruce Street?

The manse up Bruce Street, aye. Aye, Ah went up there, Ah think it was Mr Law, maybe someone before him.

But ye did get a chitty, Ah don't know if it was once a year or more often, I don't know if it was Christmas time or when it was but ye had tae go up the steps tae the hall, doon the street, beside Galloway's. You had tae– ye had tae be really needin in, ye had tae be, for someone put your name in. I know, I remember that right enough and I remember once I, we got it. Whether it was only once or no I don't know, but I remember we got it and in fact, I think it was me that went for it.

Jessie McLean

Ah can mind of folk that were puir, puir folk. Comin ower tae oor hoose at night an getting pots o soup that was left, tatties and thing. Bakin an aw, Ah can mind o ma sister an ma mother an ma granny gien different yins. Mary kens that folk cawd Rennie there's a wuman here, she was in the welfare an she says, 'De ye ken this,' she says, 'a got ma supper gey often, yin of the Rennies, fae the Jollys'. Ah says, 'Ah ken, a gien ye it'. She says, 'Yes, Ah mind o that'. Folk were puir lang ago. Oh, there was a lot o kindness, because ma mother never threw ocht oot because she gien it tae the Rennies across the road or the Garrets. Ye never threw ocht oot, ye gien tae some o them that had naethin.

Jenny Jolly

No, their pensions wisnae big but they were managers, I mean they made pots o soup and stuff like that and then they were in rented, they were old houses but they had tae pay rent. Some o them owned their hoose but still had tae pay rates.

…

Oh gosh, aye. We were poor wurselves tae, ma mother went oot and worked. Oh aye, they were– and she got a job wi the farm workers and they got their weekly pay but they got free – it wasnae, it was supposed tae be free – tatties and milk. … Ma father died, took ill, they caaed it thrombosis, no thrombosis – they ca'd it – oh, what did they ca it?

Was it tuberculosis?

Aye something like that, it was consumption, it was the auld-fashioned name for it. … He yaised to be sittin outside at the back door half the night. But ma mother, ye had tae go to the town hall, the auld toon hall, when Catyans [the lawyer] – it was him that was in it and ye had tae gaun, everybody, there wis other folk gaun as weel as you. Ma mother had tae gaun before she got a job again in Denton's and she got four shillings a week for ma sister and her, she got nothing for me, cause I'd turned 14. So Ah didnae get ocht but that's what she got a week, four shillings, it wasnae a lot o money, although things was cheaper it still wisnae, but as soon as she managed– oh, she went oot and thinned turnips and aw, crawled for extra money, she did that, though, before ma faither died. Cause ma faither liked a parlour, as he called it, a front room, a guid room, and Mrs Jolly selt lovely furniture and a mind o him getting this beautiful auld– oh, it wisnae auld, it was a kinna antique round table, but it was inlaid and it had the feet, it hadnae legs, ye ken, at the centre o it, what a beautiful table, put it in the front room for Ah used tae polish it, get sixpence worth o flooers for it, the table, every weekend.

So you felt you were less poor when your mother got the baking job?
Uh-huh, she did well. My pay was, the auld money it was paid in of course, a month was 30 shillings per month. My uncle, the McEwans that was oor cousins that was born up in Coatbridge an Airdrie an Stevenson, roond aboot there and never gied tae ma mother and right away she got money sent tae her on the spot, wired tae her, for she was, it didnae soond a lot nooadays but it was a lot in they days. They were awfy guid tae Molly and me tae, when we were at the school, for their girls was older and of course– nice clothes they hae in thae cities and we used tae get them, jist get them cut doon.

Tom McCreath and Greta Hawthorn remember how poverty was palpable at Whithorn Primary School; the state of a child's shoes was diagnostic of poverty, but the shoes' wearing life could be extended by hand-me-downs, the alternation of a good pair with a working pair, or by repairs.

Tom McCreath

I can remember in the infant class being surprised how long some of the children, often country children, came to school in bare feet and in winter they would wear clogs. But after two or three years, now I must be talking here about just pre-war, there was much less of that. But I know one, I knew of one kid who came to school, walked to school in very old shoes, but he nipped into a house in the town and changed into a better pair to go up the hill to school. There was a lot of poverty and in clothes too and of course on a wet day in the cloakroom I can still remember the smell of the coats hanging there, drying out somewhat.

Greta Hawthorn

Yes, aye, ye knew that. Ye knew even wi their schoolbags or their schoolbooks that they were never covered cos, no even wi wallpaper, because they said that you could cover– it was usually brown paper, but they said ye could cover them wi anything. But there was quite a lot o that and we had a girl in oor class that was always late, every day of the week and we knew that she would be comin but she always come at the same time but it was maybe about three-quarters o an hour later and she used tae sing at night in the streets, Cathy Garroch wis her name. I think she has jist been back once since she went away, but she seemed to be getting on, the first time that she ever was back, and she was getting on fine in

Glasgow. And we used to get food parcels from Australia to the school and there was one for each classroom and there were big tins o fruit salad, fruit, mixed fruit and the teacher would put everybody's name in tae get one an Ah won this tin of fruit and I gave them to Cathy Garroch, cause I knew that she wouldnae hae that kinna fruit; well, we were lucky at the farm, we always got apples an pears and we could get them at Glasserton Gardens for there was gardeners up at Glasserton Gardens and ye could go up and buy them at any time. So, oh she was that delighted wi this fruit, I think she ate it morning, noon and night. But it was a wee change for her tae, wasn't it? We were lucky at the farm because ye could always get rabbits or hares or pigeons or something that ye never really were hungry.

Jock McMaster

Oh, yea, definitely, aye. Some– two families in particular Ah remember, we used to feel very sorry for them because they all wore clothes that had been sort of handed to them from, I presume the council, and they were all a sort of uniform grey colour. Ah don't know what it was made of, some sort of flannel perhaps, and they were poor kids, aye, aye. They were … because that was the mid-early '50s, mid-'50s, aye, and they wouldnae have a lot, no, big families of course and farm worker wages then were very small. Nobody had a motor car, most of them had bikes, things were tighter.

Tina Soriani

And I do remember at least one boy, and I can remember his name, I'm not gonnae tell youse, but he used to come, in the summertime, he used to come to school barefoot! And very often, an excuse, if one of the pupils wasn't attending school, was that his shoes, or his boots, were at the cobblers, they only had one pair of boots or one pair o shoes. And they were being repaired so they couldn't come to school!

That these conditions existed was laid bare in John McNeillie's *Wigtown Ploughman*, which raised a particular controversy on the point as to whether the bestial behaviour of the ploughman was caused by the poverty of conditions in the farm cottages. Yet, as Ian Niall, he returned to the world of the Machars and North Clutag in *A Galloway Childhood*, seeking to return to the world which had begun vanishing, partly thanks to the changes and interventions initiated by his first novel.

Andrew McNeillie

Was there a particular reaction from the Church?
There was indeed, of course there was– the Presbytery was divided between the younger members who wanted, who had been elsewhere, had been in Edinburgh, for example, who wanted and recognised the need for reform in housing and those who didn't want to link social conditions to moral behaviour and that was the divide. Did people, was people's conduct the product of their environment or was it their own moral responsibility? That old thing that we all know about was exercised and it divided people. There was a struggle within the Presbytery for example to [unclear] the novel and whether the novel spoke true about housing conditions or whether it was not doing so. And largely it seems that the view that it spoke true won through and the verdict of the committee that was set up in the wake of the novel, set up by the Kirk, by the various [unclear] of religious institutions, whatever they were, the verdict was generally that there was a case to answer. And so that was a very priding thing I remember for my great-grandfather, that not only had the novel seemed to be the cause of this setting up of this committee, it had been vindicated by its findings that indeed, the majority of labourers, cotters, in the district, were poorly housed in the extreme so it was an interesting connection with the Kirk, I think. The [unclear] came out and condemned it as they would but I think generally speaking there were enough radical people involved to say, 'Well, this is what it's like, really, and something needs to be–'. There were people with vested interest in the County Council and so on, didn't want to own up to the situation or begin to acknowledge that it was a very poor set of circumstances and there were farmers who were probably very good in cases, providing accommodation for their workers, who didn't want to be stigmatised in this way but it just seemed to me that the balance of reactions suggests that the book was true to its criticism of social circumstances. And surely we know that it is true that in its suggestion that how we live, where we live, our circumstances, condition what we might be and what we might do. It's constantly the case, quite clearly endlessly so. Daniel Defoe wrote about this a long time ago, about criminality and living conditions and only somebody who's not very well informed, I think, would try to pretend that the way we are treated and the way we have to live doesn't condition the way we behave. He, my father, obviously saw this and believed this. It's quite to one side *Wigtown Ploughman* but my father was a huge admirer of Defoe, hugely influenced by him in his later books, of faction, he was fascinated how *A Journal of the Plague Year* is a fiction and fascinated how he might do that trick and he did a lot of factual fictions or

factions later in his life, several that were trying, I think, to learn from the brilliance of Defoe, the way that he told those stories in *The Plague Year*.

With regulation of the milk product came pipelines and water supply, which brought the new experience of on-tap water first to those closest to the dairies.

Tom McCreath

> There were some occasions where the dairyman's house was much better order than the farmer's house. And I know one house not far from here, near Whauphill, a farmer's house that didn't have running water but cottages got running water and central heating put into them and the poor wife of the farmer had to put up until they made enough money in a few years' time to get it in, running water into their own house. But the byres and everything they had to have running water and the dairyman had to have his running water and things but they're slightly remote, the farmhouse didn't have anything. So, there were great improvements and in the '50s, of course, they were putting electricity, installing electricity, in a lot of the small holdings, the government smallholdings up at Dunragit and round that area.

The reach of local government, and government in general, remained limited and its regulation confined; the community it served included the Burgh workforce, all resident within the burgh and known by their individual names, as Alex Haswell, whose father was one of a small team of workers for Whithorn Burgh Council, recalls. The burgh's centredness on itself was finally disrupted with its subsumption within the vaster unit of Dumfries and Galloway.

Alex Haswell

> But, it was a happy childhood, as I say, my father painted and decorated– originally, he worked for John Coid, eventually, he got the job working for Whithorn Town Council, and was the Burgh painter – from the mid-'60s, right through to the reorganisation of local Government in 1975. … But, the Burgh Council was quite an organisation, I think I was saying earlier on, I remember the men who worked with my father were 'Spook' McGinn, Hugh McGinn – Hugh was the dust cart man, and I do remember the original dust cart which was towed by a horse, and then we got a tractor and trailer, and that was real modernisation in Whithorn, when the dust cart [became] a tractor and trailer. And many a run I had from here to Black's Plantation, to the coup. I also remember the coup that was on the Garlieston road. It was a guy called Ambrose who was the

refuse collector at the time. But Hugh McGinn, he did the refuse, my father did the painting; there was a guy called Jimmy McWilliam, who was the joiner, and did all the joinery work; and Jim Norquoy, commonly known as Knocky Norquoy – Jim came from Orkney, but he had married a local lass and settled down here. And then there was Alec Steele, who was also a general labourer. That was the total complement of the work force, apart from the Burgh foreman. And the Burgh foreman, originally, in my mind, was a guy called Archie Frew, who became a Clerk Watch at Wigtown District Council. And then there was Johnnie Johnston, who followed Archie through, and he was also a Clerk Watch at one time. But sadly both of them have now passed away … . These weeds would never have been growing round the war memorial had the Burgh Council still been there; they had a pride in the town that I think, sadly, has been lost – not by the people – but by the fact that we're working with a huge organisation called Dumfries and Galloway Council. Whithorn Town Council had its own town clerk, who was also the local solicitor or the local firm of solicitors. And it was MacFie and Alexander. And I remember R. G. Alexander, he was a very tall, imposing man, and their office was just across the road there. And when R. G. was bought out by Ferguson and Forster, as was then, they regained the (Ian) Alexander name, the town clerk then became a guy called Bill Ray. Bill formed a friendship, of sorts, with my father, and Bill encouraged me. Bill Ray was the reason I went into law. I remember Bill telling me that his mother had scrubbed steps in Glasgow so he could go to university. So Bill's a very down to earth guy, very down to earth guy. I greatly admire him.

…

But the Town Council built most of the houses in Whithorn. The District would renovate some of them, o, but it was the town that built Kilncroft, the Town Council that built Kilncroft, they had the Crudens there already. The Park was there. I think I'd be pushed to say Wigtown district built any houses, I don't think they did. I know Loreburn built houses after 1975, but I don't think the district built houses in Whithorn. Could be wrong.

And the money to pay the burgh offices and crew came from a rate?

Yes, it would come from the rates that the Town Council would raise, they would also get fairly huge government subsidies. I mean, this was a Royal Burgh, but you could see how statures were reduced over the years, but there would be a Government grant; it would be the County Council that would raise the rates, and they would pay an amount to the Burgh Council. The Burgh wouldn't have the capacity or the capability to collect money. I mean, they collected the rents for their houses, Ron Marshall– for as long as I can remember, Ron Marshall was the clerk who collected the rents down in the office there.

And they operated from the old Town Hall?

The old Town Hall, yes, the Council chamber was in the old Town Hall, and then of course, it became the Masonic place. I think a lot of the Council's business would be done in The Grapes! (both laugh) Or wherever, public house that was the flavour of the day. I think the one at the bottom, which I think had originally been The Railway Hotel, then became The Golf Hotel, when J. B. Kirkpatrick had it – and then latterly, The Black Hawk. I think they would meet in there as well. I think it's had, I'm going to be perfectly honest here, it's had a detrimental effect on Whithorn. I think often [due to] necessity, councils work on the basis of strategy and policy, and sometimes that means that places like Whithorn do lose out. I think that Whithorn had its own identity in the '70s, certainly in the '60s and '70s. There's been a move away – but how much of that is down to the fact that local Government has moved further away, and how much of it is just down to the fact that the world has moved on – I'd need somebody to reflect that with me and have a long discussion about that.

...

I think every now and again, big Government does something that has an effect on a small community, and big Government has the ability to do that. If Dumfries and Galloway wants a couple of million quid, they can do it – in the Town Council days, they didnae have that, but what they had was the revenue to make sure the place was kept looking smart, neat and tidy. And of course, it had its own Court as well, the Burgh Bailiffs and the Burgh Magistrates. But that was a really interesting time. How someone could sit in judgement of someone in such a small community. I remember my father got fined six shillings, I think it was, for allowing his chimney to go on fire. He allowed the chimney to go on fire, and he got a fine from the Burgh Court. But I would have really been interested to see how that worked; because I when I came to Wigtown – I ran the Justices Court for Wigtown District – and I sometimes really felt that people sitting on the bench were a wee bit close to things, shall we say. Maybe that was a good thing, maybe it wisnae. It was when the late Sam Watson, who was a grocer in Sorbie; Sam was a JP and Sam was a green stick– mind you, a really good JP. But when he brought the accused over from Sorbie in his car! You started to wonder, is this a good idea?! (both laugh) I'll never forget that!

And the Burgh Court would have met at the old Town Hall building?

I think the Burgh Court would meet at the old Town Hall building, yes.
I mean, it's really a continuous tradition from medieval times; you've got that centre of justice and administration. And then in '75–

It all stopped. And the Government – and this is with due respect to all community councillors – the Government, in an effort to get the act through Parliament, to make sure there wasn't a huge [outcry], set up community councils. When you look at section 52 and 53 of The Local Government Scotland Act, which set up community councils, they didn't put a lot of thought into it. I was away from Whithorn when it happened. My first day at work was the 15th of May 1975. Which was the day Local Governments reorganised in Scotland – yeah, for the first time. So, I was away, so wasn't really aware of its going. But whether people in Whithorn noticed it – I don't think they even mourned it. There may have been one or two people in the community who thought, 'This is no gonna be a good thing'. But I don't think anybody mourned it. People don't notice.

And the Burgh Council employed, what, four people?

I think there were about six. The refuse guy, the labourer; McGinn, Steele, Norquoy, McWilliam, my father, and a foreman.

And Dumfries and Galloway Council employs?

Eight thousand (both laugh). The turnover is 360-odd million a year, the turnover of Dumfries and Galloway Council, a huge organisation. Not the biggest in Scotland, but a big organisation when you compare it with Whithorn Burgh.

Greta Hawthorn and John Wilson recall the operation of the Burgh Court and the administration of sometimes rough justice, contained within the familial setting of the burgh.

Greta Hawthorn

Yes, and Mr Alexander and Miss Hill worked wi Mr Alexander and there wis Ackie Dodds there was a lot o auld worthies in Whithorn and he had been urinating in the street and this policeman had got him and he was at the Court and Miss Hill was reading oot a his offences that he'd had, and a the dates and a the this, that and the next thing, so he was fined ten shillings so he stood up an he says, 'Thanks, ma lord, bit hoo does Miss Hill ken a these things? She must hae an awfy guid memory?' (laughter) He didnae ken that she wis readin it off a piece o paper.

John Wilson

We had two bailies and the time I was on it I don't think the– there was very little problem, very little problem, most of the crime would be drink-related and it was basically fighting, there was very little, very little thieving or anything like that went on. Even to this day there's very little thieving goes on in Whithorn. Yes, the police station was in St John Street at that time and a lot of the times the policemen would dispense justice, shall we say, the way he saw fit. There would be a lot of things that would happen that wouldn't got to court, shall we say. And that was just accepted, that was accepted and just taken on board. I think it would have to be quite serious before, a lot of them would have to be a bit more serious, before it would be taken further.

6

Here and There

In an area where people did not move far or fast, circulation of goods, services and news was achieved by other means. The travelling population, in the broadest sense, was a moving kaleidoscope which included – within a small compass – mobile businesses the pedlar with a pack, the men and women of the road who were given food and lodging, and the travelling people themselves. The visits themselves were seasonal, and for businesses, the speed with which the cycle of visits could be completed dictated the terms of credit.

Connections between people were not constant, mediated by vast networks of cables, but were instead episodic, interrupted by lapses of time and expanses of physical distance which could only be overcome by foot, bicycle or train. It was a perspective in which neighbouring towns and villages might seem very far off and the distance between arrival and departure very great.

John Scoular

> … and we were talking about the '70s now, interviewing somebody for a job in an hotel and her mother had never been out of Newton Stewart in her life. And you could have said the same thing about a number of people in Whithorn.
> …
> After that, as I say, mobility has been the key to the change, the latter change … . We're talking, well, I was born in 1931. I'm now 80 and the change in this whole area, in this whole community, and in peoples' attitudes– for all the problems that the kids have, they're in touch with the ones, the children of their own age, it doesn't matter whether they're in cities or elsewhere, they know how to use their technical equipment that every child has at its disposal, they're much more with it, their fashion is the same as the kids in the cities. … in the '30s right through to well into the '50s, very few people local to here, took a holiday or went anywhere. And the same applied to the young people, young farmers … most of them are now more acquaint with the outside world than they were then.

... And it's– the same was true right across the board, people just didn't have any contact with the outside world really, or not enough. Of course the media have a– in the days when the cinema was the only entertainment here are long gone, people can get so much access through television, radio and the printed word in a way that they didn't have.

Greta Hawthorn

We were– the furthest we were ever away was tae Wigtown Cattle Show once a year and we went on the train. And ma granny's parents and that are buried in the old graveyard near the church at Wigtown and she had a picnic and we had sheep shears to cut the grass and this wus wur yearly visit, we went on the train and we were loaded, between flowers and stuff for cutting the grave and something tae eat and everything. So we went up in the train and then we come back on the train and that was the furthest we had been for a long time.

So do you remember when you first went to Newton Stewart?

No, but I remember the first time I was ever away and we hired Mrs Bell, the Bells that have the garage, they had a hiring business, the father and the mother, and Mrs Bell had a taxi and ma mother's uncle was in hospital in Dumfries. He'd got hurt at his work and it was blood poison and we hired Mrs Bell tae take us and I thought I was never gonnae get tae Dumfries and when I was at Dumfries I thought I'd never get back hame (laughter). I thought I was miles away at Dumfries.

I suppose it was quite common for people not really to travel very far.

No, no. Well, ye couldnae afford it.

And you perhaps didn't need to?

No. Well, there was enough in the town. Ye could get anything ye wanted, whereas ye cannae even get the weans' school uniforms where ye could get that here.

The largely static population liberated an entire economy of travelling shops. In an area where travel was limited to foot, bicycle and train, businesses themselves were peripatetic and the focus for social interaction in the countryside. As Robin Kinnear explains, his grandfather's travelling business was a social circuit in the most literal sense, and the reverse of today's mobile deliveries, crossing the country via vast logistical systems, at the behest of an all-powerful consumer, who is yet entirely laid bare to the play of markets.

Robin Kinnear

A gentleman in 1908 joined the staff, by the name of Johnny Bell, and he was really like a minstrel, he would go round and they had to travel fair distances with this pony and trap and he would stay the night at the farthest point and would entertain people who were looking after him with his fiddle and had a great musical evening and they looked forward to him coming every few months and a whole day's journey was from Port William to Kirkinner and perhaps round by Garlieston, and not getting back until maybe ten o'clock at night and counting the money, which was just in coin, more or less, a big day would be maybe £6.00 or £7.00.

Kinnear's mobile business ceased in the 1980s.

Robert Kinnear

In '85, well in the '70s we would just have two vans and then in the '80s we just had the one big stock van that went round, Mr Carruthers did that, and Mr Anderson, who was the other traveller, he was based mainly in Whithorn shop and just went out on odd days to various things. But the van from Port William, it, as I was telling you earlier, it had a pony and trap where they went out with their drapery, their ladies' [unclear] socks and aprons and pinafores and things and samples of cloth for people to select suits and they did that on the pony and trap and then, when Johnny Bell joined the staff in 1908, they had an old Model T Ford and then they had a Morris 10 car and all the samples and cases were loaded in, the seats were taken out of the back and there was no front seat, there was just the driver's and all the cases were packed in there and if you had a roll of linoleum or something to deliver it was tied onto to the headlamp and the running board of the car and he would set off with these two – like cannons, coming from the front of his car over the headlights. I can remember it very well, then the first van we got after that was a wee Hillman van and then Mr Carruthers had a series of vans Ford 10 and Bedford vans, and they travelled for quite some time, from 1949 until the late sort of '70s, '80s, it was continued with just the one big stock van.

Did you go to people's houses by appointment with samples of cloth or did they find you or, how did it work?

We had a set run in the van that you would perhaps be doing the Machars area, just a certain part that Mr Anderson didn't do and then you'd move from there to Glenluce and Auchenmalg and then from there up to New Luce, up into the hills, the farms up there, and then you would do Stranraer town, Stoneykirk and Sandhead, Drummore and right down to the Mull of Galloway and they knew when you were coming, it was a set date so we didn't need to make an appointment but latterly, when people were wanting a carpet measured, then you made an appointment and it was special journey you went to see them. But it was a set run and quite a social occasion when they came because very often, he wouldn't stay in the hotel when he was away, he would stay in customers' houses. And spend the evening selling drapery, maybe arrive at the house at five o'clock just not long after the milking finished and he would have his tea and then bring in all the cases and work until maybe half eleven at night. And then they would sit and have a good crack or play music or– it was just a social evening. And this happened all the time, really quite interesting.

So, I suppose he got a lot of news on his rounds as well?

Yes, yes, he got– there was a lot of talk and very often you would maybe call … when we used to call at Parton we called at the Callander family in Parton and there were next door neighbours who would come in and this was the central point, was the Parton post office. And I've seen us arriving there at four o'clock and not getting to bed until about half past two in the morning because there were people from Drumrash would come in and from other areas. And we would maybe have, throughout the evening, we'd maybe have about twelve customers in, all wanting to buy.

It's a great way of doing business.

Yes, yes, it was lovely, it was most entertaining. But you didn't have much time for anything else. I can remember going away on the– doing the run myself down to Kirkcudbright and very, very late nights and you were really quite exhausted when you came back and you had no notion of going to a dance or entertainment when you came back home on the Saturday (laughs), it was off to bed. But it was a very interesting life and I thoroughly enjoyed it and you met so many people.

The phenomenon of the commercial traveller, circulating at intervals and filling the hotels which too are now vanished, was part of the calendar of visits at farms and shops.

Betty Murray

… [my father] talked to travellers. There were a lot of commercial travellers all the time. I think most things were ordered that way. I think there was maybe at least three biscuit travellers, one from Macfarlane Lang, one from McVities, and one from Gray Dunn. They all had their own rep, and that's the way the food was ordered. And then there were the whisky travellers, and wine.

Yes, I remember one of the deliveries – now it's coming back – from the station, a horse. And a delivery cart, it was a man called Willie McMaster. He delivered the stuff that came by rail.

34. Dodds' cart, Whithorn, Castlehill, *c.*1900.

So was he employed by the railways?

He must have been. Or was– he might have been employed by Carson, the coal merchant. For he delivered coal as well, so maybe they took the stuff from the train too.

It was farm supplies, I think, West Cumberland farmers, things like that. Wyllie, grain merchants, they all had their travellers coming round. I suppose the farms are quite lonely places now to live, at the beginning there was always men going around, and travellers coming up. There isn't that anymore. And the cottages have all been let for tourism.

Betty Stuart

His father's name was Lally Doughty. Aye, it was, it was popular and then, ye see, they had a van too, they went roond Whithorn and The Isle and aw, wi their van, Doughty's van. … Aye the van went roon aboot, there was quite a lot of vans went roond and then there was some vans came fae The Isle roond aboot here tae, like Hale, the butcher. Joe Hale, he brought his van from The Isle roond Whithorn too, and had customers here as well as in The Isle.

Jock McMaster

Oh, aye, there was the mobile shops, aye. Well, the butcher from Whithorn, Charlie Coid he came every, once a week. And Walker, the baker from Creetown, he came twice a week and Jimmy Dewar, Port William, again the grocer, now I think they handed in a list for him and he delivered it. Or maybe it was phoned in, Ah don't know. But he only got paid once every three months, Ah think. The blacksmith sent a bill every six months but the grocer, Ah think he just sent it. We just paid him once a month or whatever. There wasnae much cash changed hands. The Co-op came, the Co-op van came around, Ah remember him comin around wi groceries. Ah think that would be it, probably, so there was probably somebody every day, yes, there would be. Charlie Coid was a big hefty chap, great big podgy hands, an Ah always remember ma mum accusing him of having his thumb on the scales when he was weighing the sausages cause his fingers looked like sausages, they were great big thick, thick fingers, somebody else has probably told you that (laughter) and ma mum occasionally, 'Get yer thumb of the scales there, Charlie, ah'm just buying sausages, ah'm no buying your podgy fingers.' (laughter) His name's still on the shop at Whithorn. Aye, it's never been taken down.

The 'house call' occupied a large part of the local doctor's day, allowing a scrutiny of individual circumstances which is no longer possible in health systems which require travel to remote centres of excellence.

Guy Brown

But we did, I sometimes did up to 40 home calls a day in addition to the surgeries. And you miss going into people's houses. Because you– it's very odd, quite frequently or not infrequently, you picked up something, going in. You could see something or something they were going to tell you but they wouldn't think of coming to the surgery or calling you and going in. But things, again, have changed there and everybody goes to the surgery because there is a larger range of things they can do at the time. They'd need to carry a van full of bags with them.

The most famous of the travelling businesses was Mary Jolly's travelling dealership, selling crockery and gathering skins and furs.

Jessie McLean

Ma father was aye a dealer, general dealer. He aye dealt, he selt dishes and ornaments an a that kinna thing and they went tae the sales and bocht furniture and re-selt, he wis an unctioneer. He bocht aw thay things and ma mother carried it on efter he died.

Mary: When ma granda died when my granny was left wi what a lot, ma Auntie Mamie was only six weeks old.

Aicht o us, at the school.

Mary: An ma Aunty Mamie wis only six weeks auld jist when ma granda died. And ma granny carried on the hawkin. And every yin o her [my mother's] brothers and sisters, as they reached the age, had tae tak their turn, the sisters in the hoose an the brothers in the cairt an ma mother some o the sisters hawked an some didnae but she [my mother] could hawk.

Ma sisters, they got away fae that, they didnae dae it.

Mary: But they had tae take their turn in the hoose when ma granny was on the cairt.

Aye, tae watch the wee weans.

Mary: They'd left the school.

And did she have a shop or was it–?

Yes, we hard wur shop but we didnae sell oot o oor shop, because we were aye oot wi the cart sellin the dishes and gatherin the skins and rags.

We had lovely china an lovely ornaments, lovely dishes. Lots of folk'll hae nice dishes yet that ma mother– would buy fae ma mother.

And so you'd call at all the farms?

We went tae every farm, ye had a day in the country and a day at Wigtown and a day at [unclear] an a day [unclear]. It took ye aw day gaun roond aw the hooses an everything. But Ah can never mind, ma sister or a sister that was awfu clever at the school and the teachers wanted ma dad and ma mum tae let her gaun on at the schooling and they wouldnae dae it. Took her fae the school tae dae the hawk. And some o ma sisters wouldnae dae it, they didnae like tae dae it, but Ah did. Ah was yin that did like. Fae Ah was ony age Ah was gaitherin rabbit skins. Ah wis aye cheeky, cheeky lass. Aye, Ah was.

And did your father go out on the cart as well, or just your mum?

No, he died awfu young.

So your mother really had to make the money.

She was a good dealer. At the big sales ma mother was the main yin, she had a good heid on her, she was clever. Ah had a brother that was the same as ma mother.

Did she have her name on the cart?

Jolly, General Dealer, was her name. Mary Jolly, General Dealer.

Right. So it was probably one of the big businesses at the Top of the Town, was it?

Oh, gosh it was a big business at the Top of the Toon. We aye had guid horses. We aye kent, ma brothers aye kent a guid horse, we aye had guid horses.

Jenny Jolly, Jessie McLean's sister-in-law, explains the workings of Mrs. Jolly's brother's business.

35. Willie McGinn's cart, Whithorn, *c.1900*.

Jenny Jolly

    Oh, that was auld Wullie McGinn, 'the pedlar', they called him. He went tae America tae make his fortune, but onyway, he come back, they called him 'the pedlar' onyway. Cheeky auld rascal. And the horse was took through the blue hoose, outside it was blue, it was ca'd the blue hoose. And he used tae chap my front door, what a rattle wi the stick, he never come up the steps he jist banged it wi the stick for tatties, cooked tatties, and then he went doon and fried them or something wi them.

And he just assumed that you had to do that or did you, did he pay you?

    No, he didnae pay me, he jist thought– he was the auld uncle, he just thought he had a right tae … it was aye me he come chapping. … Mrs Jolly was a McGinn. McGinn's in aw their names tae, like Bill's. William McGinn Jolly, John, John McGinn Jolly – it's in aw their names.

And he was a pedlar going round the countryside was he?

    Rabbit skins, rabbit, ragbag. And he'd a guid ragbags, for he went tae the big hooses and got lovely claiths, he did quite well.

And they would send them up to Glasgow?

    I expect they would, they got rid o them onyway.

Betty Stuart remembers the classic Scots pedlar and the periodic circulation of supply and credit.

Betty Stuart

He came round wi big cases an that, a lot of people bought fae him because you could pay them up. Dae ye no remember his name, no? He was very popular. ... Aye Mr David. Ah bought fae Mr David for a long, long while, he used to come once a month. This was fae [unclear] he came every week and they got them– it's cawd it, then 'on tick' and paid something yince a week and then the next week he come back and paid.

And do you remember people selling things from packs round the doors?

Yes, yes. That Mrs Jones [from High Street] did, that Ah wis talking aboot. She had a pack and there was other ones come, Sammy Caldwell, he lived in Glasserton Street, Sammy Caldwell, he was a great, he was the maist favourite Ah think, Sammy. He lived in Glasserton Street, he had a pack.

Molly: So what kinna things did they hae in their pack?

Everything, drapery, everything. Onything ye wanted, Sammy Caldwell could get it. When it was time for them going back tae school they got school things in their pack. They did it so as folk would [unclear].

So, was that on foot always?

Yes, on foot. Aye he was on foot. Aye he did the whole of the town, Sammy, Sarah Holland and [unclear].

'Gaun Folk'

Mrs. Jones, who shouldered 'the pack' herself, also accommodated people of the road, in her lodging house in High Street, Whithorn; these were the section of the population who were most exposed to risk: to the chance of generosity, seasonal or surplus and casual work on farms.

Jenny Jolly

It did, oh there wis a lot on the road when I was a young lass, there was a lot o 'gaun folk' they called them, tramps like, there was an awfy lot on the road. Chappin the door for a piece and then Mrs Jones, she was a Welsh wuman, she had twa hooses, her ain hoose up High Street– they're doon of coorse years ago. Efter ye went by the [Port's Mouth]. There was the [cross?] hoose there's twa or three wee-er hooses and then there's hers, ye went up steps, and when ye're up the steps the lobby was on a slope tae. Mrs Jones, and she had a lodging hoose, I think it was a shilling a night or something she took fae them. Ah had photos o her somewhere tae, an auld Maggie Black, took them for a picnic and ma mother tae the Isle of Whithorn and Ah mind o Mrs Jones dressed up in her big hat an aw on her head, boy, she was lovely. Ah never had tasted chips, ma mother never had chips, made chips, and the first time Ah tasted chips was fae Mrs Jones. Yin day they were talkin, Ah said Ah had never had them and then she cried at me yin night tae 'Come on!' and she'd a wee bowl o them for me. They were nice, Ah was aye in aboot a lot o auld folk in they days, sitting listening tae them, but they were guid entertainment.

Betty Stuart

The lodging houses they stayed in, that was in High Street. ... She had this wee house, Mrs Jones and Tommy, that was her husband, and they sold things like combs and things, wee things, oot o their pack, they was there and next to it, ye went up the steps, and that was the lodging house, ye had tae go up the steps tae it. It was joined together but different, if ye know what Ah mean. Separate doors. She was an nice old lady, Mrs Jones. She drank but, ye seen her gaun up wi her jug tae the pub an comin back doon wi it.

And did she serve them a dinner or something?

They got something, Ah donno what they would get but the– some of the kinna worse ones that maybe wouldnae hae very much, Ah think, they kinna chapped at yer doors an asked for a piece. Snib Scott an that. ... He went to a special house doon at aboot the Port Mouth, he went in there to Mrs Begg, ye called her, an she always gien him food and he took her dog oot. Dainty, was the dog's name, he took the dog oot a walk and the big black curly dog, it was so fat wi bein fed, it couldnae move. Aye he went there.

Were there any other famous characters that you remember? Somebody's mentioned somebody called Scotch Jimmy.

Oh, Scotch Jimmy, oh Ah mind oh Scotch Jimmy. He was a kind of wee, he was a tramp, he sung or he tried tae but he had a beard richt doon an hair but, what was it he sung? Oh, *Bringing in the Sheaves*, the hymn. And Robert John Connin, he was another one, they were the famous, two famous ones fae the lodging house and he was a good singer ye ken and, as Ah say, the other one kept the Bible upside doon.

Molly: Did he get pennies for that or what?

Oh he got pennies, ay ye had tae keep a penny in the hoose for them, they aye got a, their pennies. Ah think maistly everybody would gie them a penny. But the Scotch Jimmy, was aggressive, he wisnae like the other– I think they were quite glad to get rid o him oot o Whithorn. He was aggressive, he would have fought or hit ye for nothing. He aye went tae the pub a lot, Mrs Flannighan's.

Elsie McShane

Aye, well, there was Snib Scott, he was famous. That's the only one I remember. Oh yes. He was a regular.

Did your mother give him anything?

Yes, they allowed him to sleep in the shed, overnight only – and leave your tobacco. She always fed him!

So that was pretty much expected?

It was expected, it was bad luck if you refused, yes.

Judy Brown

And he [Snib Scott] was always dressed in his oilskins and every other bit of clothing he possessed, even in the scorching sunshine, and he would say when the sun was out, 'It's a coorse nicht' (laughs). Coorse nicht. But he was just a character, he was harmless but he had the philosophy of– that you didn't need to work if your belly was full (laughs). So, if he got any – why work at all? Just go round and beg from a few people.

Was your family quite tolerant of that, did they mind giving him a bit to eat?

I don't think any of the farmers minded Snib, he was just one of these characters that, as I say, harmless and just plodded on the roads.

Jenny Jolly

There was Scotch Jimmy, Ah mind him especially, an Ah mind o auld Daisy Bell for she would have whipped ye. She used tae sing, she aye got drunk, she'd aye a guid dram, Daisy, and she never sung ocht else but 'Daisy, give me your answer do' and we yaist tae follow her a but she would have slapped ye, ye had tae get oot o the road quick wi Daisy. An she stayed in a cave, it wasnae much o a cave, at the Black Rocks, jist beside [unclear], it's no really a cave, it's a bit where she aye slept.

Cave dwellers seemed to be a phenomenon of the Machars coast between the two Wars, apparently the reverse of the peripatetic; Johnny Logie, one of the most famous, raised vegetables on the very margins of the beach, Greta Hawthorn recalls.

Greta Hawthorn

And then we had Johnny Logie that lived along in the cave off Cairndoon Bank, Cairndoon, and he went into hospital and I've got a photo of him lying in his bed wi his clothes still on and his bonnet. And he supplied

36. Snib Scott

37. Johnny Logie at the Hermit's Cave, Monreith.

The Grapes in the summer time wi vegetables, potatoes and carrots and turnips and he had a great garden and he had the water comin trickling down fae the rocks and he had a big sink, bath, and that was his water that he had tae cook wi and that. And he was spotlessly clean. And Mattie Lawrie had the grocers shop and he had a van that went round and he left Johnny Logie's messages or whatever at Cairndoon and he walked up the cliff side and got his messages every week.

In the exchange of favours between those giving and those expecting a gift of money or food at the door, though it may have been bad luck not to give, there were also repercussions if the allocated surplus were exceeded, as Jessie McLean remembers. Given the peripatetic family trade in rabbit skins, there was also no truck to be had with the travelling people who came round.

Jessie McLean

Ah can mind o the tramps fine. An ye were telt what was left oot o ocht, ye were to gie tae the tramps an ye got a guid lickin. And it was a richt guid lickin, sometimes ma granny yaised a belt. It made ye jump. If ye gien tramps mair than what they should hae got (laughter).
But you were allowed to give them something?
But ye aye gien them something and gien them a bowl o tea or a bowl o soup.
And do you remember any of the tinkers coming?
Oh the tinkers, aye, but we werenae allood tae mix wi them. They were daen us oot o business, ye see, they were wantin rabbit skins tae. So we never mixed wi them. Oh ma Granny Jolly was strict, she was a strict old lady.

A threat not only to other mobile businesses, the travelling people were, by virtue of their lack of settledness, seen as a threat within the settled community, though not by all.

Betty Stuart

And what about the gypsies or the travellers, do you remember them?
Aye, well there was some of them used tae come and they stayed in the green, the village– the green where the school used to be. They used tae and then another bit– they went up this way, up the entry and stayed in the field out here.
And were you allowed to talk to them?
Aye, they were a, some o them said they were frightened wi them but Ah

38. English gypsy children, encamped near Newton Stewart.

don't remember being frightened wi them, Ah think they– you were kinna threatened wi them if ye did onything wrong (laughter).

That's why they were frightened, perhaps.

But Ah remember them because they were in this field an aw. No this field, this field round here. … they ayeways come, aye. They had caravans an– the McMillans, the McMillans fae Stranraer, an they came wi their caravans … . Aye, the descendants o them. They were aye at– Maria, there was one o them called Maria McMillan and she, they came and they stayed an she was at the school for a while, Maria McMillan.

Molly: And what did they dae, then? Did they sell stuff?

Selt stuff.

Aye. Pots and pans and things?

Everything. Clothing tae. Everything.

People Who Left

Yet some, driven by poverty, did set their eyes on distant horizons: the port at the Isle of Whithorn, on to Liverpool and the distant Americas, were the points for a departure into the unknown.

John Wilson

Ma father was one of seven brothers and one sister. The brothers, all but two of them, emigrated to America and to– one of them went to Australia. Ma father, as I say, was in America, came back and then stayed here. … But he did say a funny thing because there was mass emigration at that time and he told us about. There was about seven or eight men sittin on the wall one night and one of the old men who lived in Glasserton village at the time came along and he went down this row o boys or men that were sittin there and he said, 'You'll go to Australia, you'll go to Canada, you'll got to New Zealand', they'd all go different places and ma father said it was unbelievable because, eventually, they all went where this old man had said they'd go. But that was the way it was. There was no work here so they had to go. Ah had an uncle in, Ah had two uncles in New York, Ah had one uncle in California and Ah had an uncle in Australia. Ma father had went abroad as well, that was five o them had gone, ma father came back and stayed, as I said, and he'd two other brothers who stayed and Ah had, there was a sister who lived at Mochrum.

People Who Came

'Incomer' is a highly charged word in the modern-day Machars, referring largely to the influx of those following the differential of property prices, but earlier influxes preceded them, following the movement of the trade in dairy and beef, sometimes literally, as incoming farmers herded their cattle on foot to new farms.

In common with many farming families, Tom McCreath's family came down from Ayrshire, first as tenants and then as owners of farms in the Machars. Many came following the opportunities in dairying, sometimes following their herds of cows on foot into the Machars. Robert Trotter's book, *Galloway Gossip*, shows that in the nineteenth century, the incomers were not viewed without prejudice by settled Gallovidians.

Tom McCreath

Well, both sides of the family had their roots in north Ayrshire, well, one in north Ayrshire, one in south Ayrshire, but my grandfather on Father's side was a Girvan man. He moved to Newton Stewart to be an apprentice ironmonger in Davidson's ironmongery and he then saw an opportunity to get a shop across the street, to set up on his own account. From there he took the rental or the tenancy of Skate farm and then Challoch farm so that his family of five sons and two daughters were brought up in farming as much as anything else and Grandfather had a very good ability in breeding Ayrshire cattle which, many of which were exported and he seemed to have a natural ability for that. On Mother's side, the family roots were really in Renfrewshire, where they were lawyers, cattle dealers, farmers, more or less, and they had friends in the Castle Douglas area so they moved down to Boreland of Balmaghie, my grandfather being the youngest of a family of 13, I think. In 1895 the tenancy of Broughton Mains farm which is in Whithorn parish, came up. The owners had gone bankrupt, sorry, the previous tenants had gone bankrupt and the tenancy was offered to the dairyman who had at least five sons, a very able man, a Mr Ramsay, but he felt the farm was just too big to take on as their first farm although, in time, he and his family bought up many of the best farms in Wigtownshire. But at that time, they were very uncertain times 'cause farming was in a depression so Grandfather got the opportunity to take it on, I think indebted to his mother-in-law, who was the daughter of, was the wife, rather, of a Clyde engineer. Father, being the youngest of the five McCreath brothers was in the First World War straight from agricultural college at Glasgow University, was in the trenches where his CO was Winston Churchill, in Belgium. I think he must have been slightly traumatised because after invalid leave for a short time he was posted to 1st Seaforths who went to Selonika and then up into Macedonia to face off the Bulgarians. But after the War he carried on his career in agricultural colleges and became principal of the East Anglian Institute. My mother's brother had also been in the War, in the Dardanelles and then in France, and again it had a massive effect on him and he rather fell out with his father, he couldn't settle, he was given the farm of Broughton Skeog but had to give it up because the money ran out so that my father married … and took over the tenancy of Broughton Mains.

Others came in as experts in the beef-rearing trade, such as Robert Galashan's father and uncle and then travelled across the Atlantic with the export trade to distant Argentina and Iowa.

Robert Galashan

Well, my father would come doon here from Aberdeenshire. He was born in Alford, and both him and elder brother come down. Brother was in Palmallet, who was called William Galashan. My father was John Galashan. And there would be, I think they would be about 16 and 17 when they came here. And they worked for a good number of years wi the Shorthorn cattle, that was their job. And then as time went on, I was born in Palmallet, and my father was shifted from Palmallet to Brownhill, and he looked after the Shorthorns there. And then after a few years I would be aboot three and a half or four, my father left and went to Mr Dron, at Cravictor at Crieff, and he took over the Shorthorns there. We were there for about, maybe two and a half to three years. My mother died when I was seven. So I came back to the uncle and aunt in Cruggleton. Uncle

39. Messenger the horse.

Thomas Buchanan, he was the stud groom for all the Clydesdales there. And that's how I came to be there. And as years went on I started in Palmallet. I wanted a job in a garage, and I wasn't, there's nothing available, and I worked for aboot four months wi the Shorthorns in Palmallet, and then I got a job up in the Universal Garage in Whithorn, and I worked there. Meantime, my father, he went to John Blackwood Hodge and Company at Baldoon, and he shifted from there tae Glasgow, and then he went to Northampton, completely out of the cattle altogether: engineering. But my uncle, he stayed, he looked after aboot 80 head o Clydesdales. And he foaled, he must have foaled aboot 40 in a year.

The beef trade at Cruggleton was such that it brought the breeders into contact with trade throughout the world and sent Robert Galashan's father to Argentina, as well as despatching young Robert to the shows round the countryside.

Robert Galashan

I stayed the night in the showground wi the cattleman, and what we did, it was like tents made right along in sections, and the bulls was there and the men had mattresses made wi straw, and you slept in there along wi the bulls.

Goodness. They wouldn't let you do that now.

They didnae bother, you know. And of course in the mornings they had tae be washed and groomed and made beautiful for the show! But Mr Marshall won a lot o honours and that. And then when he went tae sell a lot o his stock they went tae Perth bull sales in Hotham and the buyers, a lot o the foreign buyers bought them there. And then any of them that wanted to see more o the stock used to come doon, come over by plane fae different parts o the world and buy them. And then early on, my father used to go oot to the Argentine. There was so many Shorthorns would be taken out to the Argentine, and I think it's about September he would go, and they were put onto the boat and taken to Buenos Aires. And that was his responsibility fae the time he got on the boat to they were sold. And I'm quite sure there'd be a lot o Marshall's breeding still out in the Argentine.

So how did the bulls get up to Glasgow?

Oh, they would go by train.

Coming and Staying

While some moved out, others arrived: Italian immigrants came and stayed, becoming an institution in the town. Tina Soriani and Aldo Petrucci recount the arrival of their family in Whithorn.

Tina Soriani and Aldo Petrucci

TS: Right, okay, how they came to be in the south west of Scotland? Right. My mother and father got married in Italy in 1929, but my father had been in Scotland as a young boy of 15, he came to work for some far out relation in Auchinleck. And then he went back to Italy to serve in the First World War. And he eventually came back to Scotland, and we don't know exactly how he met my mother, but it must have been years later. They got married in 1929, and came back to Scotland, and worked for a while with the same relative in Auchinleck. And from there, my mother wasn't all that happy there, but they started, they went to stay with friends in Glasgow, and from there they rented a shop in Alva, Clackmannanshire, which they did, at that time, Italians would go away on holiday for a year, or six month, and hand the shop over to someone to run for them for while they were away. So they were there for a year, I was born there, and then from there they went to Motherwell where my– I have a brother that died, in '83, and Aldo were born there, in Motherwell. And they stayed there for about a year, a year and a half, I don't know exactly.

Anyway– and from there they went to Gatehouse, and rented a shop there. And it was while they were there that he wanted to move to Whithorn. Well, no he didn't want to move to Whithorn, they went to see a premises that was for sale in Whithorn and I believe it was called the Brunswick Inn, that had been closed for about two years. And my father decided to buy it. There was an Italian family there that had a shop. They had arranged, my father had arranged to buy this other friend's, well, he was an acquaintance, shop, but he gave him the sort of goodwill or something but bought the premises in the centre of the town. And that was in 1933, and from there – there were three of us at that time – and that's how we came to Whithorn. And there was a lot of work to do, it had been an inn, and derelict, empty for two years. And they put it together and slowly built up the business.

AP: I think it'd be an interesting fact that– I was going to say, that he bought it in 1933, was it, Tina? For £200, that's what the premises cost! And he must have spent quite a bit of money turning it into a cafe. And that was it, and they were there for, what, 33 years or something, Tina, 30 years?

TS: Yes, well, to '62.

And which part of Italy was that?

AP: It was about maybe 60 miles north of Florence, in the mountains. Very near a ski resort called Abbettoni, it's probably the best known area up there. But it was a little village just maybe about four or five miles south of that, still up in the mountains, beautiful area, we love even visiting it today. It's a lovely area.

And were there many families from there that came to Scotland, or were you quite unusual?

AP: A lot of them.

TS: There were actually three brothers, and one was in Creetown, one in Newton Stewart, and one in Catrine.

AP: But I read that something like 75 per cent of the Italians who came to Scotland came from a hill town called Barga. Which isn't far.

TS: In the Luca area.

AP: Yes, not very far from where my parents were born, their little village.

TS: In fact, in Barga, they have a fish and chip festival every year! But anyway, my father slowly– and you know, he used to say, I remember him saying that the tradesmen in Whithorn were very good, because he had no money left after buying the property, he'd spent his savings there, and they trusted him. … Mr. Kelly … that did all the work, it's still his work, the shelves in the shop and the floors, everything was his work. And when he paid his last payment he said, 'Mr Petrucci, you're a very honest man'. … Anyway, he slowly made alterations, slowly as he could afford them. When

we came to Whithorn there was no water. And I can remember them–
there must have been electricity came, I can remember still the gas things
hanging – well, not hanging, coming out of the wall when we arrived. And
I don't know when electricity came, because I can rememer my father
making ice cream. Ice used to come from Ayr, and he would pack a double
container with ice and salt, pack it, and he would turn it to make ice
cream. ... And he got an electric ice cream freezer, a big thing, similar to
what's there, now. But I can remember this freezer has a compressor that
has to be cooled by water, and he had a tank put up outside, a great big
tank, that had to be filled with water. And on a Sunday there was about
half a dozen young men that had a thing going, one filling the cans and
other ones carrying them to fill this tank with water, that went through to
cool the compressor of the freezer. And the same water, like the potato
peeler, the same tank of water, the peeler wasn't electric, but there was a
handle similar to what they are with the electric, exactly the same, only it
had to go with manually. And the water trickled into the peeler to wash
the skin away while he turned it.

I don't know when we started getting them from W. B. Anderson, but
anyway, they were mostly always local potatoes when we could get them.
But of course the potato harvests is finished, there used to be pickers from
Ireland come over, every summer. But they don't– they don't grow
potatoes now. I can remember a comment, because my sister was doing a
history of the family as well, and she went to– we were friendly with the
vet, who used to be the Whithorn, a Mr Edgar, Jim Edgar, they lived at
Monreith and they went to see him, and Olga was asking him about, can
he remember when my mother and father came to Whithorn? 'Oh,' he
says, 'you know I was just a lump of a boy, but I do remember an old man
saying,"Do you know who's bought the Brunswick? An Italian! He's
coming to fry chips, who the hell wants chips in Whithorn!" ' He was very
good, Mr Edgar. But anyway– so I don't know, yes, they had the brunt.
We have tae thank my parents for their way of living, they gained the
respect of the public.

...

AP: But that's all finished, because we grew up here, we married outsiders
from the Italian community, you know.
TS: And the thing is, when you come to a second and third generation
you find that their careers have all changed, they get educated and they go
into professions.

...

AP: It suited me fine because when I took over the farm it was a rented
farm on Stair Estates. And Stair Estates were so courageous, first of all, and
very kind, to give me a farm, I always say, because it could hae created a lot

of anger in some cases, and a lot of amusement in others, when someone with a name like Petrucci took over a local farm, you understand! There was something like, I believe, 70 offers for that farm, and I had been working on Stair Estates for experience, to gain experience, so they knew me pretty well. And when the time came this farm came up and I made an offer for it, and lo and behold I was successful in acquiring it, a rented farm! And I think it created quite a bit stir in the area. But I don't think I let them down, because now we've several farms.

Right, and is it dairying?

AP: Dairy farming, yes. And my son, my third son took over the farm, and he is very very good at his job. He has doubled the capacity for the cows, doubled the number of cows, and just about doubled the acreage as well. So altogether he's been very successful.

…

TS: So we ended up, there was five of us after, we had a sister and then a young brother in '42. And he was a mining engineer, and went– well, he went tae Africa first, to Rhodesia, Zambia, was it?

AP: And then, it was a time, there was a lot of upset, he didn't like what was happening over there, and he applied for a job in Canada. And got a mining engineer.

TS: My mother and father always spoke to us in Italian, and we answered back in English. First of all, sometimes, if we were wrong they would laugh, and we didn't want that. But mainly always if we had friends there, we wanted them to know, the other half of the conversation, you know.

Now, one thing I remember about my mother especially, we grew up with an inferiority complex, I think. I know my sister found that. I don't know if you found it. Maybe you went away to school and you grew out of it. Because my mother would say, I wanted to join the badminton, or the tennis, 'Oh, they don't want you there'. I says, 'What's wrong with me?'

AP: Oh, that surprises me, tae be honest, to hear ye saying that.

TS: No, we grew up with– and Olga felt the same inferiority complex and she used to say to Sandy, he was a psychiatrist, her husband, tried tae get it out of her, get her out of it.

AP: I remember, I wouldnae have said an inferiority, but I remember they encouraged us to be humble rather than, you know.

TS: Oh well, we were always humble, but we always thought everybody was better, that's what I mean. Everybody was better, was better than– I grew up with that.

AP: Probably because they considered us that wee bit different, you know.

TS: Well, yes, we were different! I always say we were a class of our own.

7

Here and Hereafter

Neither birth nor death were mystified by happening at a distance from the home nor mediated by medical systems which centred them elsewhere. Elders from within the community saw life into the world (and out of it).

Betty Stuart

When Ah lived in High Street, wi ma mother an that, we lived in High Street, ma Auntie Janet lived with us and I was in bed this night with ma granny, Ah slept with ma granny, an we heard a funny noise, like something squawing, an ma granny says, 'Whit's that noise, there?' 'Ah don't know' just at that ma mother came oot o the bedroom holding this squawy thing and put it in the couch and then she went, Ah says, 'There's another squaw' and she went back intae the bedroom and came back wi another one. That was the twins, ma Auntie Janet had had twins, and of course Ah was only nine then an Ah didnae know much aboot them. So they were put on the couch and ma granny said, 'What's gaun on here?' Ah says, 'Ah don't know, there's two things lying an they're makin funny noises (laughter) Ah don't know, they're on the couch'. Ma granny didnae even know that there was going to be because she was near her end by then. But that was it.

Was there a midwife or was it just?

No, no, it was ma mother ... but the nurse did come in. Nurse Robinson, she used tae live– she was on the go then, she used tae come in and seen tae them after they were born but they were put on the couch, one at the top and one at the bottom. And I got oot o the bed an Ah shouted tae ma granny, 'Oh, there's two wee babbies, Ah don't know where they come from but there's two wee babbies' (laughter) .... And then if somebody was gonnae have a baby, there wis an old lady called Mrs Steele, that's Sandra in the shop's great-granny, Ah think, and there was old Mrs Boyce and there was another one, I cannea mind who the other one was, three in all. Oh aye, Nannie, Tootie, and Tootie Dodds and, when onyone was havin a baby, that was the midwives that seen tae them, they didnae hae doctors or nurses, they three auld folk brocht they baby intae the world, aye.

Guy Brown

And was it often home births, did people go into hospital in your father's day?
Very few in my father's day. Forceps deliveries were at home, a doctor from the neighbouring practice would come and give an anaesthetic, well – I was a forceps delivery – along the road. And my father actually delivered me. It was Dr Duguid from Whithorn who was coming to do the delivery but things went wrong and my father was a dab hand with forceps and Dr McDougall didn't do terribly many. Father had been in Bellshill before he bought the practice here, and in the miners' rows and rickets and one thing and another, he was doing abnormal deliveries, at least one a day, in the miners' rows, so he had a good notion of what to, what to do and so they changed roles. Dr McDougall gave the anaesthetic and he turned and pulled me out.

Betty Stuart remembered a multiplicity of small schools which existed before the unifying force of the Education Authority brought all children under one roof: Betty remembers one of the schools at the Top of the Town which had existed from the nineteenth century.

Betty Stuart

There was a school up here, like, Bell's school. At the beginning o Glasserton Street, whaur there– remember there used tae be a green? Well, that was Bell's school. There used tae be a green up there. Mrs McDowell lived in it, ye'll no remember them.
But you don't remember when it was actually active as a school, do you?
Oh no, it was Bell's school, it was still there, if you know what I mean, but I don't think it was a school then …. . Ah never was at it, no, oh no, I was at Whithorn. It was still there and used for something else.

A consequence of the populousness of the countryside was the existence of rural schools, even in what are now sparsely populated and remote areas of the Machars; like the smiddies, they were the heart of all small communities.

John Wilson

Ah can remember Ah was taught at the Knock School at Monreith. In fact

Ah can remember occasionally we, I can remember once Mr Lambert who was a teacher at Glasserton School came up, Ah think maybe oor teacher was ill or something, he came in.

So it was there in your childhood?

But he was really old, he was a really old man at that time. But, no, Glasserton School was, well ma father was educated at Glasserton School and then at Whithorn.

So you were at the Knock School, that presumably had the children in from Monreith village, did it?

Yes, we were just at the outer edge of the catchment area from Monreith up to about three miles along Craiglemine was [unclear] farm which was about three miles the other way. That was the sort of catchment area, yea, there was about– there'd be about 20 of us at it possibly, about 20, 25. Some rough people, some rough, rough people. There was one lot Ah can remember still runnin aboot in bare feet.

And was there one teacher, two teachers?

It was a one-teacher school, one teacher. It had been a two-teacher school up until maybe 1930 but it was one teacher.

There'd be a lot of children from cottages and so on round about?

Yea, well this is the thing, you see, because there wis so many people. One farm, Glasserton Mains for example, employed about eleven men. So every farm had six, seven people workin about the place. It's so different now where the whole estate is ran by three men where– there was always, there was always plenty of kids around.

Jock McMaster

And was the discipline quite strict at the Knock?

Oh yes, oh yes, Mrs McCracken, that she was, was very strict, aye. Although fair, she was quite fair. … The wee ones sat at the front, Ah can remember, and as ye got older ye moved further back. You probably needed less attention as time went on. But Ah look back and remember we spent most of the time in the wood, digging leaf mould and potting plants and no electricity of course, and lighting Tilley lamps in the afternoon and pulling them up on a rope tae light the classroom. No central heating, if ye were cold she sent us outside (laughs) to run round the playground (laughter).

She didn't have a fireplace?

She had a fireplace, yea, she had a fire beside her with a– one of these enclosed– like a wood burning stove type thing that burned coke, but that kept her warm, it didn't keep us warm.

And do you remember people economising on the use of their shoes? I've heard of people who stowed pairs of shoes close to the school or who didn't have them at all in the summer.

> Right, right, Ah can, no we didn't go barefoot, no, we actually kept– we kept shoes at the school because we walked across the field, so we wore wellies or we wore boots and we kept a pair of lighter shoes, Ah think they probably, Ah think we jist called them gym shoes, plimsoll things at school to put on. But tackety boots were the things that the boys wore, Ah remember going to school wi tackety boots on and being very, unpopular because there was a slide in the winter time in the play-green with the ice and the guys slid on it wi their rubber soled shoes were fine but tackety boot, oh ho, ye ripped up the ice and spoiled the slide so Ah was banished, Ah was banished from that.

For country children, walking miles to school, and back, unaccompanied, was a commonplace of childhood. Country children, who couldn't return home for lunch like Betty Stuart, had to make do with packed lunches or something bought at the school – or better still at the bakery and cafe – as there was no generalised provision of school lunches.

Greta Hawthorn

> My sister was born there [Glasserton] as well, she was older than me. We just played about in the woods and gathered sticks in the summertime to keep the winter fuel going. Then we– the school, we walked to the school which was about three miles and in the winter time we had wur school bag, wur gas mask and we had another shopping bag and we brought two logs in it to keep the fires burning at the school. And if your clothes was wet they were put round the guard at the fire and the smell that came off them was something atrocious and yer shoes were put there to dry and you had sandshoes left in the school, to keep your feet dry.

Did every child bring fuel to the school?

> Not the town ones just the country ones. Because they were big log fires, they were put on at three o'clock in the morning, the janitor and his wife were there and they did the cleaning.

So how old were you when you were doing that? When you were walking in?

> Five. Five year old. We started the school at five, sometimes you could hang tae six but I think wi us being in the country we were ready for the school at five, to get company. My sister and I used tae walk and sometimes we used to get a cousin on the road but usually her mother took her on the back of the bike but we hadnae bikes in those days but we did eventually get old bikes and rigged them up and came to school that way. The teachers were very nice, we took a packed lunch, whit was a jeely piece, and we had

friends in the town and we walked up to them and they gave us tea at lunchtime. There was hot cocoa if you wanted it but we just went and had wur tea and then we had a heat at the fire and then we got cold again on the way back down. We had, we got out the school at four o'clock but in the winter time we got out at three o'clock so that we were home before it was dark because there was double summertime and double wintertime in those days. It was earlier dark for the people walking home.

...

Oh yes, all the farm cottages were all occupied and there was a lot of children went to Glasserton School, we went to Whithorn School, but there was a lot of them went tae Glasserton School. But when Glasserton School closed they put a bus on so I was the lucky one that was still at the school and we got the bus at the Glasserton Lodge and we got in, we had that. But other than that we had bikes at the finish up.

Jenny Jolly

... ye didnae get school meals in thae days, ye could hae got milk in the morning, eleven o'clock or something, a little bottle o milk, but it was twopence ha'penny a week if ye had the twopence ha'penny. And Denton's the bakers used tae hae thae big, lovely buns they were, just don't know if the weans would eat them nooadays. They werenae rich, rich buns but they'd fruit in them, raisins an aw – Paris buns some ca'd them and different names, they were big buns, they were a penny each and we sometimes used tae get a penny, ma mother had it for sweets and we used tae buy this big bun instead o the sweets.

So how old were you when you were walking in to school?

I wasnae very auld, don't know. Come ower in the early '30s, so I'd be what? Maybe seven or eight or something, maybe seven. Six or seven.

Aldo Petrucci and Tina Soriani, whose parents owned the Central Cafe, also recall the delicacy of the French bun, filled with ice cream.

Tina Soriani and Aldo Petrucci

TS: There was no school meals. They brought pieces with them, they brought sandwiches with them, a snack. No, we always went home. So did all the local children, went home at lunchtime.

AP: And a lot of them during the lunch break used to come down to the shop and a common question was, 'What have ye got for a penny?' What have ye got for a penny! And we would have these big toffees or something, we'd always have something for a penny, you know. I remember one boy,

> used tae go to Denton's for a French loaf–
> **TS**: No, no, a cookie!
> **AP**: No, it was a French loaf, a whole loaf. And he'd spread it with his hands, he says, 'Put an ice cream in there!' In the middle of this French loaf!

At some point, in Betty Stuart's recollection, there was provision for the country children.

Betty Stuart

> But there was later on, no much langer either because Bobby Martin [the janitor] and his wife, they made soup, they had the soup kitchen and they got– some o the– for the country yins, they got their soup, for it was a penny.

Discipline for children appears to us as brutal and basic, but applied within a culture where there was generalised acceptance of physical discipline, where the lack of enshrinement of rights in law went hand-in-hand with the proliferation of children.

Betty Stuart

> But our school, it would be more strict in my day than what it is now. You had tae watch yer. It was Miss McHarg that was the teacher when ye went on the primary one. Ye stood up whenever. And then Ah can remember ye aye had tae watch ye didnae sit doon before yer time. Ye stood up and waited until the prayer an that was past, ye aye prayed every morning.
> ...
> Well, the infants' class was packed, really. There was two entrances, ye went in the door, then you went through the next door, primary one and primary two, for the infants, so a lot. It was always full, the school was always full and then there was primary three, Miss Henderson's, great Miss Henderson, she was a terror o a body. She wisnae long oot. She gave ye the strap and when ye went intae the playground you could play until the bell rung and as soon as, as soon as the bell – it was Bobby ringing it, Bobby Martin – ye had tae stop where you were and then you walked in line. I can see them doing it noo, get intae lines, ye werenae allowed tae move until they telt ye tae go into the school. It was very strict.

Greta Hawthorn

> Oh yes, ye had tae bow to the teachers when ye met them on the street and

the boys had to salute. And they were 'Miss', they werenae by first names. But they were very good, there was a lot of people well educated. It was a senior secondary and then you went on tae the Ewart, and we've had doctors and dentists and solicitors, Alec Haswell was one of them and Johnny Stewart's son, he used to make up the exams for the Ewart, when he was at the Ewart himself, he used tae make up the exams for some o them at the Ewart. But ye respected yer teachers.

Guy Brown

And again there were– ours was a big year. We were very, in going to secondary education, we were very lucky to have a retired teacher brought out because of the War. And we had him, our class had him, for three years, primaries one, two and three, that would be three, four and five nowadays. And he, well, the first thing ye did when ye went in was mental arithmetic but there were certain people that he reckoned should be told once, they should be told how to do some new project, arithmetic or what, and if they made a mistake they were corrected once, if they made the same mistake twice, it was the belt. And the others were two, got maybe two or three warnings and some of them got four or five warnings. And the girls didn't get belted, it was just the boys. So, and then things like spelling which you never bothered to learn, mistake there and it was– I think you were allowed one mistake after that. So I was belted every day for about three years which I never, ever mentioned at home (laughter). But our class, when we sat the eleven-plus, more than half passed and went on to the Ewart and I'm sure it was purely due to this old teacher. We liked him, we weren't, we didn't have anything against him, we felt we had been doing wrong and we deserved to get it and we were really ready for the eleven-plus by the time– two years before it was due, because he kept on giving us something new once we had mastered something we wanted, he didn't bother with schedules he just did what was coming along next and he was. I think I've a lot to thank him for (laughs).

John Scoular

I have to say that I look back on the primary education in this part of the world, in Whithorn school, a lot of them– teachers were old dears who probably whose men had been killed in the First World War and continued to be– but they could teach and no child, no matter how backward they were left the school without the basic abilities to read, write and count. … They got the basics out of education and the disciplines of the school and the effect of that in the community was vast. If you had gone, then, back and told your parents that you'd got the strap or a telling off for something it would be more than likely you would get the same again from your parents right across the board. And these people could teach. I think we've over-refined our attitudes to education, if you don't have the basics you can't get anywhere.

Marion Sunderland's mother came as a teacher to the Isle of Whithorn School; the teacher like the minister, a figure with a distinct place (and occupationally tied house) within the community.

Marion Sunderland

She'd be about 30, I think, approximately. One of the reasons for wanting to live in the country was my father had been in a prisoner of war camp in Germany for four years, he had been on an oil tanker captured in the Indian Ocean, by the *Graf Spee*, I think, so she thought if she moved to the country there would be less rationing, which is true. I mean, the eggs weren't rationed around here I don't think. So that was why they came. And she was head teacher, then, of the Isle of Whithorn School until it closed. My father started a garage, a small car repair business behind the sailing club, but I don't think he was a very good businessman. So he went back to sea as a chief engineer in the Merchant Navy. And did that until he was too old to work. So that was the story of how we came.

...

I was born in what was called the schoolhouse, opposite the church. And that actually belonged to the Education Authority, that house. It was a strange house, because if you look at it, anyone who's in the village, it looks as if it's been one house. So actually the two houses share the middle window. So you could talk to your neighbour by looking sideways through the middle window, there was a gap!

...

The Isle of Whithorn School, originally children just went there until they left school, I think, I believe my mother taught 14-year-old girls when she first went there. I seem to remember her saying she had a battle with the girls, because there were dances in the village on a Friday night, would come to school with their hair in curlers! Getting ready for the village dance. Because there were a lot of Polish men living at Burrowhead, my mother in fact had an extra job teaching them English, so she was teaching English as a foreign language too. The Polish, I don't know what they were, soldiers, airmen, at Burrowhead.

...

There was the infant room, and the big room, and that was it. In the middle we had the dinner room, and by the time I was leaving primary school I think we were actually getting indoor toilets for the children. And it was a two-teacher school, I suppose, until Mrs McEwan died, Mrs McEwan who taught me and the infants was an aunt of John McWilliam, her brother was John's father, her brother Methven, whom I never really knew because he'd died in the early 1950s. Methven McWilliam was Etta's brother. But Etta I think was divorced, and had no family, and she came back to teach in the Isle with my mother, and I seem to remember. It was quite a big school, I think there were about eleven or twelve in my primary seven, much bigger than it ended up as, but there were bigger families, of course. Mrs Young had about eleven or twelve children. There were other big families as well. That's the one I particularly remember.

...

So, what do you remember of the curriculum when you started school? You can obviously compare it with the modern curriculum, so–?

Oh, there were none of the folderols! It was very very much reading, writing, arithmetic, very much so. Primary six was geared to passing the intelligence test. The intelligence test was this, I think you only sat it in primary six, I'm no quite sure, might have been primary seven. But I remember all these codes you had to break, and work out, and things like that. And dreadful things that you just learnt, like 'butterfly is to wings as fish is to – I don't know – fins'. Very useful! But the days when I was at primary school, that was in the days before topics or projects or anything, or environmental studies. That's not to say we didn't do any, I mean, on good days you were on the beach. It was a great school to be at primary school, it was wonderful. You think of where it was, you know, on the shore, right there on the shore. It was absolutely fantastic. Because of course you were allowed to go on the shore. You weren't supposed to go on the shore on high tides, because there's what we call the Island, that's the back shore, or the Stinking Port or whatever you care to call it. And on high tides you could be marooned on the island until the tide went out, unless you cared to get rather wet. So you weren't supposed to go on the island in high tides, but my brother, who was four years older than me, thought that was a great way of not going to school in the afternoon, if you could manage to get marooned on the island. My mother would just tell him to wade, paddle, get wet, get back here!

...

There was a lot of– there was physical punishment, yes, and it was pretty awful. I'm not saying the children were punished unfairly, but the method of punishment. I never agreed with corporal punishment. I think it's wrong. How can you possibly teach children to be kind and caring, and yet you hit them? No. Having said that, when I was a young teacher, it was what you did, and I did use the belt a couple of times. But I really did not like doing it, so when I was teaching primary seven in Whithorn, and there was a junior secondary school there, I used to get out of it by sending pupils to the deputy headmaster, not the headmaster, who, at the time– the headmaster at the time really probably should have retired. But we had one or two deputy head teachers at Whithorn Junior Secondary who were good, fair men actually, but didnae seem to mind the corporal punishment the way I did.

The driving necessity of assisting the family budget decided many career choices. The distance between childhood and adulthood appears short to us, because responsibility for contributing to the family budget fell earlier, even though parental authority deferred until later the self-determination which we would regard as definitive of adulthood.

Cathy Miller

No, when Ah sat the Control for tae go to the Douglas Ewart, Ah failed by one point and the headmaster, Mr Smith, and the gym teacher and a teacher from the Douglas Ewart came out to the farm to speak to ma mum and dad. And they said that they very much wished that Ah would go on to the Douglas Ewart and become a gym teacher. Because I was top of the class at Whithorn, Mum and Dad both said no, Ah was comin home. So that was ma future decided.
And did you mind that or where you quite happy?
No, Ah was quite happy, either way I would have been happy. Ah loved the farm and Ah loved the work, it was hard work cause latterly Ah was doing 84 hours a week between the milk run, and Ah was the one that brought the pigs into the world, you would maybe pig a sow from midnight to three in the morning, come in and scrub and washed and changed, get two chairs together and lie on them till about half past five, up and away.

In Sickness and Health

Prior to the advent of the National Health Service, treatments were ad hoc and visits by the doctor deferred until absolutely pressing, according to what could be afforded – and then supplemented by traditional remedies supplied by elders in the community. The visibility of the body was only skin-deep and confined to what was palpable – through the skill and touch of the doctor, as Dr. Brown's account reveals. Just as the sources of payment for medicine became less ascribable and more invisible, gradually, so it seems did the sources of pain and the nature of cures.

Jenny Jolly

>Oh ye had tae pay, aye.

Would you pay them after you saw them?

>I expect it wid be, I tell ye, folk– ye didnae gaun endlessly tae the doctor in my days. You got treated at home. Gey often ye got a dose of castor oil or something.

So was there anybody who was known for curing?

>Oh aye, all the auld folk.

You would go to some elderly person and ask for advice?

>Uh-huh, oh God, aye. And Ah used tae gaun tae an auld wuman next door tae us, auld Janet Dodds, and she yist tae send me up tae The Calcutta wi a jug, for a jug o the beer oot o the barrels jist, ye ken, straight fae the barrel, and when Ah come doon, handed it tae her, then she pit some in a wee cup and gave me a drink tae. Ah wouldnae drink beer noo but Ah drunk it then wi the auld wuman, thought this was great.

Betty Stuart

>Ye paid the doctors three and sixpence for a call. Ah can aye remember that, three and sixpence. When Dr McWhirter and Dr McDougall come tae visit ye, maybe be in for ten minutes, three and sixpence, if ye didnae pay it then ye got a bill, for some reason or other, for Ah can remember gaun and payin the bill, it was three and sixpence and the nurse, there was a nurse, District Nurse, Nurse Robertson, she went to the school and that, she wisnae liked, she was so strict. Oh, she was very, very strict. She went to the school twice a week and went through the hair and that and one thing and another. But the doctors were aw right, they were really very good. Dr McWhirter, he lived down where, right away doon where the vet is; Dr McDougall lived in the middle just doon by the Port Mooth, on the left hand side, and they were very good, the doctors.
>
>…
>
>And everyone helped each other. If anybody maybe was ill ye just automatically went. If someone was having a baby these other auld folk went. So there wisnae sae many … although we had guid doctors, there was Dr McWhirter and Dr McDougall, when Ah was young. And they were good doctors. They had so many patients each, you see, some went to Dr McDougall and some went to Dr McWhirter, they kinna– between them.

Medical payments were episodic and surgeries were thoroughly domestic, as Dr Guy Brown recounts.

Guy Brown

> Well, I was born into a medical household, four doors along. Father was GP here before me so that it was in the blood, you couldn't help it getting into the blood. He had, for years after the War, he had an assistant for– almost living in for probably about ten years, different assistants, and of course they'd both go to do their calls and discussed them over meals, what had happened that morning and who was what and why and I had– I knew everything that was going on but I couldn't say this, say a word, say a word about it, never even thought of saying a word about it. And then went off to college and university in Glasgow. After doing house jobs there, returned to join my father, as his assistant, and his health was failing so. He was with me about three years, doing less and less and less and I was doing more and more and more and then he retired. Although it was 24 hours a day, seven days a week, I joined with Whithorn. There were originally two practices in Whithorn, they had joined previously when old Dr McDougall retired and we– the patients were split so we– it was still in the private days, it wasn't Health Service, the patients were split, a lot came to Port William, most stayed in Whithorn and so we had patients in Whithorn and Garlieston and Isle of Whithorn and as far up the shore as the Crow's Nest so it was quite a– and into Kirkinner so quite a wide area. It was good fun though, I enjoyed it thoroughly.
>
> ...
>
> Well, my father came in 1936 and he had bought the practice and I've came across a letter, not terribly long ago, saying that the carpet in the consulting room didn't go with the sale, it would be removed with the fittings. And there was no electricity here at that time, it was oil lamps, didn't come till later in '36, the electricity come through. So, yes, he sent out bills once a quarter, when my mother needed some money, and even after the Heath Service came in he had a number of private patients that stayed private.
>
> The work was different then, he had three surgeries a day here: 9.00 till 10.00; lunchtime, I think, 1.30 till 2.00, and 6.30 to 7.30 in the evening, except Sundays and his half-day which was a Thursday and I don't know if he did a morning surgery on his half-day or not. Looking at the old letterheads he might not have done, there might have been no surgeries on the Thursday.
>
> ...
>
> There was a Panel, there was a Panel who would pay for patients who couldn't pay and there were a number of panel patients which the accounts

had to be sent in, probably monthly, I don't know, quarterly, and it involved all the doctors in Wigtownshire. And the Panel paid the doctor but no, a lot of people worked on the farms in the cottages and they weren't very well paid and if there was a lot of attendance in some of the cot houses the cost of the visit to the farmer was increased to help pay for that.

And was it, do you know how much your father charged? Was it, did it vary with what he was doing?

Well, I think the practice, he bought it for, I think for about £1000, I'm not sure what he charged but I do know that just prior to the Health Service, it was two and six for an extraction of a tooth without anaesthetic, five shillings with (laughter). … And the ones that had it without were either the very butch, tough nuts or the terribly terrified who wanted it out and away. But when the Health Service started the dentist did it all, the doctors stopped doing it. But, up until then the doctors pulled a large proportion of the teeth. There was no fillings it was only extractions, but he pulled quite a large number, in fact there were two full sets of tooth forceps in the surgery until I took them up to the museum at Crichton. I never pulled a tooth, I was asked once or twice and I chickened out (laughs).

But it said on every forcep what tooth it was for so you could pick the right forcep. And in the surgery I was a bit of a hoarder, I didn't like flinging things out. And there were trephines for boring into the skull, lots of guillotines for removing tonsils and all sorts of things.

Right, right. It sound as if there were quite a bit more surgery going on as well as prescribing medicine.

Well we did a lot, all the casualty was done unless it was a broken bone, very few people went to hospital. Even in my day, in earlier days, he's often going to get a consultant down to see the patient at home. Consultants were allowed to do so many home visits. And they would come and see people at home, they got paid extra for it, and you could– kept a lot of your medical patients in bed at home because there was nothing more to be gained by going to hospital. Surgical patients went to hospital, the Garrick at Stranraer who had a surgeon up until quite recently. The rest to Dumfries or Glasgow. Port William went Ayr and Glasgow, Whithorn went Dumfries. Largely, we sent patients to Dumfries as well but a lot of the Ayr consultants came down to the Garrick and it was handy for people going from here to go up the coast than inland. Previous to that they sometimes called a doctor from Whithorn, Wigtown, Stranraer, but the first resident doctors were, I think, 1830 something, 1840? And the Selby senior came in about 1870s and he had a pony and trap, I have several photographs.

…

Were there any diseases particularly associated with say, working conditions on farms, that you remember or poor housing conditions?

There must have been a lot of, there were a lot of chest infections. But a lot of them on the farms were, they were mainly dairy farms and they got their milk and they got their potatoes and they cultivated their garden, beef was probably the short, meat was probably the short straw.

And in terms of medicines that must have changed a great deal.

Out of this world (laughter). My father dispensed, I dispensed too, but he dispensed and the traveller would come round and he would send in an order and a tea chest would arrive, maybe two tea chests, with mixture A and mixture B, mixture C, and you had to add so many grains of this and so many drams of that and so many grains of something else and now everything is ready prepared. You just open– in fact it came in Winchesters for us, for me, but they all come in ready prepared bottles, there's 200ml or 300ml, off the shelf. I had one stomach mixture which was, it was a bicarbonate but not baking soda, it was a very light one and you weighed out the powder and it more– the pile of powder was greater than the size of the bottle it was going into. And you gradually popped all this, got it into the bottle, a little water to dissolve it and then ye did an anti-spasmodic which had a nice smell and a greenish colour and ye got that in and of course the patient was standing there waiting for it while you were making it up in the consultation, because they always went away with what they required, and it worked wonders. I think it was seeing all this disappearing into the bottle and they'd be– they were back for repeats but they didn't get too many repeats for it took far too long, but it cured a terrific number of patients right off. One bottle of it was fine and I think it was the watching it being made up. But then they started coming in bottles of, if it was tablets 10s, 500s, 1000s and you sorted these out but nowadays everything comes in packets of 28 or a course. You don't always, sometimes you want longer than an ordinary course, you've got to burst packets but it's much– and there are so more drugs now, there are effective drugs now, while the drugs were– you had analgesics and sedatives and stomach mixtures but there wasn't an awful lot more.

And have you noticed any change in life expectancy in this area over all your time?

Yes, it has increased, there are more elderly people and there are going to be more still. Because the more– many more people are going to hospital because there's more they can do in hospital now. They can go and get all their tests done and set up a course of treatment. We used to do it all from here by sending things off in the post, samples off in the post, bloods. and took them one day and you posted them that morning and they got them the next day at the hospital and then they analysed them and two or three days later you got the result back. Now you get the result back the same day. But there are so many tests now that can be done, it was all hands, and hands, eyes and ears previously. What you could feel, see and hear.

…

And notes are– that's an enormous difference, medical notes. I looked at my father's notes and it would be '2nd of January, right-sided pneumonia; 3rd of March, back to work'. Now if somebody had pneumonia you would probably, they would probably go to hospital but if they hadn't gone to hospital, even if they did go to hospital you've got about a page of notes to write up everything about them in case somebody, some lawyer wants to see them if. And if you haven't written them down, you haven't done them, you may well have done them.

…

Before the, in my father's day, he had a branch surgery in Whithorn which bounced around Whithorn, it was McEwan the grocer's shop and then it was down at the creamery, was it Mrs Green, Ah think it was, and latterly, in [unclear] next to the chemist, which is now part of the chemists. And it was– we had an afternoon surgery there for the Whithorn people about three, four afternoons a week. I liked it when it was Whithorn monthly holiday because sometimes nobody came and I could put up my feet and have a read or a doze. And it was quite handy because the chemist was next door and you could always get prescriptions, it was John Baxter then, from John. So I accompanied him, sometimes out in the car with him, listen to the radio while he was at his surgery and then it was as a workplace and then we joined up, as I said, when the last of my friends had emigrated, I joined up with Frank Findlay and Norman Robertson and it's been that way since.

So was your father's surgery just the room in these houses, just a room with a desk?
Initially it was his front room, you went to the house and it was the front room on the left and the back room on the left was the dispensary, it was a really dark hole, and people waited in the hall. There was a box seat in the hall and a coat rack beside it, and it would hold about two people, and the overflow sat on the stairs and apparently I occasionally gave them an impromptu concert from the landing when they were waiting, as a child. But there was one night they had– ma father had finished his surgery, nobody sitting, no one to be seen and he come through to the kitchen where ma mother was and after half an hour or so they moved up to the sitting room was up the stairs, they moved to the sitting room and as they were coming through the hall they saw a pair of feet sticking out from beneath the coat stand and on moving the coats they found that somebody had fallen asleep waiting and just slumped to the side and the coats and fallen over them (laughter). So the patient was attended to and they went up for a seat. Somewhere about the end of the War he– there

was a large room to the right-hand side of the front door and he divided that into a surgery and a waiting room and knocked a cupboard door out to make a doorway into the, which was the, where the garage was, into the garage entrance, so that the patients could come in that way. Prior to that they'd come and rung the doorbell and then shown in by the maid that they could come in. But it was all wartime material and the soundproofing wasn't particularly good and the people with the most intimate complaints wanted to shout at the top of their voices. You're trying to 'sh' (laughter) and you could often hear what was happening in the – when a stir, when something more urgent was being brought into the waiting room.

...

It was functional at the time but it was behind the times, the consulting room was lined with bottles and shelves for medicines and most people came for their repeat prescription and consultation so they got their repeat prescription at the time and that's probably most of the surgery.

...

We dispensed for all our patients except we couldn't dispense for Whithorn, I think if somebody lived within three miles of a chemist you had to give them prescriptions. So there was John Baxter and Ross, was it John Ross, on the other side of the road, down opposite the bank. And then the dispensing was, there were two ways of paying for dispensing, you could take a capitation fee of– I don't know, a very small amount, a couple of pounds, or something like that, per patient, and you didn't write, you didn't write 'scripts so they weren't priced and if you wanted anything special we had to apply in writing to Kirkcudbright where the, we were, there was. Galloway and Dumfries were two Health Offices and we were– and you had to apply in writing to get permission to prescribe the new tranquillisers and antibiotics and things like that, you got a line saying you could give them to this patient, usually had given them to this patient before, but you wouldn't be paid for them till you got the line, so that was the dispensing. He could have made a lot more money and a much better pension if he had written a prescription of everything but he couldn't be bothered with paperwork, in any shape or form, and we had to send in a return once a quarter of the number of people we had given immunisations to, the number of people who had had babies, and the number of holidaymakers we had seen, and I remember on one occasion getting a phone call from the – what would later become the Health Board – saying, 'You haven't sent in your return this quarter, what have you got?' I said, 'Dear knows.'

'How many confinements?'

'Oh maybe about four, five.'

'The same as last time?'

'Aye, well, maybe one less or something.'
'Right, and holidaymakers?'
'It wasn't a good quarter for holidaymakers, they'd be down, about the same as last year.'
'Right, and immunisations?'
'Oh, just the usual run.'
'Well, we'll pay you on that,' they said, 'and make sure you have it in next time and we'll balance it up'.

Cleanliness and Godliness

Going to church regulated the rhythm of the week and, in its calendar, cleanliness was next to godliness, as Saturday was the day for bathing and Sunday was clearly differentiated from the working week not only by church attendance, but by its clothing and its holiday atmosphere.

Betty Stuart

> Sunday was the bath day, no it was Saturday for the sake o the Sunday School in the morning. It was jist yin o they, jist an ordinary bath we had, zinc bath, one at a time.
>
> *And did you have a Sunday best?*
>
> Oh yes, and a hat. Aye, Ah can see it yet, a straw hat, and ye'd flooers alang it (laughter) and a bits hingin doon, aye. Oh, we wisnae allowed tae go to the Sunday School withoot yer hat, no in these days. Ah had one, Ah don't think ah'd hae two. A straw hat wi wee flowers and wee bits hinging doon.

Sunday was a day for congregation, in the spiritual but also in the social sense, when people who did not meet elsewhere could socialise. John Scoular's father was minister of Glasserton.

John Scoular

> I have to say that when my father was ministering to this big parish, the turnout in the churches on a Sunday was very considerable but it was part of— it was one of the few— Sunday meeting— were one of the few occasions when everybody could meet and chat and they drove in or they cycled in and what have you. And it would be quite— they'd hang about in the churchyard afterwards simply catching up on the week's events but it was a very different world. You forget how much change has been. And you think also that change before that was much slower.

40. St John Street United Free Church, Whithorn.

Established and Free

Whithorn, like other parishes in Scotland, had suffered the fragmentation of the Presbyterian Church, and at one time had a Church of Scotland, Secession Church, Cameronian Meeting House, Free Church, and ultimately a Roman Catholic Church, as well as meeting houses. The churches orchestrated not only spiritual life, but also social care, social life and poor relief.

John Scoular

> That's right. Three ministers, the cathedral church in Whithorn, Harry Law who was quite a famous preacher in the Doric. And a minister in Isle of Whithorn and Glasserton. And, as always, acrimony became involved when the various charges had to be united. It nearly broke my father and mother's heart, there wasn't a degree of Christian fellowship really that you got families split over– nobody would face up to the necessity of. Don't forget, when my father was in Glasserton he was holding services also on a fortnightly basis in Monreith and in the school at Ravenstone, as well as Glasserton Church, itself.

Betty Stuart

> We were members o the Free Kirk in St John Street. We went to the Kirk in the morning, Sunday School in the afternoon and then evening service.

And was that quite a large congregation?

Oh, yes it was, aye. And he was the Reverend Neil Campbell, always remember that, we had great times and we were takin to the shore and that for the picnics an that and burying him in the sand an aw they kinna things. They were lovely folk, his wife and that, and very good to the ones that hadnae very much and they had kinna things for. Ah don't know what they cawd it, wee kinna meetins and they got food and that, extra food and that. Also there was a church down on the road up to Vicky Wilson's. Right across fae there, that was the church.

And that was still working was it?

Oh yes, we went tae it. It was gaun.

That's known as the Cameronian Meeting House? And did they have a reasonable congregation?

Yes, but funnily enough, a lot– I'll tell ye what used tae come, the Salvation Army, an when they came they stayed there. Aye, it was a– I don't know who the minister wis but Ah remember going to it. We went tae aw the churches, there was one in Glasserton Street too, a meeting, a religious meeting place in Glasserton Street. Aye, it was in the– the garage used to be like there, Caledonian Garage, the hall was across there. We went at nights tae it. It was mostly at nights it was on.

So, on a Sunday, would you spend quite a lot of your time going to churches or meetings?

Well, when Ah was young Ah had tae because ma granny was jist church on the brain, I think. But they were very good tae ye and if they thought ye needed something, as Ah say, they had meetins, in a kina, doon there where the garage wis there was a meetin– there was a wee bit off the church I think. Ye went intae there and they got and then there was a place. Ye got lines or something, I don't know what they were called, but you went to this place, anyway, and they gave you a line and ye went– took this line and you got clothing.

Right. And did the ministers come out if you were sick, did they come and visit?

Yes, the ministers, they would, especially Mr Campbell, that was fae the Free Kirk, that's where he wis. He married ma– he christened me, Ah wis gonna say married me, he christened me, Mr Campbell. Ah've got it up the stair.

Tom McCreath

It wasn't a severe doctrine. Newton Stewart was completely divided between the Free Church and the parish church and each had their own lawyers, A. B. & A. Matthews for the parish church people and McCormick and Nicolson for the Free Church people. But that didn't apply here and Mother decided to go, with Father's persuasion, to the parish church for family unity but no, in my time, there was no animosity as there was in Newton Stewart.

In nearby Glasserton, the estate church was attended by the family from the big house and the head of the house also monitored the attendance of those who worked on the estate.

Cathy Miller

They used the far away loft for themselves and the ladies in waiting and the one across the way was Physgill. The one that was facing was Physgill. And when Ah first went to church there was a choir in those days and there was the Telfers and the Miss McTiers, and the Miss McTiers' clothes were all right down to the ground and the biggest hats you ever saw in your life and each rim of the hat touched this one and then that one, the three of them until one day they got that awkward, one went to the side seat, she had had enough of this clicking o the hats. We used to always wait to see what colour o hat she would have on.

Elsie McShane

[Looking at a photograph] Oh yes, aye. He's on the right-hand side, and the one facing him was the Physgill gallery. And this one in the middle was the workers! Yes, but he [Admiral Johnston Stewart] was there every Sunday, leaning over, to see who wasn't there (both laugh). Because if you hadn't been there on Sunday, he'd have been around to see what kept you. Either he or the minister, and the minister at that time, for a long, long time, was John Scoular's father.
And did you mind, or did you quite–?
Oh no, not at all. It was just a thing that you did, yes. My father himself was quite attached to the church. He was Beadle in Glasserton church for 50 years.

John Wilson and Cathy Miller

JW: Of course, back in the Admiral's day they were, the tenants were expected to attend church.
CM: Yes, if ye didn't ye were fined a penny.
JW: It was a duty to attend.
CM: You were fined a penny if ye didn't. Ye had tae– on a Monday morning they sent a bailiff round.

Alex Haswell

[Church attendance was] a lot higher than it is today, I would surmise. There were always the stalwarts there: the local teachers, the bank managers, the doctors. There were a lot of people that went to church. I think I saw the attendances start to drop off. I remember the Minister, Morrison, Angus Morrison. Angus did a lot of work in Whithorn, he had a youth club which he ran, at the Manse, and he tried to bring the tap and the bottom thigither. That was one of Angus' things. And they had good church attendances in those days. The best church attendance was always the Christmas Eve service of course. Which, I think, eventually became something that went over the top, on a few occasions. Everybody went to church that night, well, I think that was just because it was something to do on Christmas Eve. No, there was a big Sunday School attendance, and the Sunday School used to run, every year, it had its play – its nativity play – and I remember we used to start practicing for that in October. It was Winnie Brock, and Betty Stuart, Greta was involved in it, my father. A lot of kids went to church – and the Roman Catholic church, likewise – it had a very healthy community.

The other thing, my memory of Whithorn, was that my father was the church officer, the Beadle. We kept the church clean, and most Saturday afternoons I spent half the time helping to polish the church. And hoover it, get it ready for the Sunday. I don't know if they still have a Beadle now. But my father rang the bell, and brought the Minister in. And my mother cleaned – we had to spring clean – we kept the church neat and tidy, for more years than I can remember. From when I was fairly young, I would have said six, seven right through to my teenage years. And the year my father died, on the Sunday morning, my brother played the organ and I rang the bell for him.

Insiders and Outsiders: The Catholic Church

Whithorn's Irish connections had already set it apart from other settlements in the Machars: its history dating back to the first ever Christian Church in Scotland, the arrival of Irish immigrants in the nineteenth century, and the fact that it then became of the focus of Catholic revival under the auspices of the Marquess of Bute ensured that the Catholic Church had a much stronger presence in Whithorn than in other Machars settlements. Not only was Bute concerned with the preservation of the pre-Reformation heritage of Whithorn, initiating the first in a campaign of excavations which took place over 130 years, but he was also concerned for the well-being of the souls of Whithorn's

Catholics, left without any ministry, as correspondence preserved at Mount Stuart House confirms.

John Scoular

> Whithorn has always been an interesting case in point because it's always been virtually 50-50 and I have to say, that in my opinion, as a son of the [Presbyterian] church, the Catholics had a better attitude towards the community than the established Church of Scotland, not so much in Glasserton parish because we didn't have a lot of Catholics. My father was a fairly, a fairly wise and tolerant man but in Whithorn you'd a long period in which they seemed to specialise in appointing ministers to the Church of Scotland who were far too far to one side. It's my considered opinion that there were a lot of bad appointments in the Church of Scotland with people who were completely intolerant and completely seemed to be unaware of the fact that they lived in a community which was split 50-50 and they would have to come to terms with that, whether they liked it or not. I think there were several appointments that were too heavily biassed towards the established Church of Scotland. Whether it was a conscious decision by the Roman Catholic Church or not but they seemed to— they appointed people who had a sense of the history of Whithorn, of course and the history of Whithorn is a Roman Catholic one. But they had also people who didn't want to stir up trouble in a 50-50 community. ... The rural areas didn't really, were principally Church of Scotland, as was Isle of Whithorn, which is why they could support parish ministers, the problem was one that was in Whithorn. And you have to remember that, of course, Whithorn, from the point of view of the Catholic Church was always a very, very important place. All the years since the Reformation it really was, in a sense, the Catholic Church that was interested in preserving the history of the place and encouraging people to come on pilgrimage.

One of the features, unique to Whithorn and still alive today, was the reinstitution of the Catholic pilgrimages, revived by the Marquess, in imitation of the great mediaeval pilgrimages to the shrine of St Ninian, and making an incursion through the town, all the way from the railway station to the church at the top and St Ninian's Cave beyond.

Margerie Clark

> And then there seems to have been an opportunity to pick up the pilgrimage bit again, obviously after the hierarchy was restored, from the

41. Whithorn Roman Catholic Pilgrimage, 1932.

Catholic Church point of view, I suppose, and then the first pilgrimage we know of on record, seems to have been in 1924, the first large pilgrimage. There's talk of one in the 1870s, I think, but certainly 1924 when there were about 2000 or 3000 people came to Whithorn, and that. But of course the pilgrimage itself, although it marched up the street from the station, which was at the foot of the town in these days, the Catholic pilgrimage didn't go to the cave directly, they went to the church at the Mains, where there was an altar set up outside the church, and a canopy, so Mass was said there, a High Mass, as it was in those days, which would probably be a lengthy process. And then in the afternoon, they then made their way to the cave.

...

Whether they would process or whether they just made their way, or whether some had already maybe had to get the train to go back home. But there was a prayer was said at the cave, a form of benediction would be said at the cave for those who were there. So that was in '24. Again, we know of a large pilgrimage again in 1932. But the only ones I know about that started on a regular basis seemed to be, would be in 1953, I think it was, they had a– by then, Bishop Joseph McGee, who was the Bishop of Galloway diocese, and he said what I believe would be the first Mass at the cave, certainly from the Reformation, if at all, I don't know if there would be Masses said at the cave prior to the Reformation or not, I don't know of any records.

...

So that's when the– which is now the annual Diocesan event, as a mass at the cave, rather than going to the church at the Top of the Town and then processing to the cave afterwards. So that has carried on on an annual basis ever since. And it takes place now, it takes place on the last Sunday of August every year. I think they did have it at one time on the 16th of September, which is the Feast of St Ninian, but probably due to high tides and things it was moved to August. And then they moved the feast for a few years to the 26th of August, but they've moved him back to the 16th of September, but they've kept the pilgrimage to the end of August, probably, again, weather wise and tides.

…

We always went down on the Sunday cause the men had gone down on the Saturday and done a lot of the work, and the framework, which was a wooden frame in those days, and they would prepare the ground a bit and they would erect this wooden frame, and then this big heavy old canopy was put over it, and a wooden altar was put up, and of course this is so that the priests could stand under it out of the worst of the elements, basically. Most of the priests, not all the priests could even get in. The congregation were left to their own devices, basically. Because it's held, the altar, the canopy, the frame, is set up just in front of St Ninian's Cave, and the rocks and everything down below are basically what the people sit on, or just get as comfortable as you can. And we used to go down, so the men would do that on the Saturday, and then on the Sunday that was when Auntie Margerie, of course, as the Sacristan, of course, she'd spent the week packing the stuff that was needed in old cases and bags to take down, and Bridget Mills and Johnny would be involved in those days, and of course their children and me.

The numbers have dropped a little now, again, in its heyday in the 20s and 30s, and even looking back into the 70s and 80s we could have 2000 people down. Now we average maybe 500 or 600.

Greta Hawthorn

But the troops used tae come in on it [the train] and the pilgrimage, when the pilgrimage was on, it used to come in on it and all the people in St John Street put notices on the door if they wanted to go to the dry toilets, they were there, and Billy's mother used tae have tea for anybody that wanted a cup o tea, just on the way there and they would walk fae there tae the Glen.

And they were pretty large pilgrimages, weren't they?

Oh, they were. They would be at Denton's and they would still be, they'd be still at Denton's and were nae through the Port's Mouth end. There is pictures o them somewhere. But they were big pilgrimages and then when the trains went off they came on buses and then the buses were parked at Physgill but there wasnae the car parking. That was the dam where the car park is now, that was a dam that worked the mill wheel in the steadings at Kidsdale. There wasnae that car park then but they used tae let them get intae the farmyard or up the road, or up at Physgill.

The Catholic Church had existed, somewhat temporarily, on the brink of the town, until it became established, within living memory, in a tin-clad building on the Mains farm, which was acquired by the Marquess of Bute, just on the verge of the burgh boundary.

Margerie Clark

And there was no Catholic building, no church building in the town at all from the Reformation, they'd had no Catholic church. So I believe, in those distant days, they used a hayloft somewhere down at the foot of the town, until the Marquis of Bute in the 1800s supplied, or paid for, an iron chapel to be built down at Bishopton. Or Bishop's Town, as it was still called at that time. So that gave them a place of worship there, and then subsequently after a couple of years it was moved up to the place where it remained until it ceased to be used, up at the Mains, just outside the town. And that was the place of worship for the Catholics right up until the 1950s. But of course there was always a hope that they would one day be able to have an actual church building, but of course church finances and stuff prevailed that they didn't. But from what I can pick up they had an extremely good community. And of course it must be said that the community worked very well together. Both the Church of Scotland community, the Catholic community, in fact I think there would be two Protestant churches at that time, because there was the church down at St John's, yes. And they all seem to have worked well together. Of course things were very different, and it was like nobody darkened one another's doors, but at least we didn't have a Northern Ireland situation or anything like that. And then they managed to raise funds, and a new church was built and opened in 1960, 16th of September 1960 there was a new building opened in Whithorn itself. Because over the years they had managed to buy property where two or three houses were in the middle of the town, and they also had property donated to them by Mr J. V. Little, who was the plumber. In fact, a family of plumbers, at that time, so that helped them out a lot as well. And I think property they did buy was only for £1 or something. And then they were able to have the church built, which is the church that stands to the present day. And I think it cost £40,000 when it was built. It costs a lot more now to upkeep it!

By and large, the picture emerges of a town where religious difference was, mostly, tolerated. Betty Stuart, a member of the Free Church, remembers her visits to the Catholic Church outside the boundary.

Betty Stuart

So was it a, it was a tin building was it?
It was a tin building in these days.
And what sort of a congregation did they have?
Oh, it was packed. It was always packed they sat oot on the grass an that, it was packed.
Molly Stuart: *They did marriages up there, didn't they?*
Aye, they did at one time. And it was always packed though. And they had parties often, more often than what the Protestants had. And the children had tae take a Protestant with them. Oh Ah wis at a few o them. They invited ye, I went wi Mary, Mary Flannighan.
Molly: *Aye, yer best pal.*
And we got the same, but it was comical, they would shout, 'And where's the Proddies?' The priest would shout, 'Where's the Proddies, is the Proddies getting a bite?' (laughter). But he came every day, he cycled fae Wigtown, Father Clark, every day.
So mostly, the Catholics and the Protestants got on really well?
Well, they did. Maybe Saturday night they went to the pub it was different but most of them, in the whole— well the women and that did, you know. But the men, or that, so if they got to the pub and that I would think there were maybe have wee fall oots.
Molly: *Aboot nothing.*
Nothing, no, no, no and these parties, the parties they had for the Protestants and their own congregation were always great. And you always got something home wi ye, a wee present or something, he was a great man, Father Clark. He was a legend in— aw ower Wigtownshire. And his wee dog run wi him aw the road, he was on the bike, cycled fae— and the wee dog, a wee black and white dog ran aw the road wi him.

Jessie McLean

Aye we were aw— oh, ma Granny Jolly was an awfu Catholic. Oh, my goodness, ye daurnae miss the Sunday School or the Chapel for the life o ye. An awfu auld Catholic. Ma mither was a Protestant but ma granny wasnae, they were aw Catholics an ma faither was a Catholic. Oh aye.
And did you go to the church at the Top of the Town?
The yin up on— the tin, the tin yin in the field, that's the yin we went tae.

Went tae it aw ma life. They [her children] were aw christened Catholics.

Tina Soriani and Aldo Petrucci

> **AP**: And we used to go to Mass in our welly boots sometimes in the winter time! But the thing was–
> **TS**: And the priest cycled from Wigtown!
> **AP**: From Wigtown, and he must have been 70. I think it was every fortnight he used to come. And we'd go up to Mass. And the thing is, the church was really pretty full. I can't remember however many it held, but it was pretty full.
> **TS**: We also have to thank– my parents were very good, they made sure that we always went. But some of the older generation that were very good churchgoers helped us a lot as well.

So there was no resident priest at the time?

> **AP**: No. There was the priest, lived in Wigtown, and he had tae look after the parish of Whithorn at the same time. And he was there, old Father Clark, his name was, and he was, I think in Wigtown for at least 40 years. Now that's most unusual, most of them last three, four, five years and then they're moved. But he was there for about 40 years, and used to cycle to Whithorn I think every fornight to say Mass in Whithorn.
> **TS**: And the first resident priest was after he died, but they stayed in the Station Hotel.
> **AP**: Father McCarthy. He was the– he was Irish. There were a lot of Irish priests came over to this area at that time. And he stayed in the Station Hotel, and used to cycle, I remember, in his early days, tae Wigtown! … Oh, I can remember him cycling. And then someone bought him a wee car and he was able to make him go back and forward in a car.

So the church, it was the tin church, wasn't it? It was quite well-decorated inside though?

> **TS**: No, it was nice, there was a nice altar and it felt a church, it felt a church.

And it was well attended?

> **TS**: Yes, it was. It was always full. Always full.

And then eventually the move was to build a new one in the middle of the town?

> **TS**: That's right. That was Father Burke, he bought, first he bought a house across the road, I don't know who's in it, in the railed bit. …Father Burke bought that house, and then he built a house behind, a bungalow, behind the church as well, so he had a house and the church.

And was there fundraising from the congregation to do that?

> **TS**: Yes, mmhmm. A lot of fundraising.
> **AP**: I think we used to give a regular amount every Sunday. And this was to go towards this new church. But Whithorn could never have built that

church on its own, it must have got help from this Bishop or something, I don't know.
TS: Oh, yes, aye. But possibly it would be paid back throughout the time.
And do you remember the pilgrimages to the cave?
TS: Yes, I remember when they used to walk. There was a train came in and there was the pilgrimage started in Whithorn and we walked right to the cave.
AP: From the station right the way to the cave, which would be what, three miles? About three miles?
TS: Aye, because they used to walk from the school, from Kidsdale to–
AP: Now they all come by bus. It's still well attended.
TS: Oh, thousands used to go.
AP: It wouldn't be thousands today, but certainly quite a number.
TS: But even congregations are dwindling. In all the denominations.

Alex Haswell

Granny was the matriarch of the family, grandfather had been a Roman Catholic, and she was a Murray, so she was very much Protestant, and the agreement was that the girls would be Protestant and the boy would be Roman Catholic!
…
And what you would remember was the church here, not the tin church?
I remember they built the new church. I think there was a few people in Whithorn, tradesmen, who actually did most of the work themselves. I think the church was built by local crafts people. Ben Wilma – Ben was very heavily involved in that. In the un-politically correct days, he was Ben the Pole. I think he was one of the leading lights. But I do remember the old corrugated iron between Mulholland's shop, and the row of houses. And then the corrugated iron came down, and the Roman Catholic church appeared.

The re-establishment of the Catholic Church in Whithorn in the twentieth century received strong support through the conversion of a new Laird, son of Admiral Johnston Stewart.

Margerie Clark

The fact that Mr Johnson Stewart loaned the church the oratory. He played a big part in the parish in that he played the organ for many many years in the parish church, obviously access to and from the cave, he allowed us access. For many years we used to be allowed to park the cars, our cars, those who were helping, in his grounds, in front of Physgill House.

…

When it began that lay people could start to read some of the readings at church, the Epistle and things like that, it was his family or himself that would do it quite often.

…

I think years ago there used to be church fetes were held, cause there's a photograph, we have a photo in the family album of my granny and some of them serving at the stalls, and that was held in the grounds at Physgill. And then latterly, where the present church is, because of course the house that is there now behind the church wasn't always there, there was ground there, grass ground, and they used to have the summer fetes there. So I suppose that would be when the break would come, it would be during the summer, they would have the fetes at Physgill. And then when they had ground behind the church they moved them to Whithorn, to the ground there, which probably was easier for people to get to in those days. But they've always been– Mr Johnson Stewart and his wife were always a very important part of the parish. Of course, they were both converts, but not together, they became converts at different times. So he had a long association with the parish. In fact, apparently, in the days when [the Church at] the Mains were still on the go, he– and of course in his early days, because he would be a convert, he maybe wasn't quite as au fait with the hymns that would be looked on in those days. Nowadays we're a bit more general, but in those days there would be certain hymns that would be looked on as Catholic hymns, that would be used at Mass and that. So he would go to my granny's, maybe at the weekend, this was years ago before I was born, and before they lived at the Pend House, even. So they would go through what hymns, and my granny was very into all this, because sometimes she used to have to, before Mr Johnson Stewart played the organ, she would be the one that would maybe pick hymns, or start hymns. So they would go through the hymns, and choose whatever the hymns would be for a Sunday, and then he would play them. So there was that association. But they were always very involved and active. I suppose they wouldn't be so involved in such as the cleaning of the church and things like that. They would sit on the parish committees and things like that. But I suppose that was the way that was it in those days. They were looked on as 'the Laird and the wife,' and that was it. People didn't expect them to do that sort of thing the same. Always very faithful in their attendance.

Yet there were undercurrents of prejudice and the church, until it was embraced in the centre of the town, retained a certain otherness, beyond the burgh boundary.

Elsie McShane

Yes, I remember the pilgrimages. Bigger events than they are now. My, I remember my mother saying about them– when they marched through Whithorn people drew their curtains, drew their blinds. It was awful; she didn't like that at all.

That was because they didn't like them?

That was the religious thing. She thought it was awful. But it happened. … Yes, we were always encouraged to have friends from both [Catholics and Protestants], yes. I remember my father saying, they used to come out of the classroom – the Catholics came out of the classroom – and they got their Bible studies different from us. My father used to say that shouldn't be.

He felt that made a distinction?

Oh yes it did, right away it made a difference. He thought it shouldn't be. …

Our minister, previous to Alec Currie, our minister Campbell Cowie – did you ever know Campbell Cowie? – Well he did his best, you know. He really encouraged us. He really– he bent over backwards, Campbell did, to bring it together. To a certain extent he did succeed. He didn't like it at all, he wasn't for that. People who were joining the church – like my kids – when they came to join the church, he, part of their instruction, he took them to the Catholic church. Which is a very brave thing to do. Yes he did, and he could explain to them the stations of the cross and all the rest of it. No, he did his best. I think he made quite a good job of it. He was always very friendly with whatever Priest was here; he was always very friendly with them.

Margerie Clark

Yes, yes, there could have been [reasons for the Catholic church being beyond the burgh boundary]. That would be in the 1890s or whatever, so there may have been still – although the Reformation was long past – there would maybe still be a little bit of feeling at the time, or rules and regulations. Cause I have heard it, sometimes there would be stipulations, certain buildings, even previous, not in Whithorn but in other places, where maybe it used to be a Church of Scotland church, if it was put up for sale, there used to be a clause to say it was not to be sold as a

Catholic church, or to the Catholics, or things like that. So there may have been something like that. I honestly never heard any of my family say anything about that. In fact they were always very fond of that [tin] church, because of the– they'd known nothing else until– they were christened in it, and married in it. In fact Auntie Marjorie and Uncle Ben were actually the last couple who were married in the church at the Mains when they were married in July '57, they were married. And then I think it was knocked down in the November.

But obviously there's usually devotions, or a daily Mass or something, if there's a priest available. So for the weekday services the Laird donated this property that had been a butcher's shop, that was turned into a small oratory, and they could have devotions and a daily Mass there. And again, because my grandparents lived in the Pend House, the key for the oratory was kept there, so the result was, that's how I suppose the family got to know so many priests going in and out, because that was where they would go for the key. And again, my grandfather, who was actually Church of Scotland, he wasn't a Catholic, but he was very good at seeing to the up-keep of the oratory, if it needed any repairs doing or the sanctuary lamp, he would go and see to that, and all this sort of thing. Of course in 1920 or whenever it would be that they were married it was unusual for Catholic and non-Catholic to marry. Cause of course that was one of the stipulations, if a non-Catholic married a Catholic they're supposed to agree that the children will be brought up Catholic. So I believe from what my mother and auntie told me, he was stricter on them than my granny was, cause he said if he had any sins to answer for he would not answer for that one!

…

But I think the likes of Auntie Margerie and my mother and them, and they'd grown up with a different situation, to even I grew up with, because as I was saying earlier, the priest lived in Wigtown, so they only had Mass every fortnight, because he had to cycle from Wigtown, unless he got a lift. But most of the time they said he cycled from Wigtown. And he would cycle maybe on a Saturday and stay. There was a little room in the church at the Mains that he would sleep in, just with a curtain, I think, between him. And then they would have Mass. And of course Mass in those days was a lot longer than it is now, and they were meant to fast, I think they had long fasts, they fasted from the night before if they were going to receive communion. And he would arrive on the Saturday night and have his supper, and maybe the call would go out for confessions, because, I mean, nobody had phones in those days, but the word would go out, Father's here, and they would go. And of course they would go for Mass on the Sunday, and it was all in Latin, obviously.

And then apparently he used to go through and have a little cup of tea and refresh himself, and come back and preach. And I think they could sit for about an hour.

…

But I think Father Clark, he was 40 years here. So they grew up with Mass a fortnight, confessions were every six weeks and that, so the shortage of priests now that's making things difficult, that's what they grew up with, they were used to that. So they always used to say, when people would weep and wail, what are we gonna do if we can't get Mass every day, and we can't do this and that. And they would say, 'What are you talking about? We grew up with that, and it didn't do us any harm'. Their faith was strong, they lived by. Their church was second only to the family, I would say, to them when they were growing up. And they accepted changes that came, or had to come, and that was the way it was.

Hereafter

Death and funerals had not yet been removed from the intimacy of the family home – their physicality less mystified and less sanitised than they later became, when most took place in the less private space of hospitals and funeral homes.

Jenny Jolly

So what about in the old days if somebody died, would some women come in and help lay them out?
That's right, that's what happened.
Just neighbours or were there–?
Jist neighbours, aye. Sometimes there was twa women, they aye ca'd auld, was it Mary or [unclear]. Auld Nellie Boyce an another wuman, they were ca'd 'the sisters o mercy' for they aye liked thae jobs and that's what they ca'd them, the sisters o mercy (laughter).

Betty Stuart

The undertaker was there, aye, Charlie Hawkins. Annie Hawkins' father, he was an undertaker.
Do you remember if they had a horse-drawn hearse before a motorised one?
Aye, they had, because I can just remember that and no more, but maistly it was, I can, Ah don't know whose that would be but I can remember one, at one time seeing that, but no much aboot it.

Robin Kinnear reflects on the changes in mourning wear.

Robin Kinnear

> Yes, that's right. And this was a tremendous urgency, that it could be done for weddings and funerals, was getting a suit made up quickly if it was for mourning, you could wire through the measurements or you could phone through to Yorkshire and you would have it in three days which was really quite astonishing and of course if you wrote a postcard off on a Sunday to Glasgow, if you got it away in the post before one o'clock they would phone you up on a Monday morning enquiring about the order you had sent in and it would be sent down that day by train and would come into Whauphill Station and there was a lorry from the contractors, McLean the lorry contractor, who went three times a week to Whauphill, so these were all delivered to everyone, all these parcels, very, very rapidly so there hasn't been a tremendous improvement in post and contacts now (laughter).
> …

In terms of the mourning do you remember people wearing crepe round their hats or mourning bands, do you remember that?
> No, I can remember them wearing armbands on their jacket for several …several weeks afterwards but not wearing it. They just, the ladies just came as they would be for church in their hats and always in pretty heavy mourning. But what you did notice, if there had been a death in the family, when you walked down the street, all the blinds were drawn, were all closed and that was a sign and a lot of little cottages you would– the minister would come and would have the service over the coffin, in the house not at the church, and you would then go from that service where practically only maybe a quarter of the people actually got into the house and you would then go to the interment at the graveyard in Mochrum. But there were a lot of church services done in the houses.

The undertaker had not yet been purified of his link with the making of coffins, so that the local joiner was (and is) regularly the funeral director.

John Wilson

> Yes, that was part and parcel of the sort of agricultural joiner, or the country joiner, that initially joiners made the coffins. We, Ah think we only made one coffin, we made a coffin for a child one time, we used to get the coffins from Dumfries. The coffins were sent up on the train from Dumfries up to Newton Stewart and we'd go across to Newton Stewart

and pick them up. Ma father did that, Ah did ma first funeral when Ah was 17 year old because ma father had the flu and Ah was left at the deep end and Ah had tae get on with it (laughs) and we did that, yea.

So, your duties as an undertaker, you would have to go out and visit the family and measure up the body?

Yea, we did that, we– that has changed radically as well, we would go out and make all the arrangements, we used to hire– there is a– we hired a hearse from a man in Port William who had a hearse. We would hire a bus and the bus would go round the local area picking up the people to bring them into the funeral because people didn't have cars. So this bus would trundle round the local area, pick up people and bring them to Glasserton Church or into Whithorn or wherever. We occasionally, at the very start, we used to send out letters wi the black band round them and the black banded envelopes, we had them. That began to change as well, we had– eventually we got the coffins, the coffins were being kept– there was a firm in Glasgow had a depot in Garlieston so we could just nip down to Garlieston and get them. But in the '50s even death was looked on differently, because I can remember when Ah came intae Whithorn in 1964 and the local taxi driver would go up and pick up coffins for some o the, the undertaker from the Isle of Whithorn and it was never thought anything about it. He had a Austin Cambridge taxi and the boot on the Austin Cambridge folded down from the back, like it came doon like a lid, and he would just set the coffin on this boot lid and tied on and off he would set. So you'd see this car going up the town with a coffin wrapped, it was all wrapped up in hessian and it was just another commodity really. That is all changed now.

…

There was an undertaker, the old joiner in Port William was an undertaker, the joiner in the Isle of Whithorn was an undertaker, the joiner in Whithorn was an undertaker so, and it was simply because this tradition of making the coffins.

So, presumably in your father's day, he did make the coffin, or your grandfather's day?

Yes, oh yes, they did, they did, aye, ma father did but by the time that Ah come on the scene that, it had changed and the coffins were– we got them from Jardine's in Dumfries.

So, did a lot of the coffins start, as it were, that you would leave them in the house for the family and then go from there, because that's changed as well?

Yes, the funerals were mainly from the house at that time, yes. That began to change I would say about in the '60s, the early '60s and it got it was more convenient because, especially in Whithorn, if we had a funeral, say at the top o the town where the street's narrow, people would– the funerals were always well attended, as you know, round about here they are always well attended. And what would happen at the Top of the Town, they would stand round the doorway and the minister, we would get the minister to stand at the doorway so the people at– the relatives could hear but also the people outside could hear what was being said and inevitably there would be a big lorry would come roarin up through the town and drowned out so it wasn't very handy and especially in the wintertime as well wi bad weather and then we began then to have more and more in the church and now it's just the norm, they're all in the church. But, no, originally it was, they were all from the house.

And did your father have the responsibility of preparing the bodies before putting them in the coffins?

We– most times we did that, yea, we did that ourselves. There was a lady in the town here, if it was a Whithorn funeral, there was a lady in the town who was nicknamed 'the Angel of Death' (laughter). She would prepare them but most times it was us, we did it ourselves. And people were quite happy just to let us get on with it.

And did that change over time? Was there different ways of doing it or?

Not really, no, not really, amazingly things just stayed the way they were. People, people weren't embalmed or anything like that, that didn't happen here. And this was why the funerals were normally held within about three days. And really, there wasn't any need for it. It's different as well because we used to be able to phone the graveyard foreman and say, 'We've got a funeral in Glasserton' and arrange the date wi them but that all changed because it was too easy, it seemed to be, it was too easy. It had to be done through the council offices and then this is when ye get delays if somebody dies at the weekend. But it can now stretch out to four or five days. But before that we could always just phone the superintendent, 'Aye that's no problem' and it as done. So, aye, things change that way.

And were there– obviously the graves must have been dug by hand?

The graves were initially dug by hand, yea. And that can be hard because round about here you don't go very far before you hit rock and Ah think eventually in Glasserton they pre-dug a lot o the graves because when machinery began to be used they pre-dug them and backfilled them. But in Whithorn as well it was very, very hard, some o the graves were quite shallow and they had to, they had to bury side by side.

And was that a specific job, I mean was somebody be sexton, or the gravedigger?

No, the council, by the time Ah was on the scene and ma father was on the scene, the graves were dug by the council.

…

In actual fact when ye were talkin aboot, talkin aboot the funerals there Ah remember there was one little dog, when Ah was in Whithorn, there was one little dog who attended virtually every funeral. And we had a terrible time wi this wee dog, this wee dog arrived at ... by this time we were using the church and this wee dog arrived up at every funeral and there was another chap who, a local worthy in the town here, who liked a drink and between him harassing us, because he was always sort of banging his stick and harassing us at the Pend mouth. Every time we came out he'd be there, between him and this dog we had quite a time of it, we had a terrible time keepin this wee dog fae going into the church actually (laughter).

And were there any things, any symbols that people used in their houses if there was a funeral? Did they drape it or did they shut their curtains?

Oh, the curtains were always shut, yes, curtains were always shut. And that's another thing that ye see as time went on, people originally when I started in 1954 onwards, people always showed respect to a funeral cortege, now they don't bother. But you would see linesmen on the roads, for example, workin on the roads and if a hearse came along they stood up and took their hat off. You'd always see that and people on the streets would stop and stand up face the hearse, now they just look at it and go on, they don't bother at all. Latterly when, for example, we were going up to the crematorium, we used to use the crematorium at Ayr and you would come up to the roundabouts at Ayr and people would just cut you up, they wouldn't give way, at all, to a funeral. And that's just the difference, you know, 50 years, 60 years, how times change and it's not for the better.

And do you remember wakes being held in the houses? Was that a habit?

Some o the Irish ones did, yea, yea. Ah don't know much about that because we were never really involved in that but, aye, some o the Irish connection, connected people would do that, yea. They were always very, very well attended, you would always get 60, 70 folk at least. Because, the thing was, it was a very tight-knit community, especially in the '50s up to the '60 s, because everybody knew each other and a lot of them were related. It was actually an undertaker's nightmare to go into a house when somebody had died, you'd go into a house and there would be maybe ten, 15 folk sittin in the house and you never knew who was related and who was just the next door neighbour, so it was always quite difficult to try and work out relationships because they never, ever would tell you and Ah never really liked to ask who's related here and who's just a nosey neighbour (laughs). So that was quite difficult, eventually ye began tae know but in Whithorn, especially, there were so many people related through one way or another.

8

Incursion and Dispersion: Second World War

Into the comings and goings of this small world, the intrusion of a much wider world came with the Second World War, with its vast horizons, conscription of the labour force, logistics of troop movements, the commandeering of the great houses for hospitals, the subjection of land to national food production targets and the greater equalisation of roles between men and women. Farmers scanned the skies, not for the onset of rain which could ruin a harvest, but as members of the Home Guard scanning for enemy aircraft.

A sudden influx of newcomers came about through the establishment of military training camps and test facilities in the area; national priorities were superimposed and military zones were created disrupting ordinary travel, especially when the Mulberry harbour for D-Day was tested at Garlieston.

Tom McCreath

> Very much kept at a distance but we all knew it was supposed to be hush hush but I remember one point Father was going to the police station in Garlieston over some business and I was in the car, looked down at the harbour and it was throbbing with activity, working on components of the Mulberries, testing and developing them.

Jack Niblock

> … and of course there was the Army at Portyerrock where they were trying out stuff for D-Day.

Yes. Were there areas you weren't allowed to walk?

> Well, we weren't allowed into that area. John McGuire, the one that took over from my grandfather as coastguard, he had a permit to still fish lobsters round there and he had salmon nets round there as well.

But you needed a permit?

> You needed a permit to work out of there, even walking along the road you weren't really welcome.

But would you perhaps see things, the construction?
   Yes, you could see the floating roadway and that and one thing and another. Oh I can remember them all right.

Farms lost young men to the fighting front and Home Guards were hastily scrambled from those who remained. The decline of the great houses was confirmed when they were commandeered for convalescent homes and quarters.

Tom McCreath

   But, on our farm, four of the young men joined up, one went actually before war was declared because he was a farrier and went to the Scots Greys and then a young chap in the TA to the Army, another to the Air Force and, later on, a younger chap was of age to join the Army, he unfortunately was killed in Italy but the other three survived.
And do you remember the Home Guard in this area?
   Very much. Suddenly all sorts of people were expected to turn out after a day's work for parades. Father was second command of the Sorbie Garlieston battalion, would it be a battalion? I think it was, yes. But they took it very seriously and the first parade they had they came armed with pitch forks and scythes and you know what (laughter). Father, he couldn't believe his eyes (laughter). And later on a little, rifles came from America, they were … or from Canada, I think, Ross rifles and I can remember the Home Guard meeting down at Galloway House to clean these rifles, Father took me as a very small boy and we saw them cleaning them there. And it became more realistic when they got real rifles, I've got to say. And then they had observation posts on top of hills round about so the Home Guard would sit up, in our area it was a henhouse on top of Blair Hill, look for parachuters or goodness knows what and the very night there was a serious callout the message didn't get through and they weren't called out (laughter). It was a bit like *Dad's Army* but thank goodness we can laugh about it now but it was dead serious at the time.
And what do you remember about Galloway House during the War?
   Not a lot initially, but the Factor there was in command of the local battalion but then it became a hospital for convalescents, prior to D-Day. But because they had many fewer casualties than they expected it was fairly quickly closed down. But the maximum patients they had was 14. But in our young days that was the place where they reared pheasants and the whole countryside was moving with rabbits and pheasants and partridges in the turnip fields, trout in all the burns, it was a wonderful place for small boys and poachers (laughter).

Jock McMaster

Aye well, my father's brother who farmed with him, he volunteered and was unfortunately killed in the RAF. In, '44 so that was a big impact Ah suppose, yea. Dad was in the Home Guard and Ah know we laugh aboot it but we shouldn't, it was bloody hard work cause you were working all day. And patrolling at night looking for submarines, he told us some great, well, I wouldn't say great tales, he just told us as it was. Sitting on the hill at the golf course, presuming you could hear the engines throbbing and aw this and cycling away to the Rocks o Garheugh to report to the Glenluce contingent. A fair distance, it is, and then workin all day as well. … So what other things the War affected Ah don't really know, it was before my time. Foodwise they would have to produce a lot more food, they had to plough more. Ah think the Ministry had a system where they went round and checked up on farms to make sure they were producing food and they were told which fields to plough and get for the war effort.

Yes, yes, because presumably it was a reserved occupation?

Well, it was, aye, although a lot of them did, as Ah said ma father's brother he volunteered tae go. In fact they argued and fought as to who was gonna go and he said, 'Well, ah'm older, ah'm goin'. That was the story, anyway. So he did his training in Canada, as a navigator, his eyesight wasnae good enough for a pilot but he was a navigator. Ah would have thought the other way round, Ah would have thought the navigator would have had to be able to see where he's going, but never mind. And funnily enough part of his training was when he came back here, he was at Whitehaven and he flew over here quite regularly. We have his log, which is very interesting, and then we was stationed in the Middle East but he flew over here round the, over the Fell and Scaurs and Mull o Galloway and the Isle of Man, as part of his training which must have been good fun for him because he would know exactly where he was.

Robert Galashan was also a young boy, living on the coast overlooking all the military activity.

Robert Galashan

The only other thing on that bit that I remember was at Palmallet, but they had targets oot in the water, and it wis the time Baldoon wis on the go, as an airfield, and they used to train the bombers. The RAF fellaes, I used to go oot and help them, they used tae go and lie in the hay anad have a sleep and leave me to work this, it wis like a telescope wi a gauge on it, and they come over when they bombed them, and ye got a reading off

> the smoke that come up fae the bombs. And ye marked it doon on this sheet. So these fellas, when they got fed up o it, they said, just write it doon! They used tae bring us big blocks o cheese, drinking chocolate and aa this, fae the NAAFI, ye couldnae get it in these days, it wis rationed. And we used tae go up there. But that's the only bit. There's a big arrow in cement pointit that way to the bombing targets, they sat oot in the water. And the planes come over and bombed them. But that's the only other yin. No, I'm tellin ye wrong, there wis another yin at Sheddock, they used tae talk across tae the other yins on the phone. Aye.

The trains which were used for transporting milk were now also used to facilitate large troop movements in and out of Burrowhead Camp near the Isle of Whithorn.

Jack Niblock

> Oh yes, it had a huge impact on the village here. The two pubs, The Queen's Arms and The Steam Packet, they thrived. And of course they had the big camp up at Burrowhead. I think my mother worked in the Church of Scotland, I think she worked in the canteen there, occasionally went up as a sort of relief thing up there. I can remember the anti-aircraft training batteries up at Burrow Head camp. Because we used to watch for the target which was being towed, if it was shot down, the target was shot down, where it landed because it was silk, so we had to try and find the silk target if it came down in a field or something like that.
> ...
> During the War we had the recovery ships and the patrol ships when they were firing at the range up at Burrow Head but they weren't commercial they were there to– because the planes used to land on the sea so they picked them up from there and brought them in on *The Crescent. The Haldane* was a commercial boat just patrolled the outskirts to keep ships out of the, anything out of the area.

Guy Brown's father's medical practice felt the impact at Port William.

Guy Brown

> During the War it was very busy with planes dropping out of the sky here, though. We had one flew straight into the shack at the end of the village there. We had one landed in that field but tipped over, tipped over the wall, otherwise would have hit the houses. We had one up the Mochrum road, came down in a field, left its undercarriage in the ditch

and slid up towards Mochrum with a full load of bombs. And another one tried to land in the field in front of Mochrum schoolhouse, a Spitfire, realised he couldn't land, was going to pull back the stick, flew under the telephone wires on the Port William side of the road and managed to pull it up and go over the schoolhouse on the other side of the road and I believe the schoolmaster at that time was standing in the window and dropped with a heart attack but whether that's just a story or not, I don't know. And somebody shot up the– a lot of shooting out in the bay, targets, and somebody forgot which way they were pointing and shot at the creamery, there was bullets rattling all over the cement floor but nobody hit. But there are lots and lots and the casualties of these were all hauled into our, literally were hauled into our house and the RAF doctors arrived and it was always my mother's washing day. I peered through the banisters at what was going on. That was quite a busy, quite a busy time.

So your father had to treat people from the forces who were in the area or did they–?
No, they had their own doctors but accidents, yes. There was one, a lorry load of soldiers coming down from Stranraer and you know where the Changue farm is? Well, the lorry went on to the– being followed by a car and the car went to pass and just as the car– the lorry wobbled and saw the car and took to the beach. It went bouncing, apparently, down the beach turning somersaults and the old farmer in the car, didn't stop but he came down and rang the doorbell of my father's house, told the maid, 'There's a silly bugger doing somersaults wi his lorry up the shore, I think they might need the doctor.' (laughter) I think there were only a couple of broken bones there, it was amazingly, so there were lots of stories like that.

And of course, my father started the Home Guard here and I didn't realise, I noticed him going out, he was the MOH [Medical Officer of Health] for the Home Guard, noticed him going out regularly in his uniform but somebody sent me a book a few months ago about the – what was it – the volunteers before they became the Home Guard, the Local Defence Volunteers, it morphed into the Home Guard, and it was being formed and there was an argument what to form but it said that a lot of people had got the idea that something was to be done and Dr Gavin Brown at Port William was the first to have a bash, so he was one of the first and they were called 'Brown's Coastwatchers' apparently. And they had places, different places, up and down, up at the rocks at Garheugh, down at the golf course, other places where a band went out and looked out for Germans being landed by landing craft or whatever, plans how to block off the golf course because they were bound to land at the golf course and, aye, they had a great time. And I've came across one of the reports he had written on an exercise that they had done very well but the first aid people had stayed in their headquarters when they should have been out and when they were told it was time to get out they went off at such a state, such a pace that they drove over a bridge that had been blown up. So I think they had a lot of fun, the Home Guard.

...

So you remember Port William in the blackouts do you?
Yes, we were– there were two bombings, one that land, a land mine at Barmeal, which I remember hearing the plane going round and round and then hearing the bang.

...

And ma father remembered, ma father was wakened by this plane going round and round and he stuck his head out of the window when this 'bang' and the sky lit up and he said he didn't know whether he was blown back in the window or he came back at such a rate it took the top of his head, I think he got such a fright as he came in. So, John Kinnear, again, two doors down from him, he was the ARP man and he came, he phoned him to say, 'I think maybe we should be doing something, however, we'll need to wait till we find out where the bomb's gone off'. So there was a wee bit of a quandary what they should wear. Should they wear, Ah think ma father had two steel helmets, one with a red cross and one without a red cross, with an MO on it and the other without MO, and John Kinnear had his ARP one and would they take their gas masks or would they not take their gas masks? 'Och, I think we might, we'll maybe just wait and see what other folks are doing', so they flung everything in the back of the car and put on their bonnets and the one at Barmeal landed as near the, the gable end of the cot house, as that pole over there, onto rock, and the mark's still there and the bits of stone that went up and peppered it, turned the roof into a sieve and there were a lot of people in the house and not one was hurt. I've also, the Barmeal farm, every window on the side facing the explosion was in, blown in, with shards of glass stuck in the wall and all the furniture on the other side of the room and they were all sleeping at the other side of the house, so nobody was hurt. And shortly afterwards another stick of bombs was dropped at South Barsallach, over a stackyard which they probably mistook for tents. But they were jettisoning bombs on their way home and it was the same farmer farmed both farms and he felt that maybe the Germans had it in for him. And that's all we had during the War.

Many local girls found new romance with the incoming troops and those in ancillary trades, including Betty Stuart and Jessie McLean.

Greta Hawthorn

Oh plenty, there was a lot o people got married fae the troops. Elsie had two sisters got married, they had a double wedding, and there was a lot of romances and then the RAF were in Glasserton big house. That's where Mrs Wilmot's husband was. And there was quite a lot o the RAF were there. And the day that Burrowhead closed they invited Whithorn schoolchildren and the Isle schoolchildren to a fete day up at Burrowhead and they came in in their trucks and took us up there and ye were there fae nine o'clock in the morning tae aboot six at night and what a great sports day we had! And they had scones wi treacle and ye had tae try an eat them off this pole so ye were covered in treacle but never mind, it was a great day. Bit there was never any bother wi the troops. And then the dances were very busy then and ye could nearly feel the floor movin' when they were on it wi there big tackety boots on.

One can sense the quickening of pace and urgency, with the arrivals and departures, large scale engineering projects at the command of a distant government, and the confluence of different populations, whose brief encounter also gave an urgency to romance.

Betty Stuart

So, the War must have had quite an impact, with all the extra people coming in?
   Yes, oh it did, aye. It was something seein the boys marchin way doon tae the train an that.
That was the boys from Whithorn that were getting recruited?
   Yes. Everybody was oot at their doors and they marched right doon and then there was the ones up at Burrow Head, they didnae come on trucks, they marched fae the station to Burrow Head.
In their time off they would get to come into Whithorn?
   Oh, they came into Whithorn, for they came tae the tea room where Ah worked cause she did special meals for them, Miss Hannah, the two Miss Hannahs. It was where Katrina Keith lives. That's where it was, there was other ones, but that's the one they went to because it was aw home-made baking an it was Joanne, that was the eldest one, it was her, and she was very good to them, she gave them extras and that, and carry-outs and that tae take tae the camp. And then the officers started comin too, it was always packed.
   And ma mother used tae come down on a Saturday night and help me to wash the dishes, on a Saturday night. And then, of course, there was dances, we cawd them 'the hops' across in the hall and of course Ah had tae

42. Brass band, outside the Free Kirk, Whithorn.

work on and on and if ma mother come Ah would say, 'Would ye dae the dishes?' 'Oh aye,' she says, 'Yer gaun tae the dance' and she did ma work for me while Ah went tae the hop. We cawd it 'the hop' in these days, 'The Saturday Night Hop', Rennie McAdam's Band, Wigtown. They were a great band, Rennie McAdam had such a voice (laughter). We loved it, oh we did. And everybody loved Rennie McAdam and he was so cheery there was nae carry-on and there was nae fights. We had a good man that put them oot, that attended, Bobby Herd fae– he was the one that flung them oot if there was ony carry-on, it was great. Whithorn Saturday night hops were famous aw ower Wigtownshire, they came fae everywhere. It was very good.

Mm, but Ah had tae be home, even though Ah was a teenager, well Ah would be 18, maybe. Would Ah be? Ah had tae be in the house at a certain time and this night Ah wis goin up the street an Ah was wi a soldier (laughs) and he'd asked me ma name an Ah said, 'Violet' (laughter), Ah can remember an it would be aboot Galloway's shop an Ah seen her comin and she wisnae changed or ocht, she had the wellies on comin doon the street wi a stick and we used tae [unclear] on it. 'Is that you Betty?' An he says, 'No,' this fella, he says, 'No, sorry, this is Violet', 'Aye,' Ah says, 'Well Violet up the something street the noo or ye'll get this [unclear] ower yer back' (laughter). Ah remember that so well, aye, 'Violet'.

...

Oh yes, they used tae march fae the train, they didnae get any pick-ups then, they walked aw the way fae the train tae Burrow Head, the same tae Kidsdale.

And that's when your husband came?

Yes. Aye, he was here before that Ah think. He worked wi ... his uncle had a farm at Cairnhouse, he came from Glasgow and he went tae live wi

> Auntie Emmie and Uncle Johnny at Cairnhouse farm, he worked wi them for a while. And then he put in for a builder's job. He was a builder, his Uncle Johnny was a builder, he wasnae a farmer, although he was on the farm and he took a job as a builder wi Wimpey. Wimpey recommended him, Wimpey was a big firm in Glasgow, he worked there for a long while and he went tae Baldoon.
>
> ...
>
> Ah think he [her husband] was– wi him workin– he was working in the, like Army bases and Air Force. He worked wi them. He worked at Baldoon for a long while when he come here and in Glasgow he worked wi the big companies, Ah cannae remember them noo but it was to do wi the Army anyway.

Margerie Clark's father was at Kidsdale.

Margerie Clark

> He was ground crew. ... I think he was there sort of the middle of the war time, I believe there would be barrage balloons and such like there at the time, but he didn't. He would talk more about when he used to walk from Kidsdale down to the Isle of Whithorn and walk down to Whithorn. There was a lot of walking in those days went on! And I think one of the reasons he met my mother was that he was usually sent out to get the bakery or the rolls or things for the ones that were at Kidsdale.

Jessie McLean

> Aye, this is whaur Ah met Billy here.
>
> ...
>
> *Mary: Ye met him, he come during the War tae build the camp up at Burrow Head. So it was a wartime romance?*
>
> Yes, an Ah got a good husband. Bill was a good, kind man and clever. De ye ken I went to the school wi the vet that was here in Whithorn and he's far cleverer than the vet for the vet yaist tae come tae ask him questions. He was a clever, clever man.
>
> *Mary: He was a Bevan Boy, ma da.*
>
> He belonged tae Edinburgh.
>
> *Mary: He come fae the mines in Edinburgh an he come here tae help tae build the camp an she met him, she worked in yin o the hotels here, an he was lodging next door. And ye met him and merriet him in six weeks in Stranraer an she come hame an she went up hame tae her mother, ma granny's an he went tae his digs.*
>
> His digs, aye (laughter). Ma mither was that angry.

Mary: An then he went intae, he went intae the War and they brought him oot tae gaun back intae the pits for a couple o years, during the War.

He was really a, his uncle was a manager o a big pit and he was getting his job but Ah didnae like Donald in the pits. Ah didnae like ma wean in there.

Mary: Ma da liked here, didn't he? He didnae like– he liked doon here.

He liked it here, he liked Whithorn, jist like you like it, a stranger tae Whithorn but he liked it.

Mary: And then there was nae work an the pits kinna, there was a pit doon in Kirkconnel and different bits roond Cumnock and ye went there for work and Donnie by that time had left the school and he went intae the pit. And then he went intae the Navy. Ah wis still at the school. And them ma dad took silicosis in the pits and we moved back hame here. And then he died when he was just 50-odd.

The changes to Galloway House, Glasserton and Physgill were dramatic, and in the case of Glasserton House, led to demolition.

Greta Hawthorn

And Burrowhead Camp was the great thing to the town and Galloway House was a military hospital during the War for some folk, maybe recuperating, and they brought them in on buses and some o them from America, they had their blue tunics and everything on. And ye felt that sorry for them trying to get oot o buses and things. Billy was in the hospital at Galloway Hoose for six weeks because they thought he, he thought he was taking chickenpox or something and he telt them and so they sent him there for convalescence, he was at his mother's every day.

So, was he in the Forces?

Yes, he was in the King's Own Scottish Borders [Borderers].

Tom McCreath

What about Glasserton House during the war, was that in use?

Late on, it was, to house some engineers who gathered to form a company to plan the Mulberry harbours. And all engineering battalions were contacted to send their best men. So what did they do? They sent all the guys who had charge sheets the length of your arm, up to all the mischief of the day and they really were a collection of absolute rogues. They, I think, you know the story that they found out where the wine cellar, was which had been closed off with a welded door, so they got out picks and shovels and dug down through the kitchen floor to get at it. And in the rooms upstairs, I gather, they would have taken large logs and just laid them on the floor and fed the fire with these, they almost wrecked

Glasserton House but I've got to say that when they were in Normandy and the storm came and hit the Mulberry harbours they were magnificent. They were tough and they were dedicated and they were well led. I think I've got to say that the parents remembered the spirit that the country had in the First World War and it seemed to them inconceivable that the country would ever have the same spirit if war was declared again and how wrong they were.

Elsie McShane remembers the end of Glasserton House.

Elsie McShane

I remember my father got quite friendly with some of them, you know. And the officers were lovely, there were some very nice people. They were quite kind to us, with chocolate when nobody else had it! (laughs) But I remember it would be '42, '43, when my father, we used to talk about it afterwards, that's what it was. He had been told, in the morning of that day, that we'd be moving out, one of the officers said, 'We're moving out, we're moving out through the night'. And actually, they went to fight in North Africa; part of the North African campaign. I remember – quite vividly – my father and my two elder brothers went to the road end to see them pass by. So, then what happened after that? Well, the War came to an end, and Robin's father didn't come home then, he came home a few years later than that. But there was a housekeeper, a sort of caretaker and his wife: and their name was Jamieson. And I've spoken to the Laird when he was asking me about things, and he could tell me that Morley Jamieson is actually a playwright, and he's still going strong.

Well, it [Glasserton House] was full of dry rot, and wet rot, and everything else. They just decided that it would have had to come down. It would have taken a fortune, and they didn't have a fortune, to put it right. So it came down. That was 1948 49. … [The demolition of the house] was a bit heartbreaking. It was really sad. Have you seen photographs of the house? It was absolutely beautiful. Yes, it was beautiful. … [The stone from the house] was taken away, yes. … there was nothing left. Nothing at all. It was very sad – it just wasn't viable at all, no. I think what bits of silver there was, what had escaped the clutches of the soldiers – the good stuff – was in the bank.

Just as farms were forced to produce more from every acre, the forests were put to use to meet national targets. The land round Galloway House, once parkland for pleasure and leisure, became the centre for forestry operations to produce industrial timber; a young Jenny Jolly was recruited to work there.

Jenny Jolly

At the very start I went doon tae – it was the same firm like – but it was down tae Innerwell, right down to the Innerwell, right doon tae where the, you know, where the salmon bit is? There was a mill there and that's where Ah wis so it was a fair cycle fae Whithorn doon there. And then in a short time when they got started Galloway House Ah got transferred up tae it, so it was far enough but no ocht like Innerwell.

...

So tell me about what the timber was used for?

Oh, the wedges, oh they were nasty wee things, ma face aw chipped wi them trimming them, the wedges wis trimmed at this wee, what ye call the running-off saw, the circular saw, and they needed a terrific load o them. They went for the battleships, they needed them for getting them doon, tae launch them doon tae the water, ye see an they werenae yaised again so that's hoo they were aye lookin for them and then there was – for pallets and stuff – stobs, just different items, ye ken.

...

Well, I was daen the same work as the Timber Jills, Ah wis workin wi them, just the same. In fact I was daen mair for Ah had the big hatchet, the big axe wheeling roon aboot me trimmin the big trees while they sat, Oh God!

...

You actually climbed up into the trees, didn't you?

Some o them. The big trees, the foreman had tae tie things roon his legs, spikes, tae cut the tree, tae stick in, the spikes stuck into the tree.

So, how many years did you work on the sawmills?

Oh, gosh, I was there – 17½, I was there till I was 22.

So nearly five years, then? Pretty much the whole of the War.

The War was actually finished before Ah finished. We were still cutting wood.

And did Lady Forteviot offer her woodland or was it kind of compulsory?

I think it would be compulsory, there was jist the certain bits they couldnae touch, especially this park, but eventually they got the trees there. But to start with they werenae getting them. But she didnae come back there efter that onyway, she stayed up in Perthshire. But her nephew came and he stayed in the gardener's house.

So, how much did you get paid for the timber work, do you remember?

Oh, was it about £3.00 a week or something maybe? Something like that, Ah ken at the Catyans it was 30 shillings per month, at Jones' it was 30 shillings per month. But that was for seven days, you only got a day, an odd day off or a half-day or something. It wisnae a lot o money.

So, tell me a little bit about how you worked on the trees at Galloway House?

Well, they were, obviously they're great big trees, there's wee yins tae but they were easy. The big trees, the men had these big axes and they had tae chip them aw roon aboot before they got a cross-cut saw and they had knee pads, because they had tae go on their knees wi it tae saw it doon. And then when it was doon, we had big axes again, no hatchets, the wee yins wis nae yiss for that and a tree had tae be trimmed, aw the branches trimmed off it, and some o them was big, of coorse. Some of them had tae be cut off wi a cross-cut saw, that ye held, and then there was some ye trimmed and then ye had tae kindle a fire and burn aw the bush, aw the rubble. When we went tae another tree when the fire burned doon, ye got a big shovel and ye lifted the hot ashes and took it tae start another fire. Yince ye got the first fire gaun, after that ye just carried the fire wi the big shovel and it lay oot aw night, so did the bucket o water, only [unclear] emptied it oot an Ah was the youngest so it was me that aye run for the water for the, boilin the billy cans up and in thae days ye got a two pound tin o syrup and this is what we had. Ma mother edged it aw neatly round so that ye didnae get yer hand cut and a nail, hammer a nail hole on either side and a wire through it and ye had a big lang lump o wid, stick on the wid and ye just held it ower it and boiled it on the fire. But it was really tinker's tea cause it was smoke an aw but then ye were gled tae drink it. When Ah started at first, ye started, well ye aye started early as ye ken, cycled doon, and there was no tea breaks, and little time at dinner time and it was– ye worked a Saturday till dinner time tae and then it came oot ye got tea breaks, that come oot, and then the next thing was it was just a five-day week, eventually. They were long oors tae start wi.

Yes. So it was all manual cutting? You had no machines to cut with?

No, no in thae days, no, it was men wi big cross-cut saws, yin at either end and sometimes you helped tae but ye had a hatchet, as I say, and I still hae the big auld hatchet at the back there.

So the men who did the cutting, were they local men?

No, they were fae Wigtown, kinna all roon aboot.

So what was the name of the company that was employing you?

Oh aye, it was. They were fae Larbert, away up at Larbert, what dae ye ca [James Jones & Sons Ltd] … it was that Mr Davy Kerr was their head man, didnae … oh Jones, Jones wis the company fae up Stirling way. They'd stuff aw ower the place. It was a Caterpillar tractor an aw of coorse on the go, pu'in things oot. And it had a big chain on it for pu'in the big trees alang a bit, oot, and yin day Ah wis gaun for something, water or something, and it snapped an it just flew. It just missed me an nae mair. Everybody come tearing, runnin, they thought it had hut me cause Ah did try tae deuk and fa doon but no, it just went ower the top o me. Everybody got a fright.

So, you cut the trees down and then they were hauled to?
> They were hauled tae the mill. They hadnae a mill to start wi, though, cause Ah helped at the building o the mill, they were hauled away tae somewhere anyway. And then the big lorries used to come in tae take the props and stuff away tae different bits an the wedges tae the shipyards at the Clydebank for they could only yaise these wedges tae launch the battleship and then they couldnae be yaised again. I used to trim them at the wee runnin-offaw, there's the big saws and then there was the middle saw and then this wee runnin-off yin but the stuff in yer face, Ah had tae get goggles, tae for ma eyes wi the stuff comin off them. And as Ah say, pit props and different things and then there was firewood, we used to go roond tae Elrig selling the logs, the firewood, well there was the old village, and Ah always remember the wee houses, because a lot o them, that they had it at the Isle of Whithorn as well, roses growin up the front door, up the wa', right up.

So you helped build a new mill at Galloway House? That was to make it more efficient presumably?
> Aye, but it wis tae– they needed a roof, no right doon, but needed a roof jist fae the top o the saws and it was big sheets o tin and Ah used tae stand, they used tae hand me a bit and Ah had tae push it up tae somebody at the top that was fastening it. And there was the auld steam engine in it, there was an engineman, Ronnie McCutcheon, I mind he had a bad eye, he got hurt in an eye when he was younger but he was the engineman, had tae keep feeding it.

Feeding it with coal or–?
> Sticks and everything. Everything, for it had tae be kept blazin, ye ken. It was nice and warm in the winter time tae gae in and have yer tea (laughter).

And were there people who lived on the site to manage–?
> Yes, they built what they ca'd, well they ca'd them huts, but they were really like wee prefabs. Ah mind o Dennis Adams makin a lovely garden, he made, he cut up the wid fae the sawmill and made a fence roon it and had a lovely garden. He'd potatoes and veg in it, it was close up to the gardener's hoose. That's where the land army stayed, in thae days, and there was toilets an aw outside them and big wash hand basins and whatnot, that's where they had tae wash and whatnot.

So, how many Land Army girls were there?
> Oh, there were quite a few, just cannae mind, because they went out tae different farms. That was their base, jist and then there's a base up at Physgill House. … they had breeches an aw, the land girls, an overalls for workin in like yon brownie overalls.
>
> …

[We worked] fae eight o'clock, it wis the same when we started, there was no teabreaks, ye jist worked through and ye worked tae Saturday dinner time but then the hours got aw chynged and ye worked tae a Friday night, unless there was a big, big order, which didnae happen often.

So, how many people do you think worked on it?

There was different yins, they had wee squads that just four thegither and then four somewhere else so, and then, of coorse, there's the folk at the sawmill. But there was aye a man that was the foreman, whae ye – Jimmy Sharp, he come fae Wigtown.

While there was increase of business for teashops and cinema, rationing reached businesses like Betty Murray's parents' shop.

Betty Murray

And then Burrowhead camp was open and my father did supply a lot to the officers mess at Burrowhead. ... I can't remember exactly what was rationed first, but it was two ounces of butter, and two ounces of marg, about two or three ounces of bacon, and two or three ounces of cheese. And sugar, that was eventually rationed. Bread was rationed after a while, and they called them BU's. There was a book with tickets, and they called them BU's, and the bread was rationed. And then jam became very scarce, and I remember a big consignment of tinned jam coming into our shop, it was South African. It was the loveliest jam we had ever tasted, fruit; it was beautiful. Tinned, South African jam, and it was beautiful.
... I think people got permits for keeping bees, for harvest, and that was for extra sugar. They got permits over and above their coupons.

Blackout cloth replaced scarce clothing at Kinnear's shops, which was among those whose stock underwent strange transformations.

Robin Kinnear

Yes, well, there was– we kept rolls of blackout material and joiners made frames and then they were stuck on with drawing pins. But during the war, of course, it was all clothing coupons and it was very difficult to get any coupon-free stuff at all so my father started selling anything that they could manage to sell and he had distemper; wallpaper which we sold up until the '80s, we had wallpaper books that we sent round customers or people would come into select their wallpaper; bicycle tyres; wee battery lamps and it was terrible because there was two ironmongers as well, they were selling the same sort of thing, but my father didn't have any stuff to display really in the window. No sort of new dresses in or new cloth or things like, that it was just essentials that you bought with your coupons. He had two boxes, he was very keen on his tomatoes, growing his tomatoes in the greenhouse at home, but he wanted to grow some more so the siting of our shop faces south so we had – very bad for drapery – you had to have blinds over the windows, but he put two big long boxes in the windows, one on each window, with tomato plants in it. … But that was where, during the War where they wanted you to cultivate on every possible bit of land you could and they actually cultivated the roadsides, grew things on the roadsides. And when they were planting corn, oats and things like that, they … it was right up to the wall and all the fields had to be opened by scythe to let the binders in, there was no space for them at all. These are just some of the things but we had a very easy war here, in Port William, because there was plenty of eggs and ham and freshly made butter and milk and cream, all the farms had it for sale.

The rural economy, which had always been inventive and autonomous in regard to food production, was far more resilient than that of cities, under conditions of rationing. While the wartime Government sought to encourage thrift and self-reliance, these were already the principles on which the countryside was operating. Judy Brown confirms that there were far fewer food shortages, in an agricultural area, than in the cities.

Judy Brown

And did you find that food was shorter than before or were you ok because you produced food?
We were very much ok, we didn't, as far as I know, we didn't suffer at all because in those days if you wanted a piece of mutton or lamb then you just slaughtered one. You slaughtered a pig or you– and we had our own milk, our own cream, our own butter. We were all, again in that time, you went out and collected blackberries and you made blackberry jelly and jam and rosehip syrup and all these things that nobody does now. It was just part of life, you just did it and then of course there was the black market.
Was that quite vigorous in this area?
I think so. You would hear the odd, as kids we heard the odd goings on at night (laughs).
Would people approach you to give them extra?
No, I think it was a sort of exchange, shall we say? And the chap who made ice cream in Whithorn, at the time, he got a lot of jam sugar, so he would bring us out some jam sugar. And he would maybe get a couple of dozen eggs, you see, in its place, it was a bartering system. … I remember too,

after the War, going up to Glasgow with my parents. I followed Dad into St Enoch's Hotel and he goes up to the reception desk and asks for two rooms. 'Sorry sir, fully booked.' So he goes into one pocket and puts three eggs on the desk, goes into the other puts three. 'How many rooms sir?' So he got his two rooms for half a doz.

Jenny Jolly

So were you rationed on milk and butter even though it was a dairying area?
Oh, yes, yes. Oh yes, you were for everything, even eggs was scarce as well. The eggs in thae days [unclear] went tae the market, they were stamped lions, a lion on them, they had tae get passed through. When Ah worked in the Catyans hoose though, we did well because they used to kill a pig on the fly, they werenae supposed to. … And then she got, it was a secret though, so I never said ocht aboot it, she got auld Kennedy man – was it Bob ye ca'd im? He was a butcher, onyway, he was trained a butcher and he was a butcher wi Owen's in Garlieston and she got him across the field but he had the things an aw hid doon his jacket and here he was jist oot for a walk wi his way o it and he killed a pig, ye see ye werenae allowed tae dae that.
This was during the War?
Uh-huh. And God, we had a great time wi that pig. She was aye, ye got some guid feeds, I'm telling ye (laughter) and she made puddings, she made mealy puddings and black puddings and aw wi it. She had the things for– they were like long, that came oot o the pig, ye hung them, ye stretched them and ye hung them ower the back o a chair aw night and that's what she used for the white puddings.

Further foreign bodies were introduced to the Machars economy, with the seconding of prisoners of war to local farms.

Jock McMaster

And prisoners of war, he talked quite a lot aboot them, the Italians and Germans that they had workin in the farm, and actually they a lot o them were good workers, quite enthusiastic.
So, you had them on this farm?
Yea, yes. There was a camp at Port William, just where, nowadays, it's 3b[construction] have their workshop there, that hostel was where the prisoners were billeted although the main camp was at Minnigaff but I think they must have been a few just stayed down this end, maybe for the week, Ah don't know, before ma time. But funnily enough Ah had a

German chap came to the door, three or four years ago, and he'd been here as a prisoner. Aye, it was funny, God it was funny that day. He went into the garden here and he went, 'My goodness this garden's never changed. Your grandfather used to put me in here,' he said, 'it was like a labour camp,' he said, 'digging and digging and weeding'. (laughs) But he, it turned oot was only 18 then, towards the end of the War there was an awful lot of these young lads were captured over there so he wasnae much older than I was, to be honest, and he could remember it well.

Burrowhead eventually became a camp for Displaced Persons, which resulted in some marriages with some of the Polish inmates; but one of the best known local Poles came to Sorbie and Whithorn, of his own volition, to practise his skill as a blacksmith.

Margerie Clark

Oh yes, 'Ben the Pole', as he was known of originally. He was born and grew up in Poland, his father was a blacksmith before him, as was Uncle Ben, he trained and became a blacksmith, and then of course Germany invaded Poland, and at that time he was still quite a young lad, and I believe from what he told us he was working in the distillery at the time there, and the Resistance approached him and asked him to help them by smuggling out the pure alcohol, because it was good for medicinal purposes, for wounds and such like. And he did that for a wee while, and then I think somebody tipped him off that the Germans were onto him, so he had to escape after that. So he was actually only 17 when he left Poland. But he did join the Polish army originally. He'd actually, apparently he'd always wanted, as a boy he wanted to go into the Navy, but his father wouldn't have it. He thought that wasn't a good thing. I think they had one large training ship for the whole country, and he wanted to go to the Navy, but his father wouldn't allow him. So he joined the Polish army. He joined the cavalry.

...

I believe the day they invaded Poland one of his sisters' husbands was shot that day, almost immediately, because he was a teacher or something, so he had been shot. So as I say, Uncle Ben went through a lot of the War. I know he was in Italy for a lot of the War, he spent a lot of time in Italy. He picked up Italian, he could speak a bit of Italian. Oh, and of course he could speak German, because unbeknown to the parents– it wasn't that the parents taught them, but they had a friend, they had next door neighbours in Poland, and they were German, and they had moved in. But it helped him during the War because he was able to escape capture at one point, I think probably the Gestapo or somebody were after him. And he told us a story of, he had stolen a German uniform, German soldier's uniform, and pretended that he'd gone AWOL, a German soldier gone AWOL, so he actually did get thrown into a prison cell for a time. But not as a Polish spy or anything like that, they thought he was a German soldier. So it probably saved his life, the fact that he could speak German. He did get a bit of abuse, in the physical, they hit them and he said that one of the times it was a holiday, and they'd left them all in the cells, and the guards were going away for the holiday. And of course they'd complained, and the guard just opened the door and took the huge big bunch of keys and just whacked him across the face with the keys. Which subsequently broke his teeth. So eventually he did get away. You always got snippets of stories from him, you never got the full bit, so it's always difficult to piece together which part of the War we're at at times. I do know he went to an aunt for help, one of his German aunts, but she wouldn't even let him in the door. But subsequently he caught up with his unit again, and went through Italy, and was in Rome, afterwards, and found himself, I suppose, here. Because the time came, after the end of the war, they were all being demobbed. And they'd finished up in– a lot of the Poles finished up either Newcastle or Edinburgh, and he subsequently finished up in Edinburgh. And he was wondering about what to do, and where to go, because he knew then he wasn't going back to Poland. Although he had family there, his parents were still alive, and there was quite a large family of them I think, I don't know how many, there must have been about six or seven of them in total. But because of the Russians invading Poland he knew he couldn't go back. Or he thought he couldn't go back. So he'd been looking for work, what to do. And I think he toyed with the idea of emigrating to the States, and then he was looking on the jobs board, and saw a job advertised for a blacksmith in a place called Sorbie. And he couldn't speak English, at this point, he could speak obviously Polish, German, Italian, but he had no English at that time. But he saw the work, so he decided, cause he was fully qualified blacksmith, that he would follow up and go for that job. Which was how he ended up being in Wigtownshire. And he worked for a man by the name of Tommy Woods in the smiddy in Sorbie. And subsequently he began to pick up English. The family, the Petrucci family, who originally had the cafe– well, of course, it's still their grandson, great-grandson, who has it now. But the Petrucci family, he became friendly with them, because of course he could converse with them in Italian at least, so he wasn't completely cut off. And of course he picked up speaking English just from the locals. Which was why the result was that he spoke with a Wigtownshire dialect! And many people wouldn't believe he was Polish because of that. But that was how it came about, because he learned his English in Sorbie and Whithorn. So he'd worked for Tommy Woods for a while, and then he ended up working for– he left Tommy after, I don't know, think it was a few years, and worked for a gentleman, name of Willie Roanie, who had the smiddy in Port William. And he worked there. And the Roanie family were extremely good to him, he had actually better treatment from them than he did from Mr Woods. But he worked for them, and Willie Roanie at one point after a number of years opened a smiddy at the top o the town, in Whithorn, roughly where the island is now, up there, and Uncle Ben then worked in that smiddy for Willie for a number of years as well. And then eventually he decided I think this time he'd got married to Auntie Margerie, I think he married her in between, during the time he worked for Mr Roanie, but he'd met her, that's another story, but I'll finish the one about the smiddy. He then opened his own smiddy in Whithorn, early '60s, that would be. Barns Smithy, which is, the place is still there, and some of the buildings are still there that he had, which is where George Pattison now resides.

But he met Auntie Margerie, because she was manageress in the then Kingsway cinema that we had here in Whithorn. She wasn't one to make her mind up quickly. But when they did get married, they actually bought this house, 44 George Street, from a couple, Mary Cain, that's who they bought it from originally. So they were married in 1957, 17th of July 1957. And that was how that came about.

Evacuees from Glasgow came and went: they were the briefest of transplants to the countryside.

Tom McCreath

Yes, actually three days before the War broke out Glasgow was evacuated, as were many of the cities, and we, in this area, were scheduled to have evacuees from the Gorbals and Clydebank and known to be so-called slum areas the person who saved the day was, I think, a Miss Hopkins who was caretaker at Glasserton House who had done slumming in Glasgow and she advised people how to prepare. … The house, the farmhouse was scheduled for 16 evacuees because a fairly large house. In the event we got twelve and a teacher. They arrived, oh, they were rough, some adorable little kids, largely from Catholic families in Glasgow and, although that didn't make any difference, but Mother and Father had a tough job sort of bringing order into the house (laughter). We had been advised to take up all the carpets and move them upstairs and in our drawing room, as we called it, that was the dormitory and until we got mattresses we filled sacks with straw and then, of course, put a sheet over them but that was, that kept them going until we got mattresses, and running, feeding them was a, quite a major operation and Father was the hairdresser because they were quite heavily infested when they arrived and I won't say too much but they were adorable kids but the parents couldn't do without them and the last of them were away in six weeks. … Yes, but you'll find if you ask anyone who remembers that period that was by far the most traumatic of the whole War. They wouldn't go to sleep at night so father bought a football and ordered the teacher to keep them going until they were dead tired (laughter). He said it was the best spent money of the War (laughter).

Yes, that must have been a terrific shock for them because they probably had never seen the countryside?

Oh, they didn't know what it, a horse was. 'What's thae animals wi the fur on?' And then when the heard that cows were the source of their milk some of them went off drinking milk. … I can still remember them, they were going to form a gang so I decided, well, if they were doing that we would have to have our gang too (laughter) so I enrolled a couple of friends from the neighbouring farms and then Mother got to hear about it and that was the end of the gangs (laughter).

So if they only stayed six weeks did they start school?

Oh yes, they went to school in Sorbie, they walked it, uh-huh, and I can remember the evacuees in Whithorn school.

Did any of them stay long-term? Or did they mostly vanish?

They mostly vanished, we had correspondence from a couple who went back to Glasgow and of course the ones in Clydebank suffered that very big air raid. I think one was killed, tragically. After that we got two who stayed 18 months and they were ok, yes.

The Petrucci family, who had settled well, already running a successful business at the Central Café in Whithorn, suffered the trauma of having their father declared an alien and interned. Yet on his return, he continued in business as usual and joined the Home Guard.

Aldo Petrucci and Tina Soriani

AP: I remember coming home from school when Italy entered the War against the Allies over here. Going home from school for lunch and my father wasn't there. He had been taken away. He had been given 15 minutes to pack a case and be taken down to the prison. And from there he went to Newton Stewart as far as I know, and from Newton Stewart he was taken over to the Isle of Man, and one incident that happened while he was in the Isle of Man, they were all up, all the prisoners were lined up, and a lot of them were going. I think it was to Australia, they were going to be taken to Australia, in a ship called – what was the ship called? The name has escaped me just now. But he was in the next line to be taken. But the ship was full so he wasn't taken. I think it would be 800 prisoners. And when the ship was in the Irish Sea a German U-boat came up and sank it. And a lot of them lost their lives. And most of these people had fought on the side of the British in the First World War, you understand! So it was really very unfair, and it cost them their lives. But on the other hand, my father was saying that on the Isle of Man everyone was very nice to them, there were no hardship, they were put up in hotels that had been taken over, and boarding houses, that's where they were stationed. And the police were very good. And he was one of the very lucky ones. Wasn't politically minded, and there was always a tribunal, interviewing these people, and if they thought they were harmless they'd be sent home. And one of the ones that were sent home quite early, after nine months, was my father. Some of them spent the whole War in the Isle of Man. One Italian that I know from Kilmarnock was actually sent back tae Italy for whatever reason, I don't know.

And how did you feel about your father being taken away?

AP: Well, I was too young, I would be about nine years old and to be honest, it didn't really affect me all that much, to be honest! And I remember. I can't even say that after a while that I missed him, he just wasn't there and we accepted it. And I can remember, I must have been in my mother's bed one morning, and I woke up and this face was looking down at me, unshaven, and of course it was, after nine months, it was my father, and I hardly even recognised him, you know. So, and my mother, poor soul, was left to look after three young children and a cafe. And it must have been pretty hard for her. But she managed it, and the cafe, really, what's the word, survived, and I think was very popular in the town. I think the town would have missed it.

And was it particularly good business during the War?

AP: Yes. I remember, because this area was flooded with soldiers and airmen, West Freugh, Baldoon, Burrowhead, lots and lots of soldiers. And I can remember the shop packed with soldiers. Just about every night. So it did make the shop very busy.

TS: The family that were in Stranraer, an Italian family, her husband was interned as well. But she was, she had to be, there's a word. She had to leave Stranraer because it was a protected area. And so she came to Whithorn and stayed with a sister in law. I don't know, she stayed with us for a wee while. ... Katie, Katie Nesti.

AP: And the interesting thing during the war, there's a family in Stranraer, or was in Stranraer, Jose Adami, the Adamis, they had a cafe, right? And

Jose was old enough to be called up by the British Army, he was in the British Army.

TS: He was born in Britain.

AP: And his parents, at least his father, was his father interned, I think?

TS: But that happened with a lot of families!

AP: That happened a lot! Even the DePatells in Glenluce, were the same, their three brothers I think were all in the Army, and, it's a funny situation!

So were the people in Whithorn during the War, were they pretty sympathetic about your father being interned?

AP: Yes, generally, they were. There was always one or two once they had a drink in them. They were a bit aggressive.

TS: But we were very lucky.

AP: Very lucky, yes. Compared to other people, yes, people in general were excellent …

AP: [Talking about a film of his father leaving for internment] It was only about a minute, a minute and a half long. And it just shows my father being escorted down the pavement with his coat over his arm and the sergeant, I can't remember his name.

TS: Porter.

AP: Walking down beside him, and Jimmy Denton I think waved him goodbye, and things like that. It was only a minute.

TS: There was a very good relationship between all the businesses in Whithorn. They all helped each other during the war. My father maybe had more sugar than he needed, he would give it to the baker, and the baker would give him oil for frying, things like that.

Yes, I remember the blackout, and there was a curfew, we had to close at nine o'clock, and of course the pictures come out at nine o'clock, or whatever was on at that time, if it was bingo, and of course the people would be in the shop, and were trying to serve them as quickly as possible, and of course the police at the door, not letting anyone else in! Yes, and I remember the blackout.

And do you remember the Home Guard being active?

TS: Yes, my father was in the Home, when he came home he joined the Home Guard. They grew their own vegetables and potatoes as much as they could, I think everybody helped each other. I know we didn't eat jam, and my mother gave jam coupons maybe tae a family that had a lot of children, and things like that. But …

AP: No, it was a very stable kind of life really, and nothing extraordinary about it.

Index

'Bevan Boy' 253
'Brown's Coastwatchers' 249
'The Halfway House' 178
'The Saturday Night Hop' 252
1st Seaforths 203
A. B. & A. Matthews lawyers 227
A. J. Marshall, Bridgebank 103
A. K. Muir's delicatessen 40
Aberdeen 39, 48
Abbot's House, Garlieston 103
Adami family 266, 267
Adami, Jose 266–67
Adami's café 266
Adams, Dennis 258
Adams, Willie (policeman) 35
Africa 208
Air Force see RAF
Airdrie 180
Airlour, The 174, 175
Airriequhillart farm 30
Aitken, Maggie 82
Aitken, Wullie 82
Alexander, Ian 184
Alexander, R. G. 33, 34, 184

Alexander's rent & solicitors office 33
Alford, Aberdeenshire 203
Allan, Bob 118
Allerton hairdressers 38
Alva, Clackmannanshire 205
Alves jeweller's shop & opticians 16, 17, 32
America *see* United States of America
Anderson, Beanie 148
Anderson, Elizabeth 34
Anderson, Mr (Kinnear's driver) 190
Angus 134
Annual Foal Show 106
Arbrack farm 18
Ardrossan 44
Argentina 140, 204, 205
Army, the 245, 246, 253, 267
Attlee, Clement 175
Auchenmalg 190
Auchinleck 205
Australia 181, 201, 202, 266
Ayr 207, 221, 244
Ayrshire 57, 114, 202

Baird, Eric 35
Baird's gun shop, Eric 36
Baldoon airfield 247, 253, 266
Balnab farm 2
Barmeal farm 250
Barns Smithy 264
Barrachan 14, 82
Barrachan Home Farm 68
Baxter, John (chemist) 36–37, 223, 224
Baxter, Mrs 36–37
Baxter's chemists 36–37
Begg, Mrs 197
Belfast 44
Belgium 203
Bell, Daisy 189
Bell, Johnny (Kinnear's driver) 189–90
Bell, Lawrence 51–52
Bell, Mrs (taxi) 189
Bell, Sammy 52
Bell's Garage 51–52, 189
Bell's school 210
Bellshill 210
Bendall, Jimmy (postman) 39
Bendall, Mr (saddler) 39, 97
Biagi, Bertie 54
Bie's, Miss Winifred 31
Bie's shop 31, 49, 50, 51; *31*

268

INDEX

Bie, Peter 51
Birchman, Miss 37
Birchman, Mr 37
Bishopton (Bishop's Town) 2, 233
Black Hawk, The 38, 185
Black, Maggie 196
Black Rocks, Monreith 149, 198
Black's Plantation 67, 183
Blair Hill 246
Blairbuy farm 115, 123, 138
Blakeman, Major 133
Blakeman, Mrs 133
Borders, Scottish 15, 17
Boreland of Balmaghie 103
Boyce, Mrs Nellie 209 240
Boy's Brigade 150
Bridgebank 103
Bridgebank farm 142
Briggs, Davie 49
Brighouse 67
Brock, Winnie 229
Broll family 75
Broll, Mrs 36
Broughton Mains farm 18, 116, 203
Broughton Skeog farm 203
Brown and Charters 35, 173
Brown and Co. 44
Brown, Dave/Davie 34, 104
Brown, Dr Guy (Gavin) 36, 58, 90, 120, 176–77, 193, 210, 215, 218, 220–25, 248–50
Brown senior, Dr Gavin 36, 58, 175, 176, 210, 220, 222, 223–24, 249–50
Brown, Mrs 175

Brown, Judy 85–86, 88, 134, 136–37, 198, 260–61
– father (potato merchant) 134, 136–37, 261
Brown, Mr (schoolmaster) 65
Brown, Willie 135
Brownhill farm 63, 87, 104, 142
Brownies 150
Brunswick Inn 152, 205, 207
Buchanan Tam/Thomas/Tom (stud groom) 100–1, 103–4, 148, 203–4; *101*
Buenos Aires 205
Burke, Father 235
Burrow Head 248, 251, 252, 253, 259
Burrowhead Camp 48, 152, 156, 216, 248, 251, 252, 253, 254, 259, 262, 266
Bute, Marquess of 49, 229, 230, 233
Bute, Marquis of 233
Bysbie mill 123, 124–25

Cacks' dairy 116
Cain, Bobby 35
Cain, Mrs Mary (shoe repair) 35, 264
Cairndoon 198
Cairndoon Bank 198
Cairnhouse farm 252–53
Cairnryan 177
Calcutta, The 30, 31, 152, 153–54, 218
Caldwell, Sammy (pedlar) 196
Caledonian Garage 227
California 202
Callander family 191

Cameron's paper shop 33
Camlay's wool shop 32
Campbell, Mr (head teacher) 32
Campbell, Mrs 227
Campbell, Revd Neil 227
Canada 98, 202, 208, 246, 247
Carlisle 103, 162
Carnochan, Mrs 32
Carr, Jimmy (market garden) 61
Carruthers, Mr (Kinnear's driver) 190
Carson, coal merchant 36, 192
Carson's grocers 70
Castle Douglas 56, 121, 142, 202
Castlewigg 35
Catrine 206
Catyans House 144–46, 256, 261
Catyans lawyers 13, 179
Central Café 30, 35, 38, 48, 69–70, 213–14, 263, 265, 266
Challoch farm 202
Chalmers, Ally 104
Chamberlain, Byron 155
– father (travelling cinema) 155
Changue farm 249
Chapman, Mrs 31
Cherry Valley 59, 147
Christie, Cathy 164
Christie family 147
Christie, Miss 35
Christie, Mr (Airlour) 174
Christie, Mr (potato merchant) 135, 147
Christie's paper shop 16, 35

269

Christmas 42, 67, 158, 160, 177, 178, 229
Churchill, Winston 203
Clachan of Myrton forge 98–100; *99*
Clark, Father 234, 235, 239–40
Clark, Margerie 34, 42, 52 53, 230–32, 238–40, 253, 262–64
– family 42, 53, 239, 253
Clarksburn 100
Clatteringshaws Dam 88, 89
Claymoddie farm 92, 96, 137, 163
Clenaghan, Mrs (Kelvingrove Bar) 31
Clyde Tunnel 177
Clydebank 258, 264, 265
Clydesdale Bank 32
Co-operative 79, 193
Coatbridge 180
Coid, Charlie 11, 32, 70, 79, 80, 82, 192, 193
Coid, John 183
Coid's butcher's 11, 30, 32, 70, 79, 80, 82, 192
Colquhoun, John J. 17
Colquhoun, Marjie 17
Commercial Pub 145, 152
Connel 171, 172
Connin, Robert John 197
Cook, Mary 36
Costcutters 37, 97
Costley, Billy 150, 232
Costley, Mr 156
Costley, Mrs 150, 232
Costley's store 32, 79
Cowie, Campbell (minister) 238
Craiglemine 211; *168*

Cravictor, Crieff 203
Crawley, Annie 51
Creetown 206
Crichton Museum 221
Crow's Nest 220
Cruggleton farm 63, 93, 103, 138, 140, 142, 148, 203–4
Cruggleton forge 100–1
Cults, the 77, 79, 140, 175
Cults farm 104, 142
Cumnock 124, 254
Currie, Alec (minister) 238
Cutreoch farm 88, 137
D-Day 245, 246
Dalgety mill 126
Dalmuir 19
Dardanelles 203
David, Mr (pedlar) 196
Davidson family 36
Davidson, Mr 34
Davidson's ironmongery, Newton Stewart 202
Defoe, Daniel 182–83
Denton, Jimmy. 42, 156, 267
Denton's bakers 11, 12, 30, 36, 42, 71, 79, 179, 213, 214, 232
DePatell family (Glenluce) 267
Derbyshire 46
Dewar, Jimmy (grocer) 154, 193
Dewar's store, Port William 154
Dig, the 33, 40
Displaced Persons Camp 262
Dodds, Ackie 186
Dodds, Billy (policeman) 154

Dodd's cart 192
Dodds, Isobel 36
Dodds family 112
Dodds, Janet 218
Dodds, John 31
– market garden 31, 61
Dodds, Tootie 209
Dolly's hairdressers 33
Donnan, Jim 59, 129, 130–31
Donnan, Kennedy 58, 59, 82, 129–30, 130–31
Doric, the 226
Doughty, Cathy 39, 77–78, 78–79, 140, 171–75
– family 77–78, 140, 173
Doughty, David/Davie 33, 39, 66, 67, 174, 192
Doughty, Lally 192
Doughty's Game Dealers 33, 38, 39, 66, 67, 192
Douglas Ewart High School 52, 215, 218
Douglas Orchestra, the 34, 36, 151
Douglas, Willie (butcher) 34, 36, 151
Dourie farm 108, 185
Dourie Farming Company 126
Dowies, The 91
Drape family 32, 39, 55
Drape's *see* G. B. Drape's
Dron, Mr (Creiff) 203
Drummore 135, 190
Drumrash 191
Drumtroddan farm 100
Drury Lane farm 87
Dublin 135
Duguid, Dr 210
Dumfries 56, 176, 189, 221, 224, 241

INDEX

Dumfries and Galloway Council 183, 184, 185, 186
Dumfriesshire 57
Dunning, Beatrice 54
– family 54
Dunragit smallholdings 183

East Anglian Institute 203
Edgar, Jim (vet) 62, 207
Edinburgh 182, 253, 263
Education Authority 210, 216
Elizabeth, Queen consort 142
Elrig 64, 258
Elrig, House of 4, 169
England 138
Ersock farm 2, 87

Faldarroch 82
Farrell, Mrs 34
Farrell, Wullie 34
Fell of Barhullion 124
Fell, the 247
Felyennan, Mochrum 110
Fenwick Moor 177
Ferguson and Forster solicitors 184
Fife 136
Findlay, Dr Frank 32, 223
Findlay, Mrs 32
– wool shop 32
First World War 4, 159, 163, 170, 203, 205, 215, 255, 266
Flannighan, Mary 197, 234
Flannighan, Mr 131
Flannighan, Mrs 153
Flannighan, Pat 50, 158
Flannighan's pub 59, 98, 197

Forbes, Mrs (Glasserton House) 161, 163
Forlow family 112
Forlow, Joanne 161
Forteviot, Lady 256
France 203
Frew, Archie 184

G. B. Drape's 30, 32, 35, 36, 37, 38–39, 55–56, 97, 98; *37, 38*
Galashan, John 103, 141, 203, 204, 205
Galashan, Molly 152
Galashan, Robert 100–1, 103–4, 141, 148, 151–52, 203–5, 247–48
– family 203–5
Galashan, William 103, 141, 203
Galloway 5, 18, 27, 224, 231
Galloway House & Estate 160, 177, 246, 254 255–59
Galloway Store 32, 178, 252
Garheugh golf course 249
Garlieston 42, 46, 56, 79, 123, 125, 126, 128, 160, 183, 220, 242, 245
– harbour 92, 245
– House of 160
– mill 92
Garret family 179
Garrick Hospital, Stranraer 221
Garrick, Billy 29
Garrick's grocers 29, 50
Garroch, Cathy 180–81
Garroch, Billy/Willie (repairs, dressmaking) 38
Garrocks store 77

Gatehouse of Fleet 206
George VI, King 142
Germany 216, 262–63
Gibson family 36
Gibson, Douglas (ironmonger) 33
Gibson, Willie (ironmonger) 33
Gibson's feed store 30
Gibson's ironmongers and saddlers 33, 39, 97
Girl Guides 150
Girvan 137, 202
Glasgow 2, 13, 15, 19, 22, 41, 43, 46, 62, 65, 90, 92, 135, 136, 137, 151, 176, 177, 181, 184, 195, 204, 205, 220, 221, 241, 242, 252, 253, 261, 264, 265
– St Enoch's Hotel 261
– University of 56, 203, 220
Glasgow Herald see Herald
Glasserton 37, 90, 92, 96, 104, 118, 148, 149, 159–60, 161–68, 202, 226, 230, 243
– Church 90, 160, 225, 226, 228, 242
– Gardens 162, 165, 181
– Hill 164
– House & Estate 5, 228, 251, 254–55, 264
– Lodge 21
– Mains farm 211
– Sawmill Cottages 161–62
– School 151, 211, 213
Glen, the 232
Glenluce 190, 247
Glenvernoch 165
Golf Hotel, The 185
Goodwin, Mr (tailor, Port William) 43, 44

271

Gorbals, the 264
Grapes Hotel, The 26, 29, 32, 34, 36, 38, 47–48, 136, 152, 154, 155, 185, 200; *47*
Gray Dunn, biscuit firm 191
Greece 176
Green, Mrs 223
Greenhorn, Mrs 39
Griffin, Anton 151
Guardian, The 17

Hale, Joe (butcher) 192
Hall, Lorna 163
Hall, Mrs 32, 163
Halloween 157, 158
Hamilton, Mr (Glasserton Estate) 167
Hanlon, Sammy 63
Hannah, Miss 36
– sweet shop 36
Hannah, Miss Joanne 146, 251
– tea room 146
Hannah, Miss Molly 146, 251
– tea room 146
Hannah, Mr (chemist) 150–51
Harman, Pat 37
Haswell, Alex 51–52, 74–75, 183–86, 215, 229, 236
– family 236
– father 183, 184, 186
Hawkins, Annie 240
Hawkins, Charlie (undertaker) 240
Hawkins, Mr (blacksmith) 98
Hawthorn, Billy 39, 41; *38*
Hawthorn, Greta 29, 30–39, 41, 47–48, 53–54, 67, 70,
91–92, 96, 120, 127–28, 136, 155, 163–64, 180–81, 186, 189, 198–200, 212–13, 214–15, 229, 232–33, 251, 254
– family 113, 212, 213
Heanor, Derbyshire 46
Henderson, Miss (teacher) 37, 214
Henderson's garage 53
Henry, Mr 156
Herald, The 148
Herd, Bobby 252
Heron, Molly 38, 39
Heron, Robert, saddler 33, 39, 97
Herron, Margaret 36
High Balcraig 24
High Boreland 129
Highlands, Scottish 1
Hill, Miss 186
Hogmanay 157, 158
Holland, Sarah (pedlar) 196
Home Guard, the 245, 246, 247, 249–50, 265, 267
Honeymoon Villa 32
Hopkins, Miss (Physgill House) 171–73
Hotham 205
Hughes, Cathy 30, 34, 35
– family 68
– shop 34
Hughes, Miss 155
Huxtable, Mary 49
Huxtable, Mrs 35
Huxtable's paper shop 35

I. & R. Morley, London 46
Indian Ocean 216
Industrial Revolution 13
Innerwell Point 256
– mill 256
Iowa 140
Ireland 12, 44, 71, 136, 137, 140
Irish Sea 266
Isle of Man 247, 265, 266
Isle of Whithorn 31, 42, 90, 123, 124–25, 136, 137, 152, 192, 196, 201, 220, 226, 230, 242, 248, 251, 253
– back shore/Island/Stinking Port 217
– Hall 151
– Queen's Arms 248
– School 216–17
– Steam Packet 20, 248
Italy 205, 206, 246, 265
– Abbettoni 206
– Barga 206
– Florence 206
– Luca 206
– Rome 263

J. B. Hoyle, Hebden Bridge 102
J. B. Little's store & workshop 32, 33
James Jones & Sons Ltd, Larbert 256, 257
James Wyllie and Sons 42, 64, 122, 125, 126, 128, 131, 192
Jamieson, Morley 255
Jardine, Mr (miller) 125
Jardine's, Dumfries 242
Jibb, Johnny 45
John Blackwood Hodge and Company, Baldoon 204
Johnston, Johnnie (Clerk Watch) 184
Johnston, Johnny 50
Jolly, Annie 157

Jolly family 51, 60, 62, 64–66, 83–84, 88–89, 106–7, 179, 193–94, 200
Jolly family business 31, 51, 64, 106, 179, 193–94
Jolly, Frank (butcher) 32, 62, 65
Jolly, Jenny (Jessie Maclean's sister-in-law) 54, 67, 70–71, 72–73, 76–77, 125, 126, 127, 133–34, 135–36, 144–46, 150–51, 153–54, 156, 161, 179–80, 194–95, 196–97, 198, 213, 218, 240, 255–59, 260
– family 133, 179–80, 234–35
– mother 71–72, 77, 179–80, 234–35, 257
– sister, Molly 73
Jolly, Jessie 62
Jolly, John McGinn 195
Jolly (neé McGinn), Mrs Mary 63, 64, 66, 67, 73, 179, 194, 195
Jolly, William (Bill) McGinn 31, 72, 73, 134, 195, 253–54
Jones, Mrs (Catyans) 146
Jones, Mrs (pedlar & lodging house) 31, 196, 197
Jones, Mrs (washerwoman) 18
Jones, Tommy (pedlar & lodging house) 197
Joyce, James 24

Kane, Norah 157
Kays' dairy farm 63
Keith, Katrina 251
Keith, Sonny 36
Kelly, Mr (builder) 50, 106
Kelly's garage 53, 75, 104
Kelvingrove Bar, The 31, 153
Kennedy, Mr (butcher) 145–46, 261
Kennedy, Stevie 38
Kerr, Davy 257
Kerr, James 151
Kerr, Mr (dentist) 32
Kerr Mrs 144
Kerrs, three Misses 35
Ket Burn 5, 28, 45
Ketburn 155
Ketburn Kitchens 45
Ketview House 34
Kevans family 84
Kevans, The 63
Kevin, Emily 64
Kidsdale camp 152, 156, 252, 253
Kidsdale farm 134, 135, 137, 233, 236
Kilfillan 129
Kilmarnock 177, 266
Kilncroft 52, 184
Kilpatrick, Jack (electrician) 35
King's Own Scottish Borderers 254
King's Road Cinema 12–13
Kingsway Cinema 154
Kinnear, John (ARP man) 250
Kinnear, Robin 8, 42–47, 56–57, 63–64, 102, 104, 125–26, 138, 154–55, 160–61, 169–70, 189–90, 241, 259–60
Kinnear's drapery business 8, 30, 34, 38, 42–47, 56–57, 70, 102, 154, 160–6, 169–70, 189–91, 241, 259–60
Kirk, Mr (Grapes Hotel) 47–48
Kirk, Mrs (Grapes Hotel) 47–48
Kirk, Mrs 85–86
Kirkconnel 254
Kirkcowan 41, 139
Kirkcudbright 114, 191, 224
Kirkcudbrightshire 43, 57
Kirkinner 152, 190, 220
Kirkpatrick, J. B. (Golf Hotel) 185
Kirkpatrick (neé Hawthorn), Mrs Margaret 41
Kirvennie farm 88
Koche, David (Murray's driver) 41

Ladies' Steps 164
Lambert, Mr (teacher) 211
Land Army/Girls see Scottish Women's Land Army
Larbert 257
Laurie, Miss 145, 146
Laurie, Mr 145
Law, Harry (preacher) 226
Law, Mr 178
Lawrie, Mattie 200
– grocers & van 200
Lawrie, Mr (lawyer) 59
Little, Mr 33
Little, Mr J. V. (plumber) 41, 233
Little, Jimmy (baker, Port William) 64
Little, Maggie 41
Little White Ribboners 150
Liverpool 26

273

Local Defence Volunteers 249
Local Government (Scotland) Act 1975 186
Lodging House, The 31
Logie, Johnny 198–200; *199*
London 18, 46, 47, 169, 174, 176
Lonsdale, Carlisle 162
Longhill farm 67, 164
Loreburn Housing Association 184
Lovat, Lord 142
Low Clone farm, Port William 95, 132
Lowe, Mr 34
Lyons, Billy 38

McAdam, Rennie 252
– band 252
McAlister, Mr (hairdresser) 32
McCarthy, Father 235
MacCaulay's store 79
McClymont, Bob 126
McCormick and Nicolson lawyers 227
McCracken, Mrs (teacher) 211
McCreath, Harry 18
McCreath, Hutchison 38
McCreath, Tom 81–82, 88, 94, 95, 111, 115, 117–18, 121–23, 126, 143, 177, 180, 202–3, 227–28, 245, 254–55, 264–65
– family 115, 143, 177, 183, 202–3, 227–28, 245, 246, 264, 265
McCutcheon Ronnie (engineman) 258

McDougall, Dr 210, 218, 220
McDowall, Betty 26
McDowell, Mrs 210
McEwan (neé McWilliam), Mrs Etta (teacher) 217
McEwan's grocer's shop 223
Macfarlane Lang, biscuit firm 191
MacFie and Alexander solicitors 184
McGee, Bishop of Galloway, Joseph 231
McGeoch, Mrs (Honeymoon Villa) 32
McGhie, Alec (electrician) 32
McGinn, Henrietta 49
McGinn, Hugh 49
McGinn, Hugh 'Spook' 183, 184, 186
McGinn, Wullie (pedlar) 195; *195*
McGuffie, Mrs 31
McGuffie's shop 31
McGuire, John (coastguard) 245
McGuire, Nurse 34
McGuire, Sarah 34
McHarg, Miss (teacher) 214
McKelvie, Betty 39, 49, 50, 51
McKelvie's shop 30, 49, 50, 51; *49*
McKenzie, Phillip 64
McKie, Mary Ann 54
McKnaught's ironmongery 34
McLachlan, Hamish 154
McLean, Donald/Donnie 254

McLean (neé Jolly), Jessie 34, 39, 51, 60, 62, 64–66, 74, 82–84, 88–89, 106–7, 153, 179, 193–94, 200, 234–35, 250, 253–54
– daughter, Mary 62, 82–84, 88–89, 106–7, 179, 194 253–54
– family *see also* Jolly family
McLean, lorry contractor 241
McMaster, Jock 84–85, 89–90, 98–100, 107–11, 113–14, 115, 123–24, 128, 131, 138–40, 143–44, 157, 176, 181, 192–93, 211–12, 247, 261
– family 110, 115, 128, 139, 143–44, 157, 176, 193, 247
McMaster, Willie (station delivery man) 191–92
McMillan, Maria 201
McMillan family, Stranraer 201
McNally, Robert 154
McNeillie, Andrew 4, 6, 7, 11, 13–14, 15–16, 18–23, 24–26, 30, 182–83
McNeillie family 19–21, 22, 23–25
McNeillie, Jimmy 24
McNeillie, John (Andrew's cousin) 24
McNeillie, John (Ian Niall) 4, 5, 7, 11, 13–14, 15–16, 18–20, 21–26, 27, 30, 117, 121, 181–83
McQueen, Kate 154
McShane, Elsie 160, 161–63, 165, 198, 228, 238, 255
– father (head gardener,

Glasserton Estate) 160, 162, 228, 255
McShane, Jean 14
McTiers, Misses 228
McVities, biscuit firm 191
McWhirter, Dr 218
McWilliam, Archie (Murray's driver) 41
McWilliam, Jimmy (joiner) 184, 186
McWilliam, John 217
McWilliam, Methven 217
McWilliam, Mr (the Isle) 31
Macedonia 203
Machars, the 1, 4, 11, 13, 15, 16, 17, 18, 19, 20, 21, 22, 23, 25, 74, 108, 116, 138, 140, 151, 165, 181, 190, 198, 202, 229, 261
Maguire, Nurse 34
Maguire, Sarah 34
Mains farm 32–33, 49, 62, 233, 237, 239
Mallet Porter and Dowd, London 169
Marshall, Cruggleton 93
Marshall, Matthew 142
Marshall, Mr A. J. 'Bertie' 103, 140, 141, 142, 205
Marshall, Ron (rent clerk) 184
Marshall, Sonny 31
Martin family 112
Martin, Bobby (janitor) 214
– wife, Mrs Martin 214
Martin, Sally 112
– mother & father-in-law 112
Martin's shoe shop 12
Maxwell, Gavin 4, 15–16, 21, 174, 176
– mother, Lady Mary Percy 169

Maxwell, Jimmy 54
Maxwell, Mr (miller) 125
Maxwell, Mrs 68
Maxwell, Sir Aymer 174, 176
Maxwell, Sir Herbert 43
Maxwell, Sir Michael 176
Maybole 138
Merchant Navy 216
Middle East 247
Milhench, Jimmy (blacksmith) 98–100; 99
Milk Marketing Board 159, 177
Mill Hill 80
Miller, Cathy 59, 67–69, 79–81, 126–27, 129, 130–31, 148, 151, 168, 218, 228
– family 59, 68, 80–81, 129, 148, 218
Milligan, Miss 32
Millisle farm 41, 115
Millisle Station 92–93
Mills, Annie 76
Mills, Bridget 232
Mills, John Townsley (master flesher) 52–53, 232; 53
Mills, Willie 52
Miln ice delivery 48
Milroy, William 139
Ministry of Defence 247
Minnigaff camp 161
Mitchell, Mrs (hairdresser) 35
Mochrum 202, 248–49
– graveyard 241
– schoolhouse 249
Monreith 17, 90, 100, 108, 135, 148, 155, 165, 211, 226
– Knock School 210–12

Monreith House & Estate 108, 115, 126, 160–61, 169, 174–76, 177
Montgomery's bakery 33
Morrach farm 135, 137
Morrison, Angus (minister) 229
Morrston, Miss 44
Morton, Mr (dentist) 37
Motherwell 205
Mount Stuart House 229
Muir, Miss 35
Muir, Mrs James 16–17
Mulberry harbours 245, 254, 255
Mulhench, Mrs 149, 150
– dancing class 149, 150
Mulholland's shop 236
Mull of Galloway 57, 190, 247
Munchie, Anton 173–74
Murray (née McEwan), Betty 33, 40–42, 191–92
– family 40, 41
Murray, Ethel 32
Murray, Mrs 49
Murray, Peggy 51
Murray's store 33, 39–42, 150, 259

NAAFI 248
National Cash Register (NCR) 57
National Health Service 57, 58, 218, 220, 221
National Library of Scotland 20
Navy, the see Royal Navy
Nesti, Katie 266
New England 164
New Luce 190
New York 27, 165, 202

275

New Zealand 202
Newcastle 263
Newton Stewart 3, 12, 15, 18, 39, 79, 81, 92, 128, 140, 154, 173, 176, 188, 189, 202, 206, 227–28, 241, 265
– free church 227
– parish church 227–28
Niall, Ian see John McNeillie
Niblock, Jack 56, 123, 124–25, 245–46
– grandfather (coast guard) 245
Niblock, Mr (banker/accountant) 56
Nicholson family 112
Nicholson, Jock 68
Nicholson, John 112
Normandy 255
Norquoy, Jim 'Knocky' 184, 186
north Ayrshire 202
North Africa 176, 255
North Britain 3
North Clutag farm 4, 18, 19, 22, 181
North Wales 20
Northampton 204
Northern Ireland 233
Nottingham 46
Nummerston Loch 149
O'Donnell, Jimmy 76
Orkney 116, 184
Ormeau Park 44
Outer Hebrides 161
Owen's butchers, Garlieston 146, 261

Palmallet 35, 63, 104, 247
Palmallet farm 142, 203, 204

Parton 191
Pattison, George 264
Percy family 169
Perth 205
Perthshire 256
Petrucci, Aldo 48, 69–70, 205–8, 213–14, 235–36, 265–67
– family 69–70, 205–8, 236, 263, 265–67
Petrucci's café *see* Central Café
Pey, Johnny 114
Philimore, Mrs (Airlour) 174
Physgill House & Estate 2, 160, 171, 228, 233, 237, 254, 258
Plymouth Brethren 38, 147
Poland 262, 263
Port William 36, 43, 45, 46, 64, 84, 102, 104, 117, 118, 119, 135, 151, 154, 156, 157, 193, 220, 221, 242, 248–49, 260, 261, 264
– mill 125–26
Porter, Sergeant 267
Portyerrock 63, 125, 245
– mill 93
Potts, Mrs 33, 35
Potts' tea room, Mrs 35
Prestrie 89
Priory Antiques 35
RAF 63, 246, 247–48, 249, 251, 252
Railway Hotel, The 37, 185
Ramsay farm 122
Ramsay, Hugh 85, 92–93, 94, 96, 97–98, 104–5, 108, 113, 115–16, 116–17, 118–19
– family 85, 115–16

– father, dairyman 41, 203
Ravenstone 90, 226
– school 151
Ray, Bill 184
Reformation, the 230, 231, 238
Reid, Alastair 3, 4, 5, 6, 7, 8, 11–13, 14–18, 20, 21, 26–27, 29, 30, 54
Reid family 11–12, 13, 16
Reid, Mr (dentist) 32
Renfrewshire 202
Rennie family 179
Rennie, Jean 23–24
Rennie family 23–24
Rhodesia 208
Rigg Bay 71
Roanie, Willie (blacksmith, Port William) 264
Robertson, Norman 223
Robertson, Nurse 209, 218
Robertson's jam factory 39
Rocks of Garheugh 247
Rogers, Willie 91
Ronnie, Mr 104
Ross, John (chemist) 224
Ross' grocer's shop, Miss 32
Royal Navy 26, 254
Ruby 33
Russell, Bertrand 175
Russell (4th Earl Russell), John Conrad 175

St John's Garage 37
St Ninian's
– Cave 164, 230, 231, 232, 235
– Feast of 232
– Shrine 230
Saltcoats 44
Salvation Army 227

INDEX

Sandhead 190
Scaurs, the 247
Scott, Snib 197, 198; 199
Scotch Jimmy 197, 198
Scotland 1, 3, 17, 27, 141, 186, 205, 229
Scots Greys 246
Scottish Women's Land Army 258
Scouler, Alistair 20
Scoular, John 29, 55–56, 90, 159–60, 163, 177–78, 188–89, 215–16, 225, 226, 228, 229
– father (minister, Glasserton) 90, 159, 160, 163, 225, 228, 229
Second World War 2, 5, 26, 45, 65, 71, 81, 88, 90, 95, 106, 111, 112, 121, 122, 136, 139, 143, 146, 162, 165, 169, 171, 178, 215, 220, 223, 245–67
Selby senior, Dr 90, 221
Selkirk 17
Selonika 203
Sharp, Jimmy 259
Sheddock farm 87, 108, 248
Sheffield 39
Shennanton Estate 177
Skate farm 202
Skeogs, the 2
Smith, Bob (steam mill) 126–27
Smith, Hugh/Hughie 126, 133
Smith, May (steam mill) 126–27
– father, mill man 127
Smith, Mr (headmaster) 218
Smith, Mrs 156
Snowdonia 21

Sorbie 79, 111, 121, 126, 262, 263, 264, 265
– creamery 117–18
Sorbie Garlieston battalion 246
Soriani family 33
Soriani, Paul 33
Soriani, Tina 48, 69–70, 181, 205–8, 213–14, 235–36, 265–67
– family *see* Petrucci family
south Ayrshire 202
South Barsallach farm 250
Southern Uplands 5
Stair Estates 207–8
Star Inn 152
Station Hotel 235
Steele, Alec 98, 184, 186
– father 98
Steele, May 91
Steele, Mrs 209
Steinbeck, John 22
Stellock farm 115, 157
Stevenson 180
Stevenson family 123
Stewart, Admiral Robert Johnston 159–60, 163, 167–68, 228, 236
– son (Laird) 236–37, 239, 255
– daughter-in-law 237
Stewart, Mrs 160
Stewart, Robin 162, 163
Stewart's Johnny (hairdresser) 35
– son 215
Stirling 257
Stoneykirk 190
Stranraer 12, 39, 103, 142, 190, 221, 249, 253, 266
Stuart, Betty 29, 30, 36, 49–51, 58, 59, 60–61, 72,

75–76, 87, 91, 98, 127, 144, 146–47, 149–50, 153, 157–58, 167–68, 178, 192, 195–96, 197, 200–1, 209–10, 214, 218, 225, 226–27, 229, 234, 240, 250, 251–53
– daughter Molly 59, 60–61, 72, 127, 147, 149, 150, 158, 234
– family 59, 251–53
Stuffit, Mrs [upholstery] 35
Sunday Mail 24
Sunderland, Marion 216–18
– family 217
– mother (teacher) 216, 217
Telfer family 228
Temperance pub 152
Templeton, Willie 36
Territorial Army 246
Tonderghie Estate 90, 160
Torhousemuir 144
Torrance House (Hoose) *see* Calcutta
Torrance, Miss Maddie 31, 153–54
Torrance, Miss Margaret 31, 153–54
Trotter, Robert 202
Tunder's Bridge 92
Turner, John 133, 134

Ulster 18
United States of America 165, 195, 201, 263
Universal Garage 104, 204

Vance, Madge 25
Vance, Mrs 33
Vance's shoe shop 33
Vietnam War 165

277

W. B. Anderson potato suppliers 207
Wales 20
Walker, baker, Creetown 192–93
Walker, Mr H. H. 43
Wallace, Mrs 156
Watson, Mrs 34
Watson, Sam (grocer, Sorbie & JP) 185
Watt's bookstore, Julia Muir 32
West Cumberland 192
West Freugh 129, 266
Whannell, Jimmy 37
Whannell's shop 37
Whauphill 154, 183
– Hall 151
– Slaehabbert 129
– Station 241
Whitefield 115
Whiteford, Joe 33, 37
Whitehaven 247
Whithorn 1–10, 11, 12, 13, 15, 17, 26, 27, 28–56, 60–63, 67, 68, 69, 70, 71, 75, 76, 77, 78, 79, 81, 82–84, 88, 89, 91, 92, 104, 117, 118, 119, 120, 122, 125, 126, 129, 131, 133, 135, 148–58, 159–60, 178–187, 188, 192, 193, 196, 197, 203, 204, 205, 206, 207, 210, 220, 221, 223, 226–27, 228, 229–40
– Army drill hall 4
– Back Row 59
– Belmont Hall 158
– Blacks Wood 77
– British Legion Hall 35
– Bruce Street 178
– bruising mill 125

– Burgh/Town Council 75, 178, 181, 183–86
– Burgh Court 185
– bus station 53
– Cameronian Entry 50, 61
– Cameronian Meeting House 226, 227
– carpet factory 54
– cathedral church 226
– Church of Scotland 226, 230
– cinema 154, 156
– Clone, The 63
– Common Park 33
– creamery 223
– cross-house 42
– Cross House, The 42, 51, 52
– Crudens, The 52
– Dinnans, the 104
– Dorans, the 52
– fire station 54, 125
– Garliestion Road 62, 183
– George Street 28, 51, 60, 70, 78, 145, 264
– Glasserton Street 49, 53, 196, 210, 227
– Green Lane 52, 59, 98
– Health Clinic 36
– Heid Pump 51, 52
– High Street 49, 50, 51, 52, 98, 196, 197, 209
– Isle Street 62, 68
– John Street 36, 51
– King's Road 54, 158
– library 37
– Manse, the 4, 11, 12, 13
– medieval ports 1, 2
– Moss, the 82
– old Town Hall building 185
– Panel, the 220–21

– Park, The 155, 184
– Pend House 237, 239
– Pend, The 12, 28, 154, 244; *34*
– police station 156, 186, 245
– Port's Mouth, the 31, 49, 196, 197, 219, 232
– Priory 28
– railway station 120, 230, 236, 251
– Roman Catholic Church 32–33, 226, 229–40
– pilgrimages 230–31, 235, 238; *231*
– Royal Burgh 28
– St John Street 186, 232
– St John Street United Free Church 38, 226–27, 233; *226, 252*
– schools 11–12, 52, 180–81, 211, 213, 214, 215, 217, 218, 265
– Secession Church 226
– slaughterhouse 28, 45
– south port 29, 48
– Top of the Town 29, 48, 49–52, 54 210, 264; *9*
– town hall 150, 179
– war memorial 33, 184
– Wards, the 68, 133, 157
– Windmill Stump 48, 54; *55*
Wiffy Keith 75; 76
Wigtown 3, 33, 56, 152, 154, 221, 234, 235, 252, 257
– Cattle Show 189
– church & graveyard 189
– cinema 154
– District Council 52
– District Justices Court 185

Wigtownshire 90, 203, 221, 234, 252, 263
– County Council 182, 184
Wilma, Ben 'the Pole' (blacksmith) 53, 100–1, 104, 152, 236, 239, 262–64
Wilma, Marjorie 232, 239, 264
Wilmot, Dorothy 35–36
Wilmot's boutique, Dorothy 35–36
Wilmot, Marjory 156
Wilmot, Mr 251
Wilmot, Mrs 251

Wilson, John 45, 60, 78, 79–81, 92, 96–97, 130–31, 149, 152, 155–56, 165–67, 186, 87, 201–2, 210–11, 228, 241–44
– family 201–2
– family's joinery business 92, 96–97, 165–67, 241–43
Wilson, Vicky 227
Wimpey 253
Woodfall Gardens 167
Woods, Tommy (blacksmith) 100–1, 121, 263, 264
Wordsworth, William 21

Wyllie's, Wyllie's grain merchants or Wyllie's mill *see* James Wyllie and Sons
Wyllie, Frances 149
Wyllie, Mr 125
Wyllie, Mrs 125
York 142
Yorkshire 170, 241
Young, Mrs (teacher) 217
Zambia 208
Zola, Émile 22

Other titles in the
Regional Flashback series
and the Flashback series

———

Stranraer and District Lives : Voices in Trust
edited by Caroline Milligan

First book in the EERC research programme of oral interviews 'Dumfries and Galloway: A Regional Anthology Study'. Themes include: Tattie Howkers / Tramps and Travellers / Agriculture and Farming / Community Life / War / Ghostly Happenings.

pbk / 235x156mm / 232pp / 52 b/w photos / 978 1 910682 11 1 / £12.99

The Making of Am Fasgadh: An Account of the Origins
of The Highland Folk Museum by its Founder
Isabel Frances Grant

The collections in Britain's first mainland open-air museum, now housed on eighty acres in Newtonmore, Inverness-shire, were begun by Isabel Grant (1887–1983). They illustrate a complex history of farming and fishing, crofting and domestic life.

pbk / 198x129mm / 192pp / 26 b/w photos / 978 1 905267 20 0 / £8.99

From Kelso to Kalamazoo:
The Life and Times of George Taylor, 1803–1891
edited by Margaret Jeary and Mark Mulhern

This son of a Border shepherd became a horticulturalist and moved to Kalamazoo, Michigan. In his memoir he comments on matters such as the Church of Scotland disruption, the temperance movement, slavery and the Great Fire of Chicago.

pbk / 198x129mm / 176pp / 11 b/w photos/illus / 978 1 905267 27 9 / £8.99

Scotland's Land Girls: Breeches, Bombers and Backaches
edited by Elaine Edwards

The first book about Girls who served in the Scottish Women's Land Army, in their own words. We hear of tearful goodbyes to childhood, joyful encounters with Royalty and cocktails, and of hard physical work – sowing, harvesting, calving, shearing.

pbk / 198x129mm / 144pp / 24 b/w photos / 978 1 905267 32 3 / £8.99

An Orkney Boyhood
Duncan Cameron Mackenzie

Entertaining reminiscences of a post-war childhood on Burray in the Orkney Islands – including the town hall cinema, neep hoeing competitions, cutting peats and the New Year's Day ba' game ('more like a small-scale civil war').

pbk / 198x129mm / 112pp / 21 b/w photos / 978 1 905267 54 5 / £8.99

Showfolk: An Oral History of a Fairground Dynasty
Frank Bruce

The story of the Codonas – a fairground dynasty in Scotland for over two hundred years – structured around interviews with current family members and including tales ranging from visits to Glasgow Fair to finding fame as far afield as Hawaii.

pbk / 198x129mm / 288pp / 43 b/w photos / 978 1 905267 45 3 / £10.99

Galoshins Remembered: 'A penny was a lot in these days' edited by Emily Lyle

Galoshins was a folk drama performed on Hallowe'en or Hogmanay in the south of Scotland around 100 years ago. These oral reminiscences were collected in the 1970s for the School of Scottish Studies Sound Archives.

pbk / 198x129mm / 192pp / 35 b/w photos/illus / 978 1 905267 56 9 / £10.99

From Land to Rail: Life and Times of Andrew Ramage 1854–1917
edited by Caroline Mulligan and Mark Mulhern

Andrew Ramage worked in the Lothians and Berwickshire at a time of great social and economic change. From his memoir and diaries we learn of the uncertain realities of rural employment and dwelling which challenge the bucolic image often attached to descriptions of 19th-century country life.

pbk / 198x129mm / 254pp / 53 col + b/w photos / 978 1 905267 69 9 / £10.99